60 Hikes Within 60 Miles: WASHINGTON, DC

60 Hikes Within 60 Miles:

WASHINGTON, DC

Paul Elliott

1st Edition

MENASHA RIDGE PRESS
Birmingham, Alabama

Library of Congress Cataloging-in-Publication Data

Elliott, Paul, 1955–
    60 hikes within 60 miles, Washington, D.C./by Paul Elliott.
        p. cm.
    Includes index.
    ISBN 0-89732-333-5
    1. Hiking—Washington Region—Guidebooks. 2. Washington Region—Guide
books. I. Title: Sixty hikes within sixty miles, Washington, D.C. II. Title.

GV199.42.W17 E44 2001
917.5304'42—dc21

                                                                    00-068366

Cover and text design by Grant M. Tatum
Cover photo by Kevin Adams
Photo on page 76 by A. Glenn; photo on page 179 by M. C. Wolter
All other photos by Paul Daren Elliott
Maps by Steve Jones, Bud Zehmer, and Paul Daren Elliott

Menasha Ridge Press
PO Box 43673
Birmingham, AL 35243
www.menasharidge.com

Table of Contents

Table of Contents (cont.)

MAP LEGEND

Main Trail

Alternate Trail

Interstate Highway

U.S. Highway

State Highway

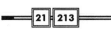
County Road

Forest Service Road

Local Road

Unpaved Road

Direction of Travel

Board Walk

State Border

County Border

Power Line

Park-Forest Boundary
and Label

Trailhead
Locator Map

Water Features
Lake/Pond, Creek/River,
and Waterfall

capitol, city, and town

Peaks and Mountains

Footbridge/Dam,
Footbridge, and Dam

Tunnel

Swamp/Marsh

35: Name of Hike

Map Scale

Compass, Map Number,
Name and Scale

Off map or pinpoint
indication arrow

Caution/Warning

Trailhead
for specific Maps

Ranger Station/
Rest Room Facilities

Ranger Station

Rest Room Facilities

Shelter

Structure
or Feature

Monument/
Sculpture

Parking

Recreation Area

Metro Rail

Shuttle
Dropoff

Campgrounds

Picnic Area

Gate

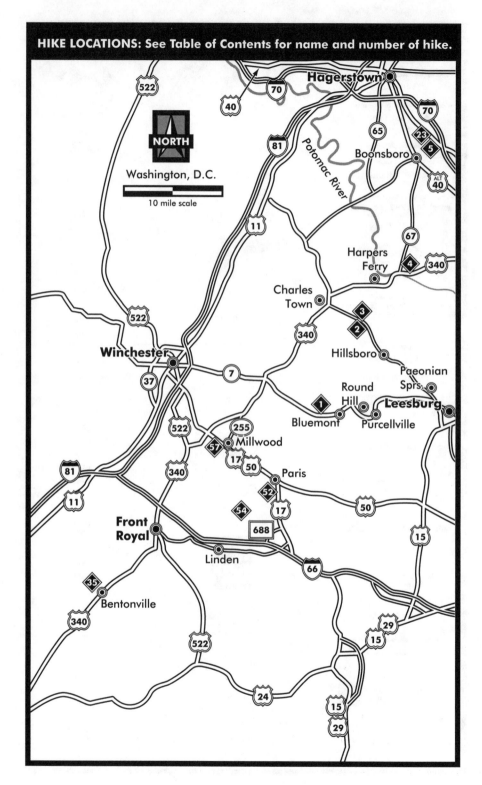

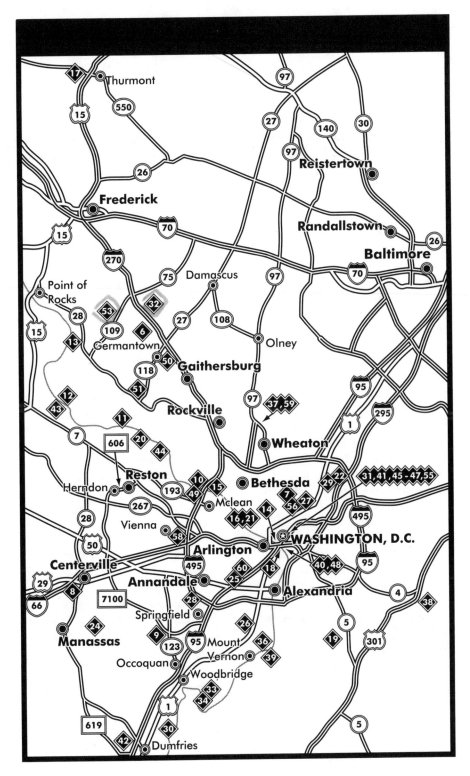

Acknowledgments

This book's contributors are too numerous and difficult for me to identify individually. They're the architects, bards, hikers, history makers, landscape shapers, rangers, teachers, and writers whose paths I crossed or may have crossed on my way here. Some I know, most I don't, but all have my collective thanks.

Twenty-one, though, have helped me in specific ways—and I know their names. Margot and Paul Edelman, Ellen Kohn, Janis Knorr, Jennie Alwood, Steve Benka, and Bud Zehmer formed the chain that led me to Menasha Ridge Press and this book. Springfield Ray Abercrombie, College Park Scott Wilson, and far-from-home Birmingham Bud Zehmer generously re-scouted hikes for me. My Sierra Club co-leader Carol Ivory joined me to take initially unsuspecting groups on test hikes. Camera-equipped Annie Glenn and Brigitte Savage went along too.

And two of hiking's grand bold men each added something special: Springfield Cliff Noyes supplied the hike-and-paddle outing (hike no. 35), and Dick "Iron Legs" Terwilliger loaned me what may have been George Washington's measuring wheel. I would also like to thank those who worked on the project in Alabama:

Menasha Ridge Press editors Bud Zehmer and Russell Helms and cartographer Steve Jones for their many efforts.

To conclude, I dedicate 1.89 percent of the book to each of the following co-owners of the environment and prospective hikers, in the expectation that when they run things, the national flower will no longer be the concrete clover leaf: Aidan Mantho, Alissa Rumon, Austin Grant, Becca Estes, Brent Vanderheyden, Cailin Lechner, Cate Perakslis, Cecilia Sherland , Claire Wolter, Cloé Berge, Cody Perakslis, Danilo Zak, Derek Vanderheyden, Dillon Ramsey, JD Corrales, Emma Estes, Evan Lechner, Erik McIntosh, Francie Zehmer, Gabriel Mouellem, Gabriel Zak, Garrett Harrison, Hannah Edelman, Hillary Lynch, Isabelle Wolter, Jack Holt, Jamie Zehmer, Jonathan Edelman, Johnny Estes, Joshua Rose Schmidt, Kai Knorr, Kasper Rapkin, Katie Clark, Katie McIntosh, Lauren Ramsey, Leah Rumon, Loïc Khodarkovsky, Lucas Farr, Luciano Mantho, Lucy Frost-Helms, Monica Moore, Morgan Edelman, Peter Manthos, Philip Hepworth, Philip Manthos, Rigel Farr, Sandra Kohn, Sean Edelman, Sophie Hepworth, Tanya Whisnant, Toma Meyer, Tyler Thornton, and Wyatt Moore.

Foreword

Welcome to Menasha Ridge Press's *60 Hikes Within 60 Miles,* a series designed to provide hikers with information needed to find and hike the very best trails surrounding cities usually under-served by good guidebooks.

Our goal was simple: First, find a hiker who knows the area and loves to hike. Second, ask that person to spend a year researching the most popular and very best trails around. And third, have that person describe each trail in terms of difficulty, scenery, condition, elevation change, and all other categories of information that are important to hikers. "Pretend you've just completed a hike and met up with other hikers at the trailhead," we told each author. "Imagine their questions, be clear in your answers."

An experienced hiker and writer, author Paul Daren Elliott has selected 60 of the best hikes in and around the Washington, DC metropolitan area. From urban hikes that make use of parklands and streets to flora-and-fauna-rich treks along the Potomac to aerobic outings in the mountains, Elliott provides hikers (and walkers) with a great variety of hikes—and all within roughly 60 miles of DC.

You'll get more out of this book if you take a moment to read the Introduction explaining how to read the trail listings. The "Topographic Maps" section will help you understand how useful topos will be on a hike, and will also tell you where to get them. And though this is a "where-to," not a "how-to" guide, those of you who have hiked extensively will find the Introduction of particular value.

As much for the opportunity to free the mind as well as to free the body, let Paul Elliott's hikes elevate you above the urban hurry.

All the best.
The editors at Menasha Ridge Press

Living in the Washington, DC, area in the late 1980s, I got outdoors quite frequently to go biking, play tennis, and run around a volleyball court. Hiking seemed such a pointless pastime, and occasionally I would make gentle fun of a friend who was an ardent and long-time hiker. Eventually, to humor her, I went along on an autumn hike in suburban parklands. Physically, it was nothing more than a long and easy walk, but I took note of the interesting social dynamics on a group hike.

The following spring, I joined a group of people climbing Old Rag, a popular destination in Shenandoah National Park. That outing agreeably combined physical exertion with vistas, wildflower discoveries, and camaraderie, and also taught me what not to wear and carry (such as old work boots).

My third hike occurred that summer, when I joined a big group doing Signal Knob, in the Massanuttens. On that adventure, I discovered the perils of dehydration, the generosity of hikers who already knew, the pleasures of outdoor discovery and of pushing oneself hard, and the benefits of day-long mountain jaunts with trail-savvy and intellectually curious companions. So it was that I slowly came to realize that

Lincoln Park includes both this 1974 work and an 1876 statue of Abe Lincoln.

hiking is an activity that gratifyingly involved a lot more than getting exercise and staying fit.

I was hooked, and one hiking thing led to another. During the 1990s, as both a social and solo hiker, I explored much of the outer Washington metro area. I also eased into organizing hikes, informally at first and then more conventionally as a leader for the Sierra Club and Appalachian Mountain Club. I slowly learned—mostly on repeated trips to San Francisco and other Western cities—that hiking is also a great way to get around in and get to know cities, especially small ones and parts of larger ones. So I began to add the inner Washington metro area to my hiking territory.

Hiking is now my chief outdoor avocation—and basic means of moving around Washington neighborhoods. And with this book, hiking has finally become an integral part of my vocation too.

I've written it for two basic reasons, other than the obvious ones (wealth, a chance at a Pulitzer prize, more wealth from the movie rights).

One is to tell or remind people about the remarkable hiking opportunities available year-round in the Washington, DC, metro area—and not just in exurbia and suburbia, but also in the city itself. When contemplating her next residential move, writer Katherine Anne Porter once said that she wanted to live "in a world capital or a howling wilderness." She settled in and for Washington (a suburb, actually), evidently not realizing that she could have had both if only she'd been a hiker.

Wilderness can certainly be found in the metro area. The Blue Ridge accounts for much of it, as you can quickly discover by sampling the various Appalachian Trail hikes I describe, and by following the trillium-rich circuit through the Thompson Wildlife Management Area. The wildest outing in

the book, though, is an out-and-back ridgetop trek on Massanutten Mountain (and the "back" part is a canoe ride on a scenic, unspoiled, and rapids-stippled river). But pockets of wilderness exist in areas closer to the city, and I have incorporated some of them into several closer-in hikes, such as those involving Sugarloaf Mountain, Catoctin Mountain Park, and Prince William Forest Park. There are yet other places where nature rears its impressive head only a few miles from the city proper—or even within the city limits (as you can discover if you scan the marshlands from the end of the boardwalk at Kenilworth Aquatic Gardens or explore a side trail in the northern section of Rock Creek Park).

What's more, as a world capital and simply as its 200-year-old self, Washington offers a rich array of nonwilderness pleasures for inquisitive and adventuresome hikers. Roaming the city on foot is one of the best ways of getting to know it, as Goethe and Dickens demonstrated long ago in Europe and Alfred Kazin did more recently in this country (he once defined city walking as "an exercise in human delight"). Today, urban walking seems to survive largely in the form of tourists taking short guided walking tours of well-known neighborhoods.

Roaming the city in the hiking mode, though, is an even better way, in that hikers are accustomed to covering more ground, walking fast or faster between stops, wearing protective footwear, and practicing self-sufficiency by carrying raingear, food, and water. In the past few years, I have found that in-city hikes are not only popular but also prompt many participants, including longtime residents, to admit not having been to or known about certain buildings, parks, or trails. I've heard such confessions not only in the US National Arboretum and the Brookland section of Northeast Washington, but also in parts of

Rock Creek park and other fashionable Northwest districts.

All in all, the Washington metro area has something to offer to just about anyone with an interest in hiking. Taken together, these many somethings reflect the area's remarkable and rich diversity of landscape, parklands, trails, wildlife, city life, historical heritage, cultural resources, and recreational opportunity, as well as its modest but fortuitous tradition of preservation.

Judging from anecdote and trail traffic, hiking in the metro area is conventionally taken to be a one- or two-season affair. But like some of my fellow hike leaders, I see it as a four-season enterprise. As tourists and hikers both know, the area is usually favored with a glorious spring and a splendidly burnished fall—and as some hikers also know, there are ways of enjoying those seasons away from the madding crowds. Area summers indeed tend to be hot and muggy, but there are places where shade, breezes, and crowdlessness make hiking a rewarding activity, albeit not sweat-free. As for winter, that season is usually mild enough and leafless enough to make the views striking, the trails people-free and bug-less, and the hiking wonderful.

My other reason for writing this book is to provide people with a reliable means of doing hikes in the metro area without benefit of having a leader. If I've succeeded, then when they go hiking with this book as a guide, they will have an on-course and enjoyable outing. And it shouldn't matter whether they're novices or veteran hikers, or natives or newcomers. I'm assuming, of course, that they'll choose their hikes wisely, accouter themselves appropriately, read attentively, and always hike with a compass and at least one companion (and perhaps a cell phone too). Oh yes, and they also need to remember that permanent trail signs sometimes disappear and that trails sometimes get rerouted.

Lincoln still stands tall at Fort Stevens.

The 60 hikes I describe are a sampling of what the metro area and I collectively have to offer. Given that I'm following in the bootsteps of other writers, my choices fall into three categories. They are variants on traditional hikes in already well-known popular hiking areas or on well-established trails (such as the Mount Vernon Trail, Greenbelt Park, and the C&O Canal towpath), new hikes in those areas (such as Columbia Island and the hike entitled Lincoln Memorial to Lincoln Park), and new hikes in underused areas (such as Brookland, the Northwest Branch parklands, the Virginia State Arboretum, and Seneca Creek State Park's Greenway Trail).

The book's hikes range in location from the central city to and through the suburbs and beyond to the foothills and mountains in the west and the lowlands in the east (with modifications in the perimeter of the book's coverage to allow for the publisher's existing guide to Shenandoah National Park and pending guide to the Baltimore area).

The hikes range in difficulty from a 1.4-mile meander through a little-known suburban botanical preserve, to several challenging up-and-down mountain hikes, to an arduous power hike on the C&O Canal towpath that's flat all the way but 62.5 miles in length (that's not a typo).

Each hike is identified by a specific difficulty factor given in the Key-at-a-Glance Information box. To help you understand what I have in mind and to decide what you want to do, I have developed and applied the following rating scale (based on similar scales used by the Sierra Club and other hiking organizations):

Very easy	under 5
Easy	5 to 7.9
Easy/moderate	8 to 10.9
Moderate	11 to 13.9
Moderate/difficult	14 to 16.9
Quite difficult	17 to 19.9
Difficult	20 to 22.9
Very difficult	23 to 25.9
Extremely difficult	26 or more

To determine the rating for a hike, I count 1 point for each mile of distance and 1 point for every 400 feet of elevation change (up or down).

In addition to including much information that is intended to be clear and useful, I have also surreptitiously threaded the text with unidentified quotes and paraphrases from published sayings, poems, and other writings on the chance that some of you also like to work on puzzles as you hike—or at other times. See if you can identify these semiburied items and, if you feel like it, tell me who said or wrote what—and in what work each item appeared, and do so by the end of 2002. As an inducement to try the puzzle, I offer to take the winner on any Washington metro area hike—either from the book or not—of the winner's choice. Send your solutions to me at either MetroHiker@ yahoo.com or P. D. Elliott, POB 9781, Alexandria, VA 22304.

As for the book itself, may it please you.

Paul Daren Elliott

Hiking Recommendations

(*Note*: Number preceding hike name indicates hike number.)

Introduction

Welcome to *60 Hikes within 60 Miles: Washington, DC*. If you're new to hiking or even if you're a seasoned trail-smith, take a few minutes to read the following introduction. We explain how this book is organized and how to use it.

Hike Descriptions

Each hike contains six key items: a locator map, an In Brief description of the trail, an At-a-Glance Information box, directions to the trail, a trail map, and a hike narrative. Combined, the maps and information provide a clear method to assess each trail from the comfort of your favorite chair.

Locator Map

After narrowing down the general area of the hike on the overview map (see pp. viii–ix), use the locator map, along with driving directions given in the profile, to find the trailhead. At the trailhead, park only in designated areas.

In Brief

This synopsis of the trail offers a snapshot of what to expect along the trail, including mention of any historical sights, beautiful vistas, or other interesting sights you may encounter.

At-a-Glance Information

The At-a-Glance Information boxes give you a quick idea of the specifics of each hike. There are 13 basic elements covered.

Length The length of the trail from start to finish. There may be options to shorten or extend the hikes, but the mileage corresponds to the described hike. Consult the hike description to help decide how to customize the hike for your ability or time constraints.

Configuration A description of what the trail might look like from overhead. Trails can be loops, out-and-backs (that is, along the same route), or figure eights, or any of those in modified form. Sometimes the descriptions might surprise you.

Difficulty The degree of effort an "average" hiker should expect on a given hike. In this book, the author has used a standardized range of terms—from "very easy" to "extremely difficult" that are explained in the Preface.

Scenery Summarizes the overall environs of the hike and what to expect in terms of terrain and land use

Exposure A quick check of how much sun you can expect on your shoulders during the hike. Descriptors used are self-explanatory and include terms such as shady, exposed, and sunny.

Traffic Indicates how busy the trail might be on an average day. Trail traffic, of course, will vary from day to day and season to season.

Trail surface Indicates whether the trail is paved, rocky, smooth dirt, or a mixture of elements.

Hiking time How long it took the author to hike the trail.

Access Notes times of day when hike route is open, days on which it is officially closed, and when fees or permits needed to access the trail.

Maps Which maps are useful in the author's opinion, for this hike. See Appendix B for places to buy maps.

Facilities Notes any facilities such as rest rooms, phones, and water available at the trailhead or on the trail or nearby.

Special comments Provides you with those little extra details that don't fit into any of the above categories. Here you'll find reminders about such matter as park or road gate closings that could trap you or your car, trails that are susceptible to flooding, and hunting seasons that could affect your hiking.

Directions

Check here for directions to the trailhead. Used with the locator map, the directions will help you locate each trailhead.

Description

The trail description is the heart of each hike. Here, the author has provided a summary of the trail's essence as well as highlighted any special traits the hike offers. Ultimately the hike description will help you choose which hikes are best for you.

Nearby Activities

Not every hike will have this listing. For those that do, look here for information on nearby dining, recreational opportunities, or other activities to fill out your day.

Weather

The best time to go hiking in the Washington, DC, area is any time you can. If you make prudent decisions about which of these 60 hikes to try, what to take with you, and what the weather is likely to be, you can count on being able to get out and

hike enjoyable and safely on most days of the year.

The area has a generally temperate climate that favors year-round hiking, although deep freezes occur from time to time in the winter and the often hot and humid summers do take some getting used to. During the winter, morning temperatures are usually in the 30s, and frosts are not uncommon. If that's too cold, wait until the middle of the day and you're more likely to have temperatures warm enough to go hiking. Also, help yourself by selecting hikes in sheltered areas or, if there's no wind, hikes where you'll be out in the sunshine. Make allowances for the occasional winter storms that lash the Washington area.

Average Daily (High/Low) Temperatures by Month, Washington, DC

Month	High	Low
January	50	70
February	52	72
March	56	76
April	61	82
May	67	88
June	73	90
July	74	90
August	74	90
September	73	89
October	66	84
November	57	77
December	52	72

On the hottest days of summer, from late July to early September, go hiking first thing in the morning and look for hikes that have heavy shade—or for trails in the mountains, where temperatures are somewhat lower. Keep in mind that even if you wait until late in the day, the temperature and humidity won't have dropped enough to be really comfortable. Also be aware of the possibility of thunderstorms; they're the area's worst weather hazard (short of hurricanes), and you need to be careful not to get caught by one when you're out on a trail.

All in all, the best hiking weather in the Washington area occurs in the fall and then again in the spring. Autumn can be glorious, especially from September to early December, during Indian summer, when the light pours down like melted butter and covers everything in a kind of golden glow just before sunset.

Even a mild Washington winter tends to be a gray winter of short days, and so the period from about mid-March to mid-May brings not only balmy weather but also the reawakening of nature as plants start to bloom, migrating songbirds start to appear, and a fresh hiking season gets underway.

Maps

The maps in this book have been produced with great care and, when used with the hiking directions, will help you get to the trailhead and stay on course. But as any experienced hiker knows, things can get tricky off the beaten path.

For even more information on a particular trail look to the United States Geological Survey's 7.5 minute series topographic maps (topos). Recognizing how indispensable these are to hikers, many outdoor shops now carry topos of the local area.

If you're new to hiking, you might be wondering, "What's a topographic map?" In short, topos indicate not only linear distance but elevation as well. One glance at a topo will show you the difference: contour lines spread across the map like dozens of intricate spider webs. Each contour line represents a particular elevation, and at the base of each topo a particular contour interval designation is given.

Let's assume that the 7.5 minute series topo reads "Contour Interval 40 feet," that the short trail we'll be hiking is 2 inches in length on the map, and that it crosses 5

contour lines from its beginning to end. What do we know? Well, because the linear scale of this series is 2,000 feet to the inch (roughly 2.75 inches representing one mile), we know our trail is approximately 0.8 miles long (2 inches are 2,000 feet). But we also know we'll be climbing or descending 200 vertical feet (5 contour lines are 40 feet each) over that distance. And the elevation designations written on occasional contour lines will tell us if we're heading up or down.

In addition to outdoor shops and bike shops, other places in the Washington metro area likely to carry topos are major universities, some public libraries, and the Library of Congress, where you may be able to photocopy the ones you need to avoid the cost of buying them

Trail Etiquette

Whether you're on a city walk or on a long hike, remember that great care and resources (from nature as well as from tax dollars) have gone into creating the trails and paths. Taking care of them begins with you, the hiker. Treat the trail, wildlife, flora, and your fellow hikers with respect. Here are a few general ideas to keep in mind while hiking:

1. Hike on open trails only. Respect trail and road closures (ask if you're not sure), avoid trespassing on private land, and obtain any required permits or authorization. Leave gates as you found them or as marked.

2. Leave no trace of your visit other than footprints. Be sensitive to the land beneath your feet. This also means staying on the trail and not creating any new trails. Be sure to pack out what you pack in. No one likes to see trash someone else has left behind.

3. Never spook animals. Give animals extra room and time to adjust to you.

4. Plan ahead. Know your equipment, your ability, and the area in which you are

hiking—and prepare accordingly. Be self-sufficient at all times; carry necessary supplies for changes in weather or other conditions. A well-executed trip is a satisfaction to you and not a burden or offense to others.

5. Be courteous to other hikers, bikers, and all other people you meet while hiking.

Water

"How much is enough? One bottle? Two? Three?! But think of all that extra weight!" Well, one simple physiological fact should convince you to err on the side of excess when it comes to deciding how much water to pack: While working hard in 90-degree heat, we each need approximately 10 quarts of fluid every day. That's 2.5 gallons—12 large water bottles or 16 small ones. And, with water weighing in at approximately 8 pounds per gallon, a 1-day supply comes to a whopping 20 pounds.

In other words, pack along one or two bottles even for short hikes. Most—but not all—of the hikes in this book have water at the trailhead or along the way. But if you must use water that's not from a tap, make sure you purify it. If you drink it untreated, you run the risk of disease.

Many hikers pack along the inexpensive and only slightly distasteful tetraglycine hydroperiodide tablets (sold under the names Potable Aqua, Globaline, and Coughlan's, among others). Time for these tablets to work their magic is usually about 30 minutes—the colder the water, the longer it takes. Some invest in portable, lightweight purifiers that filter out the crud. Unfortunately, even the best filters only remove up to 98 to 99 percent of all those nasty bacteria, viruses, and other organisms you can't see.

Tablets or iodine drops by themselves will knock off the well-known Giardia. One to four weeks after ingestion, Giardia will have you bloated, vomiting, shivering with chills, and living in the bathroom.

But there are other parasites to worry about, including cryptosporidium. "Crypto" brings on symptoms very similar to Giardia, but unlike that fellow protozoan it's equipped with a shell sufficiently strong to protect it against the chemical killers that stop Giardia cold. This means either boiling the water or using a water filter to screen out both Giardia and crypto, plus the iodine to knock off viruses.

Some water filters come equipped with an iodine chamber to guarantee nearly full protection. Or you can simply add a pill or drops to the water you've just filtered (if you aren't allergic to iodine, of course). The pleasures of hiking—and the displeasure of getting sick—make this relatively minor effort worth every one of the few minutes involved.

First-Aid Kit

A typical kit may contain more items than you might think necessary. These are just the basics:

Sunscreen
Aspirin or acetaminophen
Butterfly-closure bandages
Band-Aids
Snakebite kit
Gauze (one roll)
Gauze compress pads (a half-dozen
    4 in. x 4 in.)
Ace bandages or Spenco joint wraps
Benadryl or the generic equivalent—
    diphenhydramine (an antihistamine,
    in case of allergic reactions)
A prefilled syringe of epinephrine (for
    those known to have severe allergic
    reactions to such things as bee stings)
Water purification tablets or water filter
    (on longer hikes)
Moleskin/Spenco "Second Skin"
Hydrogen peroxide or iodine

Antibiotic ointment (Neosporin or the
generic equivalent)
Matches or pocket lighter
Whistle (more effective in signaling res-
cuers than your voice)

Pack the items in a waterproof bag such
as a Ziploc bag or a similar product.

Hiking with Children

No one is too young for a nice hike in the
woods or through a city park. Parents with
infants can strap the little ones on with
devices such as the Baby-Björn Baby Car-
rier® or Kelty's Kangaroo®. Be careful,
though. Flat, short trails are probably best
with an infant. Toddlers who have not
quite mastered walking can still tag along,
riding on an adult's back in a child carrier.

Children who are walking can, of
course, follow along with an adult. Use
common sense to judge a child's capacity
to hike a particular trail. Always rely on the
possibility that the child will tire quickly
and have to be carried. When packing for
the hike, remember the child's needs as well
as your own. Make sure children are adequately clothed for the weather, have proper shoes, and are properly protected from
the sun with sunscreen and clothing. Kids
dehydrate quickly, so make sure you have
plenty of clean water and other drinks for
everyone.

Depending on age, ability, and the hike
length/difficulty, most children should
enjoy some of the short hikes described in
this book. To assist an adult with determin-
ing which trails are suitable for children, a
short list of hike recommendations for children is provided on pages xix–xx.

The Business Hiker

Whether you're in the Washington, DC,
area on business as a resident or visitor,
these hikes are the perfect opportunity to
make a quick getaway from the demands of
commerce. Some of the hikes are located
close to government buildings and other
office areas classified as urban and are easily
accessible from downtown areas.

Instead of a burger down the street, pack
a lunch and head for a nearby trail—the
National Mall and other federal parklands
are a good bet, as are state and regional
parks—to take a relaxing break from the
office or that tiresome convention. Or plan
ahead and take along a small group of your
business comrades. A well-planned half-day
getaway is the perfect complement to a
business stay in Washington or any of the
other close-in communities in the metropolitan area.

60 Hikes Within 60 Miles:

WASHINGTON, DC

IN BRIEF

Along the Virginia/West Virginia border north of Snickers Gap, AT hikers can experience the Roller Coaster, Crescent Rock, and other local Blue Ridge treats.

DIRECTIONS

Car shuttle is required, so first drive to car drop-off and then convoy to trail-head. From Capital Beltway (Interstate 495) in McLean, Virginia, take Exit 45 to get onto Dulles Toll Road (VA 267) heading northwest. That feeds into Dulles Greenway (another toll road), which reaches VA 7 at Leesburg, about 28 miles from beltway. From Leesburg, proceed west on VA 7 about 12 miles to and past Purcellville. Just beyond, take Business VA 7 Exit onto Round Hill. Turn right onto VA 719 (Woodgrove Road) and proceed for about 3.2 miles. Then turn left onto VA 713 (Appalachian Trail Road) and follow it for about 2.5 miles to drop off car at park's Blackburn Trail Center. To reach trailhead (roughly 20 minutes), head back down VA 713. Turn right onto VA 719, go about 1.5 miles, and turn right onto VA 711 (Williams Gap Road). Proceed for about 3.5 miles and then turn right onto VA 7. You'll pass Bluemont within a mile and then climb through Snickers Gap. Half a mile past VA 601, turn right onto VA 679, and pull immediately into parking lot on right—the trailhead. If it's full, use commuter lot back at VA 7/

KEY AT-A-GLANCE INFORMATION

Length: 7.3 miles

Configuration: One-way

Difficulty: Quite difficult

Scenery: Mountain woodlands, steep slopes, boulder field, farmland views

Exposure: Mostly shady; less so in winter

Traffic: Usually light; somewhat heavier on warm-weather week-ends, holidays

Trail surface: Chiefly dirt and rocks (both loose and embedded); some grassy patches

Hiking time: 4.5–5.5 hours

Access: No restrictions

Maps: USGS Charles Town, Round Hill; PATC Map 7

Facilities: None at trailhead; water, phone at Blackburn Trail Center; toilet at nearby campground

Special comments: Be careful or stay away during hunting season (see text)

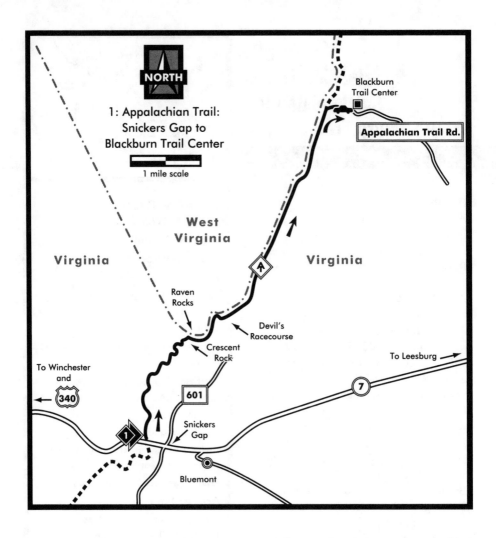

1: Appalachian Trail: Snickers Gap to Blackburn Trail Center

1 mile scale

NORTH

Blackburn Trail Center

Appalachian Trail Rd.

West Virginia

Virginia

Virginia

Raven Rocks

Devil's Racecourse

Crescent Rock

To Winchester and **340**

601

7

To Leesburg →

Snickers Gap

1

Bluemont

VA 601 intersection and walk 0.5 miles to trailhead.

DESCRIPTION

Hikers eager for, say, 4,800 feet of elevation change should try this one-way, 7.3-mile Appalachian Trail outing. Over half of it is on the aptly nicknamed Roller Coaster. It also provides seasonally diverse woodland landscapes and time on one of North America's greatest hiking trails.

The AT was conceived in the 1920s by a forester, planner, and visionary named Benton MacKaye. A primitive version was in place by 1937. But it took

decades to refine the route, secure public ownership, and arrange permanent maintenance. Officially called the Appalachian National Scenic Trail and owned by the National Park Service, the AT is managed by the Appalachian Trail Conference (ATC). Local organizations and their volunteers do the maintenance. The Potomac Appalachian Mountain Club (PATC), for example, handles the Mid-Atlantic States.

Nonstop end-to-end hiking of the AT's 2,000-plus miles—"thru-hiking"— began with Earl Shaffer's pioneer trek in 1948, which he repeated in 1998.

Currently, thousands try it each year; only hundreds succeed. Many others are "section hikers," who hike it a section or two a year. And literally millions of people hit the trail each year as day hikers.

The venue for this hike consists of part of the Blue Ridge area along the border between Virginia and West Virginia, some 55 miles northwest of Washington. The trailhead lies near Snickers Gap, long an important pass through the "Blew Ridge" (as early settlers wrote).

Trees dominate the hike, helping anchor the mountain soil, shelter the area's bountiful wildlife, shade the trail, and make hikers appreciate the overlooks. Oaks and hickories are common, but you'll also encounter maples, black tupelos, and pines. In the understory, dogwood blossoms—plus myriad wildflowers and migratory birds—brighten early spring; mountain-laurel leaves offset the pallor of winter, and poison ivy lurks year-round. The rocky trail can be slick when wet or icy, so be prudent when scheduling or doing the hike. Also, wear orange in the fall; the AT's no-hunting-allowed right-of-way is narrow. Try this hike in September, when the leaves are starting to turn and only migrating birds are in the air.

To get started from the trailhead, head for the nearby bulletin board to access the AT. Follow the white blazes generally northward on the Roller Coaster. Pace yourself, especially during hot weather. After crossing a stream, pause at a couple of overlooks to catch the view and your breath. Pressing on, cross another stream and then start a rocky half-mile ascent that'll take you into West Virginia and on to a clifftop overlook known as Crescent Rock. It's the hike's best overlook. In clear weather, panoramic views of the Shenandoah Valley and its serpentine river will greet you. Nearby, note the great stone shaft called Pulpit Rock.

After the incline, the trail levels off, curls around an outcropping called Raven Rocks, and then slides downhill. At the bottom, you'll find—and have to cross—a boulder field called the Devil's Racecourse. After that, head uphill on the last of the Roller Coaster for about a mile. For the next 3 miles, the AT stays close to the Blue Ridge crest, and you'll skip back and forth across the state line. A few breaks in the tree cover reveal the farmlands below, especially in winter. After about a mile, descend into Wilson Gap on a trail that swings left along an old road for about half a mile before returning to the ridge.

About half a mile farther on, turn right onto a blue-blazed side trail. Follow it downhill for a third of a mile to the Blackburn Trail Center, a multi-use facility owned and run by PATC. There, in summer, you're likely to meet thru-hikers and section hikers staying overnight. Linger to chat, and to look through the ever-fascinating logbook (trail register).

For more information on the hike route and current trail conditions, contact the ATC office in Harpers Ferry, www.appalachiantrail.org or (304) 535-6331. For information on Blackburn Trail Center, contact PATC in Vienna, (703) 242-0693.

NEARBY/RELATED ACTIVITIES
After the hike, detour off VA 7 to explore Virginia's Loudoun County. In the Round Hill area check out Between Two Hills, a farm that produces an inventive line of pepper-based sauces and salsas. Call for directions, (540) 668-7160. In Purcellville, visit family-run Crooked Run Orchard, where you can pick and buy produce. Call (540) 338-6642

#2
Appalachian Trail: Keys Gap to Blackburn Trail Center

IN BRIEF

On the Virginia/West Virginia border just south of Harpers Ferry lies an AT segment well suited to hikers keen on moderation. It's moderately long, challenging, and scenic—the basis for a pleasant mountain outing that neither raises nor dashes expectations.

DIRECTIONS

Car shuttle is required, so first drive to car drop-off and then convoy to trailhead. From Capital Beltway (Interstate 495) in McLean, Virginia, take Exit 45 to Dulles Toll Road heading northwest. That feeds into Dulles Greenway (another toll road), which reaches VA 7 at Leesburg about 28 miles from the beltway. For a toll-free, shorter, but slower route to Leesburg, get onto VA 7 (Leesburg Pike and then Harry Byrd Highway) at beltway Exit 47A.

From Leesburg, head northwest on VA 7 for about 3.5 miles. Just before Paeonian Springs, turn right onto VA 9 (Charles Town Pike) and drive about 8 miles to just past Hillsboro. There, turn left onto VA 719 (Woodgrove Road) and proceed generally south for about 3.5 miles. Then turn right onto VA 713 (Appalachian Trail Road) and follow it for about 2.5 miles to Blackburn Trail Center. Park there, at car drop-off. Then drive to trailhead (roughly 25 minutes), as follows. Head back to Hillsboro on VA 713 and VA 719. Turn left onto VA 9 and go northwest for about 5 miles to Keys Gap. Driving up to

KEY AT-A-GLANCE INFORMATION

Length: 7 miles

Configuration: One-way

Difficulty: Moderate/difficult

Scenery: Mountain woodlands, farmland views

Exposure: Mostly shady; less so in winter

Traffic: Usually very light to light

Trail surface: Mostly dirt, with much rock (loose and embedded); some grassy patches

Hiking time: 4–5 hours

Access: No restrictions

Maps: USGS Charles Town, Round Hill; PATC Map 7

Facilities: None at trailhead; toilet at David Lesser Shelter; water, phone at Blackburn Trail Center; toilet at nearby campground

Special comments: Be careful or stay away during hunting season

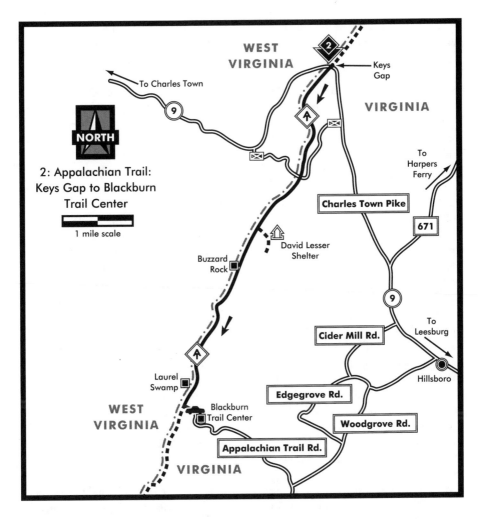

2: Appalachian Trail: Keys Gap to Blackburn Trail Center

1 mile scale

Keys Gap, watch for a large green sign on right. Just beyond it, turn right into Keys Gap parking area—the trailhead. *Note:* A shorter and possibly quicker way to reach trailhead from Washington's northern Maryland suburbs is to use I-270 and US 340 (see hike no. 3, p. 7), or to use River Road and then take ferry across Potomac River at Whites Ferry, near Poolesville, to slip into Virginia.

DESCRIPTION

Located in the Blue Ridge some 55 miles northwest of Washington, this one-way Appalachian Trail excursion is a north-to-south outing from Keys Gap to the Blackburn Trail Center. Think of it as transitional between the easier AT outing just to the north and the tougher one just to the south.

This 7-mile outing undulates through predominately oak/hickory upland woods, with roughly 3,000 feet of elevation change. The long-distance scenery, best in leafless months, includes farmland valleys to the east and west. Close-up offerings include an old house site and wildflowers and wildlife that are in season and sight. Watch your step when the trail is wet or icy, especially when you're on rocks. Wear orange in the fall; the AT's no-hunting-allowed right-of-way is narrow.

To get started from the trailhead, cross the highway carefully and pick up the white-blazed AT in a level, grassy area on the far side. Within 200 yards, the grass gives way to open woods, and the trail swings to the left and heads uphill. It's possible to go astray in this area, so watch for blazes, ignore side trails, and head generally southward. Also avoid the poison ivy.

Continue upward through the woods for a couple of miles. Pay attention to the blazes when you arrive at two successive trail forks; go left at the first one, right at the second. Also watch your step, because the trail is rocky and steep in places. That upward haul delivers you to a spot where, on a clear and leafless day, you'll have a fine view to the east of the farmlands of Loudoun Valley and, beyond, the hulk of Short Hill Mountain. Both that mountain and the Blue Ridge underfoot—plus the intervening valley—lie within the Blue Ridge physiographic region. So be careful how you use the term "Blue Ridge."

A mile farther along the undulating trail, a blue-blazed side trail leads left to the David Lesser Shelter. A 100-yard detour will reveal various amenities, including the shelter logbook (trail register). Along the full length of the AT, such logbooks offer an entertaining mix of observations, opinions, practical advice, doggerel, and seemingly encrypted messages. The writers use either first names or trail names (the aliases adopted by many thru-hikers).

Back on the main trail, continue for about half a mile and then turn right onto another blue-blazed side trail.

Follow that rocky path for about 200 yards to Buzzard Rock. That's roughly the hike's halfway point and definitely its best viewpoint. Watch for buzzards, as turkey vultures are popularly called. On a clear day, expect a panoramic view of the curlicue Shenandoah River and its peaceful valley. Return to the main trail.

The second half of the hike ascends and descends frequently, sometimes steeply on a rocky woodland trail. Along the way, there are two noteworthy locations roughly a mile apart. One is Laurel Swamp. There's mountain laurel there, but no sign of a swamp. Strangely, the most common plant is vinca, or periwinkle, a hardy ground hugger with shiny evergreen leaves and small violet-blue flowers. Look closely to see the remains of a stone-walled house amid the vinca, and a spring nearby. The second location is a roomy place with a view, to the right of the trail. Peer westward to see the river and its meanders. Then, proceed about 200 yards and turn left onto a blue-blazed trail. Take it downhill a third of a mile to the hike's end at the Blackburn Trail Center.

For more information on the hike route and current trail conditions, contact the Appalachian Trail Conference office in Harpers Ferry, (304) 535-6331 or www.appalachiantrail.org.

NEARBY/RELATED ACTIVITIES

Explore Hillsboro, a small and pleasing Loudoun County community on your travel route. If you're there late in 2003, watch for signs of Hillsboro's joining in the national celebration of the centennial of the Wright Brothers' first flight. Their mother, Susan Koerner, was born there in 1831, as a quaint roadside sign attests.

#3
Appalachian Trail: Keys Gap to Weverton

IN BRIEF

On this eclectic three-state trek, hikers spend time on the AT, in Harpers Ferry, and on the C&O Canal towpath. Along the way, they're exposed to scenic diversity, historical edification, and easy exercise.

DIRECTIONS

Car shuttle is required, so go first to car drop-off and then to trailhead. From junction of Capital Beltway (Interstate 495) and I-270, proceed northwest on I-270 for about 32 miles to Frederick, Maryland. Swing onto I-70, proceed west for 1.3 miles, and take US 340 west toward Harpers Ferry for 15.3 miles. Then turn right onto VA 67 at Weverton. Go roughly 200 yards and then take first right. Proceed for about 200 yards to unmarked parking area near guardrail on right. Park there, at car drop-off. Then convoy to trailhead (roughly 20 minutes), as follows. Get back on US 340 heading west (toward Harpers Ferry) and proceed for 1 mile, crossing Potomac River. Turn left onto Harpers Ferry Road (VA 671) at traffic light just before gas station, on left. Head south for 7.4 miles. Then turn right onto Charles Town Pike (VA 9/WV 9) and proceed roughly northwest for 3.2 miles. Just beyond large green sign on right, and in West Virginia, turn right into Keys Gap parking area—the trailhead.

KEY AT-A-GLANCE INFORMATION

Length: 10.6 miles

Configuration: One-way

Difficulty: Moderate

Scenery: Mountain woodlands, farmland views, townscapes, river views

Exposure: About half shady; less so in winter

Traffic: Generally very light; much heavier in Harpers Ferry, especially on warm-weather weekends, holidays

Trail surface: Chiefly dirt, with rooty, rocky, grassy stretches; pavement in town; hard-packed dirt on towpath (muddy when wet)

Hiking time: 5–6 hours (including sightseeing)

Access: No AT restrictions; towpath open daily, dawn to dusk

Maps: USGS Harpers Ferry, Charles Town; PATC Map 7

Facilities: None at car drop-off, trailhead; toilets, water, phones in Harpers Ferry

Special comments: Be careful or stay away from AT during hunting season

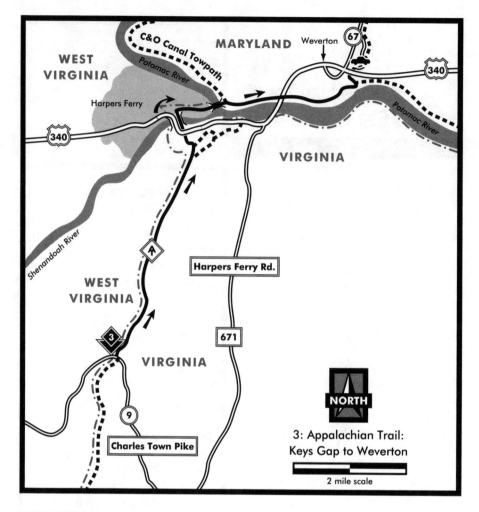

WEST VIRGINIA

C&O Canal Towpath

MARYLAND

Weverton

67

340

Potomac River

Harpers Ferry

340

VIRGINIA

Potomac River

Shenandoah River

WEST VIRGINIA

Harpers Ferry Rd.

671

VIRGINIA

9

Charles Town Pike

NORTH

3: Appalachian Trail:
Keys Gap to Weverton

2 mile scale

DESCRIPTION

This 10.6-mile hike is the least rigorous of my Appalachian Trail outings. It's a one-way trek on an AT section with only about 1,200 feet of elevation change, and most of that is downhill. As a bonus, it takes you right through the history-drenched town of Harpers Ferry, West Virginia, some 60 miles northwest of Washington,

The town lies on a promontory bounded by the Potomac River and its chief tributary, the Shenandoah River, just upstream from where the Potomac punches through the Blue Ridge. A fed-

eral arsenal was built there in the 1790s. The arrival of the railroad and C&O Canal early in the nineteenth century spurred the town's growth as an industrial center and transportation hub. In October 1859, abolitionist John Brown led a raid on the arsenal to initiate his campaign to free Virginia's slaves. The raid fizzled, but helped ignite the Civil War less than two years later. During that conflict, Harpers Ferry was taken and retaken by both sides enough times to leave much of it in ruins. The town never recovered, and over the years was battered by further floods. In the 1940s,

Congress stepped in and designated much of the community as a National Monument. In 1963 the area became the Harpers Ferry National Historical Park.

The park now covers 2,500 acres in three states, and the town itself is West Virginia's most visited tourist attraction. Its restored and replicated buildings form a quaint and industry-free mini-version of the grimy antebellum community. This hike can be rewarding year-round. Late spring is colorful on the out-of-town trail segments, thanks to trees, wildflowers, and migrating birds. Summer is colorful in town, thanks to bedecked tourists. Fall paints pretty pictures on the upland trail segments (wear something orange; the no-hunting-allowed AT right-of-way is narrow). Winter is more monochromatic, but a light dusting of snow can be a lovely accompaniment to solitude, silence, and leaf-free views.

To get started at Keys Gap, head for the nearby bulletin board, turn left, and hike north on the white-blazed AT. For the first 4 miles, the trail undulates gently as it crisscrosses the Blue Ridge crest, itself the unmarked border between Virginia and West Virginia. The ridge slopes are well wooded, largely with oaks and hickories, plus some maples and conifers. Expect to encounter wildflowers, birds, other wildlife, and maybe a few thru-hikers in summer. But avoid the poison ivy and continue to follow the white blazes.

After almost half a mile, go right when you reach a trail fork. A mile farther on, pass through an intersection where the woods open up to provide some good views, especially to the east (on your right). Thereafter, step carefully as you negotiate 1.5 miles of rocky trail. On reaching a junction, shortly after passing a large brown sign, take the left-hand fork. (The right-hand one is the blue-blazed

Loudoun Heights Trail; it was part of the AT until the AT was re-routed through Harpers Ferry in the mid-1980s.) The national historical park starts at the fork.

You'll descend, steeply in places, for close to a mile. Halfway down, be careful when crossing Chestnut Hill Road (WV 32). Continuing, pass through a handsome stand of hemlocks and get some good views, especially in winter. If it's a frosty day, maybe a crow will shake down on you the dust of snow from a hemlock tree.

You'll finally reach level ground, where US 340 crosses the Shenandoah River, at the hike's 5-mile mark. There, take an underpass beneath the heavily traveled highway and then a bridge walkway across the river. Walk along US 340 for about 100 yards, cross Shenandoah Street, and then turn right and uphill onto a white-blazed trail that's initially dirt surfaced but becomes paved. Follow it eastward into the lower town.

Turn left when you reach a white-blazed brown sign. Then continue to follow the white blazes so that you swing right at a fork and go straight through a four-way intersection. Proceeding downhill, veer right to visit flat-topped Jefferson Rock. The view impressed prepresidential Thomas Jefferson in 1783: "The passage of the Potowmac through the Blue ridge is perhaps one of the most stupendous scenes in nature." The Potomac is no longer clearly visible, and the rock itself is probably not the one Jefferson knew. But the view of the Shenandoah remains splendid.

Back on the main trail, continue downhill. Take a flight of steps hewn in a great sloping slab of rock, passing Harper House on the left. Completed around 1780, it's now the town's oldest existing house and open to the public (take a peek). Owner Robert Harper ran a flour mill nearby, provided ferry service for his farmer customers, and is commemorated in various local names in addition to the town's (those rock steps, for instance, are carved in Harper phyllite). At the bottom of the steps, turn right onto High Street. On reaching Shenandoah Street, turn right to get to the park's information center, in the exhibit-filled Master Armorer's House. Nearby are small museums, souvenir shops, and eateries.

Then walk back along Shenandoah Street, reach the old federal armory, and turn right under a trestle to reach a spacious overlook. There views of the river junction and slopes rise on all sides. Note the obelisk marking where an army colonel named Robert E. Lee captured John Brown.

Head for a bulletin board on the Potomac side of the overlook area and get on a brick walkway that leads to a footbridge across the river. On the far and Maryland side, you'll find the C&O Canal towpath and rarely more than a few tourists. Turn right onto the towpath, which, for the next 3 miles, doubles as a weirdly flat stretch of the AT. Passing Loudoun Heights to the right, you'll see off to the left the ruined canal and what Jefferson called "the terrible precipice hanging in fragments over you"—meaning Maryland Heights.

Pass towpath mileposts 60 and 59 (milepost 0 is in the Georgetown section of Washington). In Weverton, turn left at a bulletin board and AT signpost

pointing left. Use a grade crossing—over an active railroad line—to get to a road that turns sharply left. Walk across or around a grassy triangle and pick up the AT on the far side. The trail heads uphill and under US 340. At the next intersection, go left and follow the customary white blazes. Take your leave of the AT where it passes close to your waiting car.

For more information on the AT in general, visit or contact the Appalachian Trail Conference's information center in Harpers Ferry, (304) 535-6331 or www.appalachiantrail.org. The center houses AT-related exhibits, publications, hiking accessories, and a helpful staff. ATC has maintenance responsibility for the entire AT, under the National Park Service. For information on Harpers Ferry National Historical Park, visit or contact the information center there, (304) 535-6029 or www.nps.gov/hafe. For more information on the hike route and current trail conditions, contact the ATC office in Harpers Ferry, (304) 535-6331 or www.appalachiantrail.org.

NEARBY/RELATED ACTIVITIES
During or after the hike, explore the lower town more fully. Also check on ranger-led tours and other events. And remember that NPS copes with the warm-season parking problem by funneling tourists to an upper-town visitor center and parking area (there's an admission fee). Free shuttle buses link that area and the lower town.

#4
Appalachian Trail: Weverton to Gathland State Park

IN BRIEF

This AT outing on South Mountain in western Maryland offers hikers superb views as a reward for a strenuous climb. It also includes an easy ridge-top segment, plus an unusual memorial.

DIRECTIONS

From junction of Capital Beltway (Interstate 495) and I-270, drive northwest on I-270 for about 32 miles to Frederick, Maryland. Swing onto I-70, proceed west for 1.3 miles, and take US 340 west toward Harpers Ferry for 15.3 miles. Then turn right onto MD 67 at Weverton. Go about 200 yards and take first right, onto Weverton Road. Proceed for about 200 yards to unmarked parking area near guardrail on right. Park there.

DESCRIPTION

South Mountain forms part of the Blue Ridge portion of Maryland and adjoining Pennsylvania. Logged and fought over in the nineteenth century, much of it is now protected within Maryland state parks known collectively as the South Mountain Recreation Area. Threading through the area is a 40-mile strip of the Appalachian Trail.

This somewhat rigorous one-way, 13.8-mile AT hike features South Mountain's southernmost portion, which rises above the Potomac River in a series of high cliffs. The area, broadly

KEY AT-A-GLANCE INFORMATION

Length: 13.8 miles

Configuration: Out-and-back

Difficulty: Difficult

Scenery: Mountain woodlands, farmland views

Exposure: Mostly shady; less so in winter

Traffic: Usually light; heavier, even heavy, in cliffs, state park areas on warm-weather weekends, holidays

Trail surface: Mostly dirt, with rooty, rocky, grassy stretches; pavement in park

Hiking time: 6.5–8 hours (including cliff time)

Access: No AT restrictions; Gathland State Park open daily, sunrise to sunset

Maps: USGS Keedysville, Harpers Ferry; PATC Map 6

Facilities: None at trailhead; toilet at trail shelter; water, phone, warm-season toilets at Gathland

Special comments: Be careful or stay away during hunting season (see text)

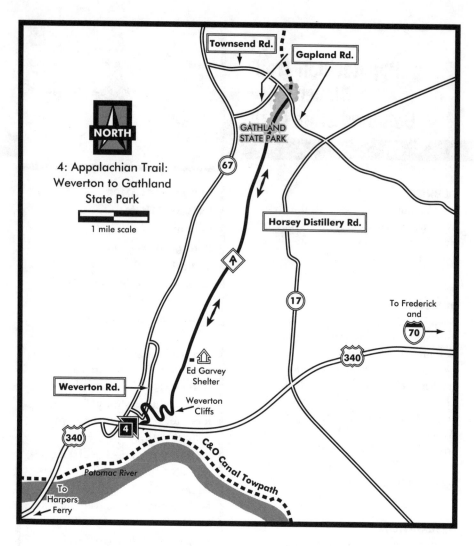

NORTH

4: Appalachian Trail:
Weverton to Gathland
State Park

1 mile scale

Townsend Rd.

Gapland Rd.

GATHLAND
STATE PARK

67

Horsey Distillery Rd.

17

To Frederick
and

70

340

Ed Garvey
Shelter

Weverton Rd.

Weverton
Cliffs

4

340

C&O Canal Towpath

Potomac River

To
Harpers
Ferry

straddling the line between Washington
County and Frederick County, lies
roughly 60 miles northwest of Washington. The north-to-south hike accumulates about 3,000 feet of elevation
change between the foot of the mountain and Crampton Gap.

The gap was the site of a September
1862 engagement that was one of several
known collectively as the battle of South
Mountain. Two decades after the Civil
War, the Crampton Gap area was bought
by a wealthy writer and ex-war corre-
spondent named George Albert

Townsend, who turned it into a mountain retreat of eccentric design. He named
it Gathland, based on his pseudonym,
"Gath" (his initials plus "h") and the bib-
lical city of Gath. He later spiraled into
poverty and died, as did his estate. Eventually acquired by the state, it became
135-acre Gathland State Park in 1958.

The hike route passes through mostly
deciduous woodlands that provide shade
and greenery during the growing season,
later turn beautifully autumnal, and then
open up in leafless winter. Flowers, ferns,
and wildlife add to the seasonal variety.

So does, dubiously, poison ivy, so stay on the trail. My preferred fall clothing color is orange; the no-hunting-allowed AT right-of-way is narrow.

To get started at Weverton, go to the eastern end of the parking lot and take the path that leads just a few yards to the white-blazed AT. Turn left onto the trail and follow it to Weverton Road. After crossing the road (carefully), head for the utility pole that marks the spot where the AT plunges into the woods and then starts going uphill. The trail ascends 500 feet as a mile-long series of switchbacks.

En route, detour onto a rocky, blue-blazed side trail on the right. Follow it downhill for about 200 yards to Weverton Cliffs, which has, in the late Ed Garvey's words, "one of the most spectacular views along the entire [AT]." On a clear day, you'll see a panoramic view of the Potomac River Valley and environs, especially if you have binoculars. In the fall, watch for migrating hawks. When a strong northwest wind is blowing, they stream by in great waves, sometimes at eye-to-eye level. Retrace your steps to the AT.

Continue up the trail as it rises steadily for several hundred feet over the next mile to reach and follow South Mountain's narrow crest line. After about a half-mile more, you'll see, to your right, one of the overnight shelters that dot the AT. Stop to take a look and check out its logbook (trail register). Completed in 2001, the Ed Garvey Shelter honors a man who lived, breathed, supported, worked on, thru-hiked, and wrote up the AT for half a century. Volunteers organized by Bowie Frank, who has a passion

for constructing such structures, built the shelter and its matching privy (which qualifies for a write-up in *Outhouse Beautiful*). The Ed Garvey Shelter is his second, and he has plans for a third.

Beyond the shelter, the trail pitches up and down a bit as it threads through the ridge-top woods. Here and there, a fleeting view is to be had, usually in winter, but the basic scenery is of the restful green-tunnel variety. You may see deer and wild turkeys—or evidence of them.

Be sure to stay with the white blazes. Ignore the occasional side trails, as well as what's left of an old unpaved road. Eventually, the trail noses gently downhill into Gathland State Park. There, follow a paved roadway for a few hundred yards to reach a 50-foot-high structure that marks the hike's turn-around spot. Townsend (Gath) erected it as a memorial to his fellow war correspondents. Then return to Weverton. En route, revisit the cliffs to see how the play of sunlight across the landscape has changed.

For more information on the hike route, trail conditions, and AT in general, contact the Appalachian Trail Conference in Harpers Ferry, (304) 535-6331 or www.appalachiantrail.org. For more information on Gathland State Park, contact the South Mountain Recreation Area office in Boonsboro, (301) 791-4767.

NEARBY/RELATED ACTIVITIES

During or after the hike, explore Gathland State Park and its collection of Townsend memorabilia. Contact the South Mountain Recreation Area office for details, and to order a free copy of the annual *Adventure Guide*.

Appalachian Trail: Interstate 70 to Turners Gap

IN BRIEF

The northernmost of the AT excursions, this hike covers the central portion of South Mountain in western Maryland. It provides a ridge-top woodland outing, a George Washington monument that doubles as an observation tower, and the chance of an indoor lunch.

DIRECTIONS

From junction of Capital Beltway (Interstate 495) and I-270, drive northwest on I-270 for about 32 miles to Frederick, Maryland. Swing onto I-70 and continue northwest for about 15 miles. At Exit 42 in Myersville, turn right onto MD 17 (Wolfsville Road). After going just over 1 mile, turn left onto US 40 and proceed for about 3 miles. Just before US 40 crosses I-70 (they don't connect there), pull into roadside parking area.

DESCRIPTION

This AT hike focuses on the part of South Mountain that lies roughly 20 miles north of the Potomac River and some 60 miles or so northwest of Washington. The hike route extends southward from where I-70 and US 40 cross the mountain. The trail winds serenely through the woods, undulating enough to accumulate about 3,200 feet of elevation change. It also passes through Washington Monument State Park, where you can stand atop the monument and practice your vista vision (take along binoculars).

KEY AT-A-GLANCE INFORMATION

Length: 10.2 miles

Configuration: Out-and-back

Difficulty: Quite difficult

Scenery: Mountain woodlands, panoramic farmland vista from tower

Exposure: Mostly shady; less so in winter

Traffic: Mostly light; heavier in state park on warm-weather weekends, holidays

Trail surface: Mostly dirt, with rocky, rooty, grassy, and paved patches

Hiking time: 5.5–6.5 hours (including tower time)

Access: No restrictions on AT itself; state park open daily, 8 a.m.–sunset

Maps: USGS Myersville, Middletown; PATC Map 5

Facilities: None at trailhead; toilets, water, phone near trail in state park

Special comments: Be careful or stay away during hunting season (see text)

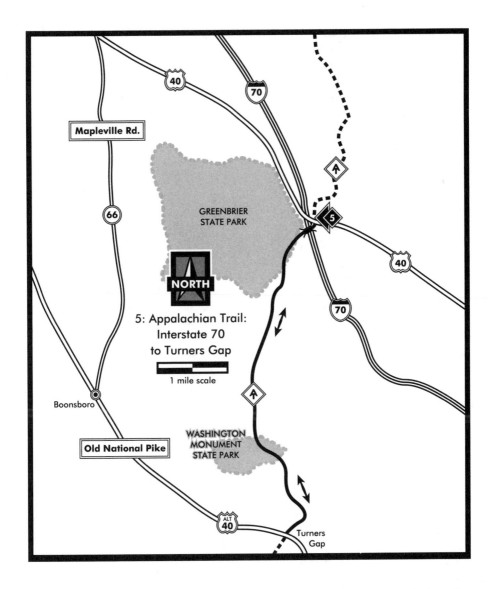

5: Appalachian Trail:
Interstate 70
to Turners Gap

1 mile scale

What you'll see most on this 10.2-mile, out-and-back hike are deciduous trees, especially oaks and hickories, and seasonally colorful rhododendrons and mountain laurels. Also watch for wild-flower blooms, poison ivy, and wildlife. The autumnal hawk migration can be spectacular. Deer bound, abound, and are legally protected along the AT. But the trail right-of-way is narrow, so sport orange during the fall hunting season.

To get started from the roadside trail-head, head for a nearby information board and go past it to pick up an old road. After roughly 50 yards, swing left onto a blue-blazed trail and follow it for 200 yards until you reach a footbridge. The southbound AT comes in from the right to reach the bridge across I-70's traffic lanes. Walk across the bridge, turn left, ascend some steps, turn right, and proceed along the white-blazed AT.

For the next 2.5 miles, walk along a trail—consisting mostly of old dirt roads—that eases up and down quite gently. Within the first mile, you'll enter the woods, pass Greenbrier State Park, and twice cross a paved road (that's Boonsboro Mountain Road). Listen for the lovely sound of silence as you move away from thunderous I-70.

Soon after you cross a power-line right-of-way, head uphill into Washington Monument State Park (like Greenbrier, one of several state parks making up the South Mountain Recreation Area). The rocky and steep trail leads a third of a mile to the monument's base. Climb the stairs within the squat, 30-foot-high tower. At the top, on a clear day, you'll find one of the best vistas along Maryland's share of the AT. To the west, you'll see the Hagerstown Valley farmlands and ridges beyond. And if it's early fall, watch for hawks.

Below and roughly 2 miles due west, you'll see Boonsboro, whose citizens once decided to honor of the country's first president. Erected in 1827, their Washington memorial was the country's first. Later, it was used as a Civil War observation post, fell into disrepair, was restored, and then fell down again. The present structure dates from the mid-1930s.

Leaving the tower, go back downhill for about 100 yards, and turn right to return to the main trail. Continue downhill for half a mile, leave the park, and hike uphill and then downhill for 1.25 miles to reach Turners Gap. There, 5.1 miles into the hike, is the turn-around spot, US 40A, and Old South Mountain Inn. Cross US 40A (carefully) to learn about the inn's colorful 250-year history and have lunch, but call ahead, (301) 432-6155. Or return by road for dinner—by reservation.

Returning to the trailhead, I paused next to a pointed fir tree I didn't remember passing. I realized that ou-and-back hikes always provide refreshingly new views on the return trip. You might want to stop at the Washington Monument, as I did, to take a fresh look at the sky and scenery.

For more information on the hike route, trail conditions, and the AT in general, contact the Appalachian Trail Conference in Harpers Ferry, (304) 535-6331 or www.appalachiantrail.org. For more information on Washington Monument State Park, contact the South Mountain Recreation Area office in Boonsboro, (301) 791-4767.

NEARBY/RELATED ACTIVITIES

If you do this hike in summer, cool off afterwards at nearby Greenbrier State Park (see hike no. 23, p. 81). It has beaches, canoe rentals, and a swimming-is-allowed lake.

Explore nearby Boonsboro. It has ambience, novelty, Doug Bast's remarkable history museum, (301) 432-6969, and the Turn the Page Bookstore Cafe, (301) 432-4588, run by a novelist and her family. Or sample Boonsboro's weekend-long National Pike Festival, held each May, (301) 733-4876.

#6
Black Hill Regional Park

IN BRIEF

Black Hill Regional Park features a large lake, rolling woodlands, meadows, and a seasonal variety of views. Situated in northern Montgomery County, Maryland, it's an attractive locale where hikers can vigorously roam suburban parkland.

DRIVING DIRECTIONS

From junction of Capital Beltway (Interstate-495) and I-270, head northwest on I-270 (toward Frederick) for about 18 miles. Get off at Exit 18 and turn left onto Clarksburg Road (MD 121). Proceed generally southward for about 1.6 miles. Then turn left onto West Old Baltimore Road. Go east for 1 mile, and turn right into park. Take Lake Ridge Drive for 1.9 miles to visitor center parking lot. Arrive early to beat the warm-weather crowds.

DESCRIPTION

Located about 21 miles northwest of Washington, Black Hill Regional Park covers 1,854 acres of rolling woodlands, meadows, and water. Little Seneca Lake, the metro area's largest lake and the multi-use park's chief attraction, occupies almost a third of it. For hikers, the park remains largely uncrowded.

   Three decades ago, the area consisted of privately owned fields, woods, and streams. Then the metro area's water authority and Montgomery County agreed to create a dual-use, emergency,

KEY AT-A-GLANCE INFORMATION

Length: 11.6 miles

Configuration: Modified loop

Difficulty: Moderate/difficult

Scenery: Woodlands, meadows, stream valleys, lake views with and without houses

Exposure: Mostly shady; less so in winter

Traffic: Usually light; heavier on warm-weather weekends, holidays, especially on hiker/biker trail and near visitor center

Trail surface: Mostly pavement; some dirt, grass

Hiking time: 5.5–6.5 hours

Access: Open daily, 6 a.m.–sunset, March–October (7 a.m. in other months)

Maps: USGS Germantown; sketch map in free park brochure

Facilities: Toilets, water in visitor center, at boat dock, parking lot 5, picnic shelters (warm-season), phones at entrance kiosk, visitor center

17

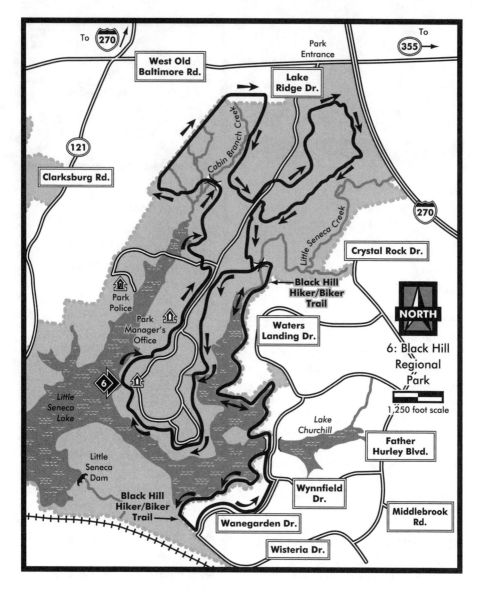

To 270

West Old Baltimore Rd.

Park Entrance

To 355

Lake Ridge Dr.

121

Clarksburg Rd.

Cabin Branch Creek

Little Seneca Creek

270

Crystal Rock Dr.

Park Police

Park Manager's Office

Black Hill Hiker/Biker Trail

NORTH

Waters Landing Dr.

6: Black Hill Regional Park

1,250 foot scale

6

Little Seneca Lake

Lake Churchill

Father Hurley Blvd.

Little Seneca Dam

Black Hill Hiker/Biker Trail

Wynnfield Dr.

Middlebrook Rd.

Wanegarden Dr.

Wisteria Dr.

water-supply reservoir and park. Little Seneca Creek was dammed, stream valleys filled up, and farmers left. Opened in 1987, the park now has both farmlands and residential areas for company. But the park itself retains an abundance of plants and animals.

The 11.6-mile hike route with about 2,200 feet of elevation change uses the park's main trail network, both near and away from the 505-acre lake. The paved and unpaved trails are unblazed but generally well signposted (except at the hike's start). Use the signs in conjunction with my trail directions, and stay on the trails to protect the habitat and avoid the poison ivy.

To get started, face the visitor center and look for a white trellis on the left. Take the paved trail nearby. Heading downhill, quickly turn right and then right again to access the paved Black

Hill Trail. That will take you between the visitor center on a knoll to your right and the lake to your left. For the next half-mile, stay on the paved, unshaded, and undulating trail as it pulls away from the lake. In spring, it's a bushy avenue of color and fragrance, thanks to wild-rose, blackberry, and honeysuckle blossoms.

At the park office, take a 30-yard detour to the left to see the site of a one-time gold mine. George Chadwick bought the land in 1947 as a summer retreat, dubbing it Gold Mine Farm. In the 1950s, as the Cold War escalated, he converted the mine into a bomb shelter.

Retrace your steps to the main trail and continue to the nearby road (Lake Ridge Drive). Turn left and proceed along the open grassy shoulder for almost half a mile. Then turn left onto the shoulder of Black Hill Road and walk downhill. After 200 yards, cross the road carefully and head across the grass onto a woodland trail at a "Hiking Trails" sign. Note the nearby sign that promises that "You can take a walk around this trail and turn it into a voyage of purist discovery."

The dirt-and-grass surfaced trail winds gently downhill and then levels off close to the lakeshore. A 75-yard detour to your left will give you views of an arm of the lake. Then press on until you get to a trail junction. There, turn left onto the Cabin Branch Trail. The half-mile-long trail undulates as it curves through the woods. It can get muddy as it crosses several small streams. A mini-suspension bridge spans the largest one, Cabin Branch Creek.

When you reach an unsigned junction, stay left and on the descending main trail. At an orange pole, turn right onto a utility right-of-way. Stay on the broad, pole-dotted, and dirt-and-grass woodland path for over half a mile as it crosses several small streams. The path

forms part of the park's boundary line, and even wanders out of the park, as you'll see when you turn right at the next signpost, pointing to the Cabin Branch Trail.

The mostly level trail parallels Cabin Branch Creek, off to the right. When you reach a trail fork, stay left and head for what the signpost identifies as the entrance road. At the road—it's Lake Ridge Drive again—turn left and walk along the open grassy shoulder for about 200 yards. When you're abreast of a yellow and dark-green gate, check for traffic, then cross the road back into the woods and onto the Field Crest Spur. You'll be on the mostly shadeless trail for nearly half a mile. It follows the edge of the woods, then swings to the right to cross overgrown fields dotted with bluebird boxes. Stay or go left at the first two trail junctions you reach. At the third junction, turn right onto the Hard Rock Trail and follow it into the woods.

The trail is aptly named, and it traces an undulating semicircle before returning to the fields. It's also scenic, but the traffic noise from nearby I-270 can be intrusive. Stay left at the next two intersections so that you remain on the trail. At the third intersection, go straight and slightly uphill (ignore the signpost).

Stay on the trail as it dips into and out of a stream valley and reaches a trail junction very close to Lake Ridge Drive. There, turn left, in the direction of the Black Hill Trail (as the signpost says). Cross a utility right-of-way and tilt gently downhill. Go left at the next junction, then follow a short trail section steeply down to Little Seneca Creek. Finally you'll reach the Black Hill Trail.

Take the bridge across the creek—the hike's halfway point. Then head away from the bridge, and go sharp right at the fork onto a short side trail. Where that trail starts uphill, look on the right for a skinny path leading a few yards to the nearby mossy ruins of an old gristmill and sawmill. The mill was abandoned a century ago, after almost a century's service. Walk carefully to avoid slipping on the moss—and into the poison ivy.

Get back on the side trail, then turn right to rejoin the main trail. Stay on that for a hundred yards or so until you reach an intersection. There, turn right onto the paved and mostly sunswept Black Hill Hiker/Biker Trail. The trail follows the creek and then hugs the shore of a large lake arm for just over 2 miles. Admire the lake views, but also notice, on your left, the houses lining the trail. Anytime you reach an intersection, turn right. Also turn right after crossing the causeway, which separates the lake arm from privately owned Lake Churchill.

The hiker/biker trail ends by rising to meet Wisteria Drive. I then like to loop through a handsome residential community to get back to the causeway. It has stylish houses set at angles to the street (a rare touch in the metro area), plus lots of trees and kempt shrubbery. Staying on the sidewalk or shoulder, turn left along Wisteria Drive, left along Wanegarden Drive, left along Wynnfield Drive, and then reach the causeway. Try the loop. Or, if field trips in upscale suburbia don't appeal, just remain on the hiker/biker trail.

After you recross the Little Seneca Creek bridge, stay to the left and head uphill on a rocky path. At the hilltop intersection, turn left to begin the last leg of the hike—a 1.6-mile stretch of the Black Hill Trail. The first part, unpaved, is an old road through the woods. Stay to the left at each intersection. The road gives way to a narrow and undulating dirt trail with intermittent lake views.

Just after the trail swings to the right and pitches steeply downhill, detour on a short side trail to a lovely spot at the water's edge. Back on the main trail, you'll arrive at a paved section. Turn left there and keep asphalt underfoot for the hike's remaining 0.75 miles. When you reach the dock area, head uphill to the visitor center and trailhead. For more information on the park, contact the park manager, (301) 972-9396.

NEARBY/RELATED ACTIVITIES
At any time of year, linger on the visitor center's observation deck for panoramic views of the lake. In winter, watch for bald eagles and ospreys; don't forget your binoculars. In warm weather, explore the lake by rental boat. Also explore the park's separate western portion (not covered here). Call the park manager for details.

#7
Brookland

IN BRIEF

Brookland, in Northeast Washington, is an unusual community of religious and educational institutions, residential areas, and cemeteries. It's a rewarding hiking locale for those who like to use their powers of locomotion, observation, and reflection.

DIRECTIONS

From downtown Washington, access New York Avenue (US 50) heading out of town. Soon after passing New Jersey Avenue NW, turn right onto M Street. Go 0.3 miles and turn left onto North Capitol Street. Go about 1.4 miles and turn right onto Michigan Avenue. Go 0.6 miles and then turn left onto Harewood Road and left again into the basilica parking lot (closes at 6:30 p.m.). If lot is full, park on Harewood (3-hour limit on weekdays; no limit on weekends, holidays).

Or use Metro to do hike. Take Red Line train to Brookland-CUA Metro station. Start hike there (see text). Or walk 0.5 miles to trailhead: Leave station through university-side exit on John McCormack Road, and walk across CUA campus to basilica parking lot. Contact Metro, (202) 637-7000 or www.wmata.com.

DESCRIPTION

The Brookland section of Northeast Washington is a distinctive area that feels more like a separate community than an

KEY AT-A-GLANCE INFORMATION

Length: 8 miles

Configuration: Figure eight

Difficulty: Moderate

Scenery: Edifices, campus areas, local streets, cemeteries

Exposure: Mostly open

Traffic: Usually very light to light

Trail surface: Nearly all pavement

Hiking time: 4.5–5.5 hours (by staying outside)

Access: Monastery grounds open daily, 9 a.m.–5 p.m. (except for Jan. 1, Easter Sunday, Thanksgiving and Christmas Days); Rock Creek Cemetery open daily, dawn to dusk; National Cemetery open daily, 8 a.m.–5 p.m. (7 p.m. on Memorial Day)

Map: USGS Washington East

Facilities: Toilets, water, phones, cafeteria near trailhead (inside basilica); toilets at Rock Creek Cemetery parish hall; toilets water, phones elsewhere en route, including monastery and cultural center

Special comments: Finish hike by dusk; CUA campus roadways are not named or signposted.

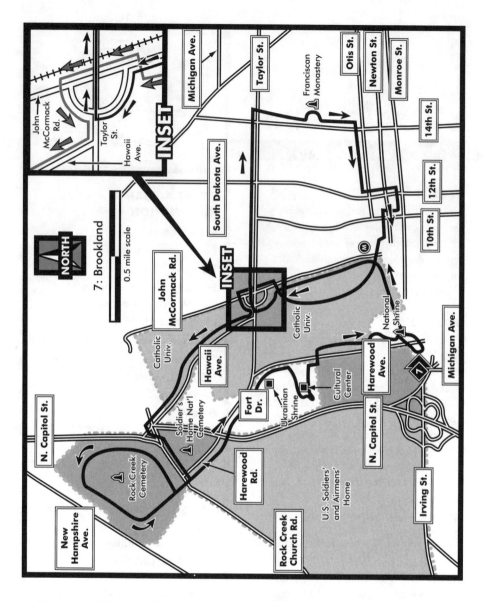

INSET

NORTH

7: Brookland

0.5 mile scale

outlying part of the nation's capital. Heavily Catholic, it's a fascinating, multi-ethnic expanse of campuses, religious institutions, residential neighborhoods, and historic cemeteries. Roaming there on foot, I've come across unusual places, friendly people, and much local pride. Brookland may be one of the city's best-kept secrets.

This hike traces an 8-mile figure eight through the community. It's fairly flat,

but hilly enough to provide about 800 feet of elevation change. And it's mostly a street outing, so you should make wise use of sidewalks, traffic lights, and your senses. En route, savor the striking exteriors—and consider re-turning another time to explore the interiors.

The hike starts at the Basilica of the National Shrine of the Immaculate Conception. The colorfully domed,

The basilica ranks as DC's second tallest masonry structure

Byzantine-style basilica ranks as the world's eighth largest church and the largest Catholic church in the Americas. Built over four decades starting in 1920, it ranks second only to the Washington Monument among the city's tallest masonry structures. Its 329-foot-high bell tower contains a 56-bell carillon and an active peregrine falcon nest.

From the basilica parking lot, cross Harewood Road and take a nearby ramp up to the basilica. Go past the entrance and head east across the Catholic University campus. Pass Gibbons Hall, then swing right onto a descending roadway. At John McCormack Road turn left, near the Brookland CUA Metro Station, onto the Metropolitan Branch Trail, here disguised as a sidewalk.

Head north, beside the Metro tracks. Just before an overpass, turn left to cross the street and go uphill on a side road to Taylor Street. There, turn right, and head east on Taylor through a residential area. Then, turn right onto 14th Street and walk uphill. Near the top, turn to visit

the Franciscan Monastery Memorial Church of the Holy.

Founded in the late 1890s, the complex is the US headquarters for Franciscan activities in the Near East, chiefly the preservation of Christian shrines. The grounds include copies of shrines and the famed Lourdes grotto, as well as flowerbeds that fill the main courtyard with color each spring.

Entering at the main gates, turn left to walk along the Rosary Portico. Follow the portico as far as you can, then step into the courtyard. Swing left to go around the front of the church, then pass through the portico on the far side to descend to the lower garden. Circle it, then head uphill on a paved path and turn right at a junction to return to the portico. Go through to the courtyard, turn left, and walk to the main gates.

Leaving, turn left and continue along 14th Street, which heads downhill. Turn right onto Otis Street, then left onto shop-lined 12th Street, and then right again onto Monroe Street. Going right once more at 10th Street, veer left to see one of Brookland's oldest surviving buildings—the Brooks Mansion. A War of 1812 veteran, Jehiel Brooks, built it in the 1840s on his country property. Originally called Bellair, it remained the family home until Brooks died in the 1880s, when the estate was replaced by subdivisions. The mansion itself was converted into a Catholic school in the 1890s, when CUA was being planned, and later served as a convent. It then lay derelict for decades until community action helped stave off the wreckers. Restored, it now houses a television cable company.

On 10th Street, turn left onto Newton Street and head for the Metro station. Cross to the station's east entrance and disappear underground at the hike's 3.2-mile mark. Follow the passageway to the west entrance and emerge to again cross John McCormack Road.

Back on the CUA campus, head uphill on the same roadway you used earlier to get to the station. Swing right around the end of Pangborn Hall, and follow a walkway north. Then turn right and go down a few steps onto another walkway leading to a grassy circle. There, turn left and proceed northward on a walkway bordering the law school, which began as an evening program for World War I veterans (as a detailed wall plaque explains).

Continuing north, turn left along a roadway, walk 20 yards, and turn right onto another roadway heading uphill. At the top, turn right onto a brown walkway and go down some steps to a diagonal concrete path that eases downhill. At the bottom, swing left and proceed on a concrete path alongside Ryan Hall and Regan Hall. Turn right onto a sidewalk leading out to John McCormack Road. Turn left and follow that road northward. But this time, go under the

overpass and turn left onto a short road leading to the far side of Taylor Street (roughly the hike's halfway mark). Turn right onto Taylor, and then right again onto Hawaii Avenue. Walk uphill to Hawaii's intersection with Alison Street and Clermont Drive.

Cross Clermont and follow Alison uphill to where it joins Rock Creek Church Road. Veer left there to follow that road uphill to its junction with Harewood Road. There, cross Rock Creek Church Road, turn left and proceed to Rock Creek Cemetery

The city's oldest cemetery (1719), it's an intriguing, 100-acre area enveloped in history. Get a map from the cemetery office and plan a perimeter circuit with side trips. You'll cover up to about 1.5 miles. Count on being surprised, as I was my first time. Some grave markers are works of art, some are bizarre, and some exude an air of mystery.

Don't miss the memorial to Marian "Clover" Adams (section E), marked by a now-famous statue created by Augustus Saint-Gaudens. As decreed by her grieving husband, writer and diplomat Henry Adams (later buried alongside her), the memorial has no inscription and the statue is nameless. But the hooded figure is often referred to as Grief, allegedly because Mark Twain said it embodies all human grief. When Twain asked Adams what it meant, Adams replied that any 12-year-old would know.

To exit, head for the cemetery gates, turn left and return to the corner of Rock Creek Church Road and Harewood Road. Cross to get onto Harewood. Head downhill and turn left to enter the US Soldiers' and Airmens' Home National Cemetery. The nation's oldest national cemetery, it dates from 1861, when the Soldiers' Home set aside 9 acres as a burial ground for Civil War soldiers. Its filling up so quickly led the government to start Arlington National Cemetery. Although expanded to 16 acres in the 1880s, it's now almost full again.

Start your 0.4-mile tour by turning left to loop clockwise through the tree-dotted cemetery of regimented rows of mostly identical white markers. Turn or stay left at each roadway junction. Near the end of the half-mile loop, detour across the grass to the left to see some of the oldest graves, although the original wooden markers were replaced with marble ones in the 1870s.

Leaving the cemetery, turn left to continue along Harewood Road, with the Soldiers' Home on your right. After crossing North Capitol Street, proceed on Fort Drive, passing Archbishop Carroll High School, named for John Carroll (the country's first Catholic bishop).

At a road fork, swing right onto another length of Harewood Road, which marks CUA's western boundary. Note the Ukrainian Catholic National Shrine of the Holy Family. Opened in 1979, it's an imposing edifice with gold domes, and best seen from the sidewalk.

Next, leave the sidewalk to circle the ultramodern Pope John Paul II Cultural Center, opened in 2001 as a museum and research center. Take the long driveway to the rear parking lot. There, climb a grassy slope to savor the view. Then descend, swing right onto the grass, and walk past the center to follow the edge of the woods to Harewood Road.

Cross the road, turn right, and continue downhill. After passing the Gilbert V. Hartke Theatre, named for the priest who ran CUA's celebrated drama program for four decades, turn left, cross a parking lot, and head up a grassy slope. At the top, turn right onto a campus roadway. Follow it to the basilica. At a sign for St. Mary's Garden, turn right onto a paved path.

At the next path junction, stay left, rather than going to the garden. Follow the path counterclockwise past the north end of the basilica and then along its west side where the path becomes a broad terrace.

At the south end, walk down the steps, turn right, and take the exit ramp to Harewood Road, where you'll be only a few careful steps across from the trailhead parking lot.

NEARBY/RELATED ACTIVITIES
Sample Brookland's other temptations: Try dining on crab cakes at the Hitching Post, (202) 726-1511, lingering in summer at Island Jim's, (202) 529-4002 (this book's only cool eatery with beaches and banana trees), or attending a performance at the Hartke Theatre, (202) 319-5367, or avant-garde Dance Place, (202) 269-1600).

#8
Bull Run–Occoquan Trail

IN BRIEF

The Bull Run–Occoquan Trail winds across the wooded hills and floodplains of southwestern Fairfax County, Virginia, providing a challenging and picturesque hike.

DIRECTIONS

Car shuttle is required. From intersection of Capital Beltway (Interstate 495) and Braddock Road (VA 620) at beltway Exit 54A in Annandale, drive west on Braddock for 1.8 miles. Turn left onto Burke Lake Road (VA 645) and go 4.8 miles. Turn left onto Ox Road (VA 123) and go 1.3 miles. Turn right onto Henderson Road (VA 643) and go 2 miles. Turn left onto Hampton Road (VA 647) and go 1.5 miles. Then turn right into Fountainhead Park and proceed 0.6 miles to car drop-off—parking lot on right. Drive to trailhead (30–40 minutes), as follows. Return 2 miles to junction of Hampton and Henderson. Turn left onto Henderson and go 6.4 miles. Turn left onto Clifton Road (VA 645) and go 2.3 miles, traversing Clifton (where road becomes Main Street). Turn left onto Compton Road (VA 658) and go 6.9 miles (passing under I-66). At "Bull Run Regional Park" sign, turn left onto Bull Run Drive and go 0.9 miles to entrance kiosk. Continue on road for 1.6 miles. Then turn left into parking lot for swimming pool and mini-Frisbee course.

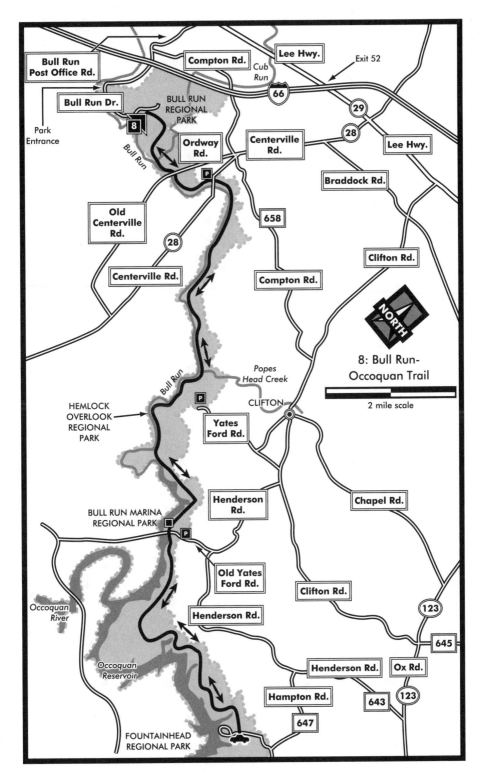

Bull Run
Post Office Rd.

Compton Rd.

Lee Hwy.

Exit 52

Cub
Run

66

29

Bull Run Dr.

BULL RUN
REGIONAL
PARK

8

28

Park
Entrance

Bull Run

Ordway
Rd.

Centerville
Rd.

28

Lee Hwy.

Braddock Rd.

Old
Centerville
Rd.

28

658

Clifton Rd.

Centerville Rd.

Compton Rd.

NORTH

8: Bull Run-
Occoquan Trail

2 mile scale

Bull Run

Popes
Head Creek

CLIFTON

HEMLOCK
OVERLOOK
REGIONAL
PARK

Yates
Ford Rd.

Henderson
Rd.

Chapel Rd.

BULL RUN MARINA
REGIONAL PARK

Old Yates
Ford Rd.

Clifton Rd.

123

Occoquan
River

Henderson Rd.

645

Occoquan
Reservoir

Henderson Rd.

Ox Rd.

123

Hampton Rd.

643

123

647

FOUNTAINHEAD
REGIONAL PARK

DESCRIPTION

For a very scenic, long, and rigorous hike within an hour's drive of Washington, try this one-way trek on the Bull Run–Occoquan Trail. Located about 25 miles southwest of the city, BROT is the only nearby, lightly used trail on which you can hike in roughly the same direction for 18 miles in a rural setting.

The trail follows the valley carrying Bull Run and the Occoquan River to the Potomac River. It winds through wooded hills and floodplains, and is marked by a rich assortment of flora and fauna, including large stands of hemlocks and springtime bluebells.

Before setting out, check by phone on trail conditions. Be prepared to turn back if you encounter flooding. Also be prepared for about 3,400 feet of elevation change. Plan to follow BROT's blue blazes (it's also called the Blue Trail) and its double-sided mileposts giving distances from each end.

To get started from the parking-lot trailhead at Bull Run Regional Park, walk to the entrance road, turn left, and hike along the shoulder toward the warm-season camp store for about 150 yards. Watch and head for a sign on the right marking the BROT. Then cross a small arched bridge onto the blue-blazed trail. The trail curves across a broad and often soggy floodplain under an open tree canopy. On reaching Cub Run, swing right to follow it downstream for over half a mile. In April the surrounding area is covered by millions of blooming Virginia bluebells. This bluebell stand is said to be one of the largest in the eastern United States.

Continuing, you'll reach Cub Run's mouth on Bull Run and a T-junction. Turn left to stay on BROT and, a mile into the hike, take the bridge across Cub Run. With Bull Run on your right, head downstream. Within the next mile, you'll pass beneath a couple of bridges spanning Bull Run and then be on a hilly woodland trail.

After passing beneath a railroad bridge and through a rocky section (watch for the stone foundations of a bridge destroyed in the Civil War), you'll reach the mouth of Popes Head Creek, a major Bull Run tributary. That's about 6.5 miles into the hike. Follow the blue blazes as the trail crosses the steep-banked creek on concrete pillars.

Then, step into Hemlock Overlook Regional Park. For half a mile, the trail goes between Bull Run and a magnificent stand of eastern hemlocks lining the bluff. Continuing, traverse a picturesque woodland clearing and then pass the ruins of a nineteenth-century hydroelectric power plant.

For the next mile, stay close to Bull Run as BROT follows the meandering stream across the floodplain. But then the trail parts company with the stream to swing to the left and uphill into the woods. Be sure to stay with the blue blazes as BROT jogs up and down for a mile on dirt paths and old roads as it passes through the wooded hills.

Follow the blazes out into the open and along the edge of several fields. After passing a Bull Run inlet and stepping across a bridged creek, you'll reach milepost 10/8 and see a broad expanse of playing fields ahead of you.

Head for a blazed post 45 degrees to your right. Then follow more posts—and the marked sidelines—straight across the fields. Turn left at a post topped by an owl, pass two white sideline shelters, and get onto a gravel road, keeping the wooden fence to your left. Near a parking lot, turn right and cross a little creek by bridge. Follow the blazes along the edge of a small playing field and then slide under the tree canopy on a dirt trail.

The hiker's way across the mouth of Pope's Head Creek is set in concrete.

Back in the woods with the comforting blue blazes, watch for a sharp turn to the left and uphill. Pass through Bull Run Marina Regional Park's grand stand of mature hemlocks. Then, getting back close to Bull Run, follow the blue blazes to reach the marina, which has a warm-season snack bar.

From the marina, follow the entrance road out to heavily traveled Old Yates Ford Road (it's the only road spanning the waterway in over 20 miles). Cross carefully to pick up the trail, which jogs to the right and heads downhill. Then turn left to follow it along Bull Run, which is now part of a huge reservoir.

Stay close to the reservoir for almost half a mile, then follow the blue blazes back into the wooded hills, where you'll zigzag on a mix of dirt trails and old roads for the hike's remaining 6 miles. You'll go up and down a lot, cross several small creeks, and catch a few glimpses of the Occoquan Reservoir.

At milepost 18/0, you'll emerge from the woods at the car-drop-off. If you're tempted, turn right and walk 0.4 miles to the marina building, where the observation deck provides nice reservoir views.

NEARBY/RELATED ACTIVITIES

Return to Bull Run Regional Park in April to see the Virginia bluebells in bloom. Take your own walk and time, or go on the annual, ranger-led Bluebell Walk. Call the park for details.

Visit the Manassas Industrial School/Jennie Dean Memorial in nearby Manassas. A landscaped 5-acre urban oasis, the memorial commemorates northern Virginia's first African-American school and its founder, a remarkable woman, born a slave, who opened it as a private boarding school in 1894. Contact the Manassas Museum, (703) 368-1873.

Between mid-May and early June, visit the old-rose garden at Ben Lomond Manor House, in Manassas, to experience the vivid colors and fragrances of 200 kinds of rose from the pre-hybrid-tea-rose era. For information and directions, call (703) 368-8784.

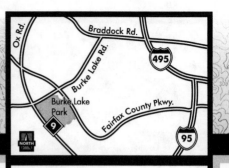

#9
Burke Lake Park

IN BRIEF

Burke Lake Park is a multi-use suburban recreation area in south-central Fairfax County, Virginia. It's an agreeable setting for a brisk and hill-free lakeside hike.

DIRECTIONS

From intersection of Capital Beltway (Interstate 495) and Braddock Road (VA 620) at beltway Exit 54A in Annandale, drive west on Braddock for 1.8 miles. Turn left onto Burke Lake Road (VA 645) and proceed for 4.8 miles. Turn left onto Ox Road (VA 123), go 0.6 miles, and turn left into park's main entrance. Drive roughly 0.3 miles to marina parking area. Go early on warm-weather weekends and holidays; if parking area is full, return to Ox Road, turn left, go several hundred yards, and turn left into a little-used parking lot. Make that your alternative trailhead.

DESCRIPTION

Located some 20 miles southwest of Washington, Burke Lake Park consists of a 220-acre man-made lake enveloped by almost 700 acres of woodlands. It's popular, especially on warm-weather weekends and holidays, for its family-oriented attractions, such as camping and picnic areas, miniature railroad, marina, and fish-inhabited lake. Hikers can appreciate that campsites are laid out spaciously, mostly screened by trees, and limited to the entrance side of the park.

KEY AT-A-GLANCE INFORMATION

Length: 5.1 miles

Configuration: Loop

Difficulty: Easy

Scenery: Woodlands, lake glimpses

Exposure: Mostly shady; less so in winter

Traffic: Usually light to moderate; heavier in marina area on warm-weather evenings, weekends, holidays

Trail surface: Mostly fine gravel; some dirt, sand

Hiking time: 2–2.5 hours

Access: Open daily, sunrise to sunset; entrance fee for nonresidents of Fairfax County on warm-weather weekends, holidays

Map: USGS Fairfax

Facilities: Toilets, water, phones at marina; toilets off trail at campground, picnic area

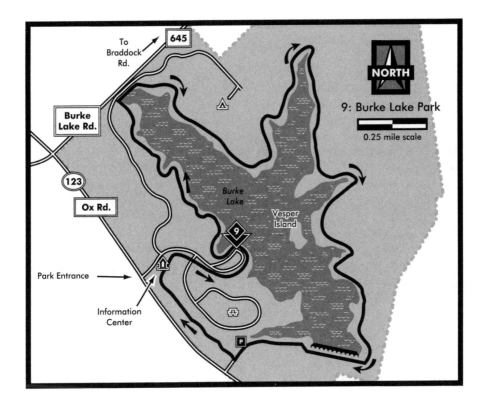

To
Braddock
Rd.

645

Burke
Lake Rd.

123

Ox Rd.

Burke
Lake

Vesper
Island

9: Burke Lake Park

0.25 mile scale

Park Entrance →

Information
Center

Remarkably, much of the 40-year-old, county-managed park remains undeveloped and unvisited. Its main path primarily follows the lakeshore, so that hikers encounter few other people, except for some local cyclists, joggers, and strollers.

This hike is a 5.1-mile clockwise loop consisting of most of the lakeshore path followed by a brief detour. You'll spend most of your trail time in the woods, surrounded by young oaks and other deciduous trees, as well as a scattering of conifers. In the warm-season months, expect to have wildflowers and birds for company (the island in the lake is a state waterfowl refuge).

To get started from the trailhead parking area, walk to the boat launching area, just to the left of the marina. Then turn left and left again onto a sandy trail that bears right and leads onto the main path rimming the lake.

The path is well maintained, level, broad, and surfaced with fine gravel or dirt. Watch for half-mile posts—green plaques on redwood-colored posts—showing cumulative mileage (going clockwise) from the parking area. Ignore other numbered posts.

Once past the 0.5-mile marker and nearby Burke Lake Road, you'll be free of traffic noise until near the end of the hike. Bear or stay right at trail junctions. Keep close to the shoreline (usually less than 30 yards from the trail), and don't wander off the trail into the poison ivy.

When you pass the 2.5-mile marker, you'll be just over halfway through the hike. Shortly thereafter, watch for a spot with good lake views. After that, the trail veers deeper into the woods. Roughly a mile later, it emerges into the open and crosses the broad-topped impoundment dam.

Beyond the dam is a shady paved path that follows the high bank of an inlet. Note several stubby paved piers jutting waterward. They're fishing platforms for anglers in wheelchairs, and the paved path links them to a nearby parking lot (also an alternative trailhead; see Directions).

Then start a final-mile detour. Leave the main trail and follow the parking-lot access road gently uphill for about 200 yards. Turn right onto a narrow dirt trail marked with a horseshoe sign, indicating that it's also an equestrian trail.

Follow the little-used trail through the scrubby woods, then emerge and turn right to follow the edge of the woods downhill alongside a playing field. Watch out for flying objects on the Frisbee golf course just before you reach a paved road. Turn right onto the road, stay on the shoulder, and continue to the marina parking area.

For more information on the park, contact the Fairfax County Park Authority, (703) 324-8700 or www.co. fairfax.va.us/parks.

NEARBY/RELATED ACTIVITIES

If you're still feeling frisky after the hike, take a rental rowboat out on the water, especially in the fall. Out there one fall afternoon, I was transfixed by formations of Canada geese honking their way across a crimson cloud-streaked sky. That still ranks as my best time on the water in the metro area.

#10
C&O Canal Towpath: Carderock to Great Falls

IN BRIEF

The C&O Canal towpath provides hikers with scenery, exercise, and glimpses of history—and is on the level. This close-in segment in Maryland features great falls, wide water, a canal boat, a museum, and spectacular cliff trails.

DIRECTIONS

Starting from American Legion (or Cabin John) Bridge on Capital Beltway (Interstate 495), proceed north on beltway for about 100 yards and exit at Exit 41. Bear left at small "Carderock" sign onto Clara Barton Parkway heading west. Go 0.9 miles to first parkway exit. Ascend short ramp, turn left at stop sign, and cross over parkway. Follow road as it swings right into Carderock Recreation Area and then swings left and goes through underpass. Go right at T-junction. Then take first left into parking lot, 0.4 miles from parkway.

DESCRIPTION

From 1850 to 1924, the 185-mile Chesapeake and Ohio Canal carried boat traffic between Washington, DC, and Cumberland, Maryland. Mule teams plodding along a towpath powered the boats. The US government acquired the flood-devastated and abandoned property in the 1930s, and made it a national historical park in 1971.

Today, the park, which preserves the left bank of the Potomac River, is a prime metro-area recreation resource.

KEY AT-A-GLANCE INFORMATION

Length: 11.7 miles

Configuration: Modified out-and-back

Difficulty: Moderate

Scenery: River/canal views, woodlands

Exposure: Mostly open

Traffic: Usually light; heavier on warm-weather evenings, weekends, holidays, especially on Billy Goat Trail and around Great Falls

Trail surface: Hard-packed dirt on towpath, with rocks, grass, sand, pebbles, mud in places; dirt, rocks, roots on Billy Goat Trail—dangerous when wet, icy

Hiking time: 7.5–9 hours

Access: Open daily, dawn to dusk

Maps: USGS Falls Church, PATC Map D

Facilities: Toilets, water, phone at trailhead, off-trail at Great Falls (plus warm-season snack bar); water at Lock 10; off-trail toilets, phone at Cropley

Special comments: For more information on the park/hike, visit or call NPS's Great Falls visitor center, (301) 299-3613, or call the park's headquarters office in Sharpsburg, (301) 739-4200

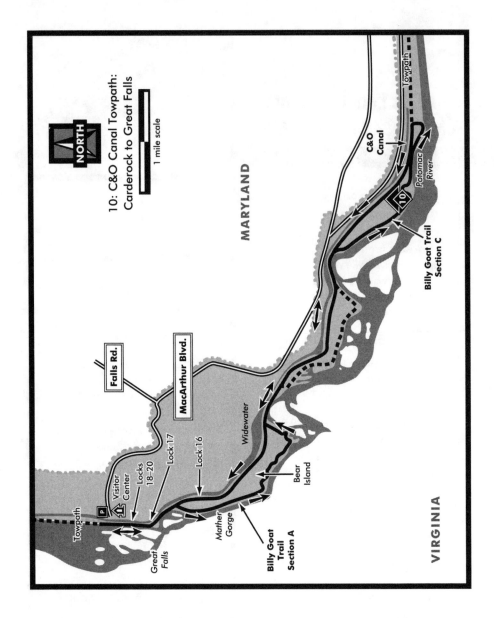

10: C&O Canal Towpath: Carderock to Great Falls

NORTH

1 mile scale

MARYLAND

VIRGINIA

Falls Rd.

MacArthur Blvd.

C&O Canal

Potomac River

Towpath

10

Billy Goat Trail Section C

Widewater

Bear Island

Visitor Center

Locks 18–20

Lock 17

Lock 16

Mather Gorge

Billy Goat Trail Section A

Towpath

Great Falls

The restored towpath is a multi-use trail, and its lower 22 miles border a rebuilt and scenic canal section.

This 11.7-mile, modified out-and-back hike starts with 4 miles along the canal just outside the beltway. The return leg features four detours, including a close look at thundering Great Falls and two sections of the rugged Billy Goat Trail.

From the parking-lot trailhead at Carderock, cross a grassy strip, then cross a nearby road. Follow a woodland trail (marked by a notice to cyclists) about 150 yards to reach the towpath. Turn left and head northwest, keeping the water-filled canal on your right.

Half a mile along the broad and level towpath, pass milepost 11 (the path is studded with mileposts, starting in

Washington). Pressing on upstream, reach the Cropley area, about a third of a mile past milepost 12. A footbridge there provides access to MacArthur Boulevard.

Continuing up the towpath, pass a mile-long lake flanked by rocky cliffs and woodlands. On a waterway averaging less than 6 yards in width, this stretch, up to 200 yards wide, is aptly known as Widewater.

The adjoining towpath is narrow and rocky. Near the end of Widewater, it becomes a jumbled line of rocks that serve as stepping stones across a shallow channel prone to flooding. If the water level is too high, go back to the other end of Widewater. There you'll find an alternative route called the Berma Road. It rejoins the towpath upstream near Lock 16.

After the stepping stones, pick your way across bedrock along the water's edge. Watch for an alternative, dirt-surfaced trail to the left; it has some rocks and roots, but is easier going. After that, head down a short wooden walkway onto the usual dirt-surfaced towpath.

Lock 15 begins the mile-long Six Locks area that ends at Great Falls. Originally built around 1830 of red sandstone quarried upstream at Seneca, the locks have been much rebuilt and repaired.

Just past Lock 16, where there's also a surviving 1830s lock house, is a curious canal-straddling structure. It's a reconstructed stop gate, designed to divert floodwater out of the canal. The walkway atop the gate leads to the Widewater detour, a half-mile stretch of towpath with great views of the rapids-filled side channels. The main falls, on the far side of Olmstead Island, are not visible, but the signposted walkway leading to an overlook is.

Between Locks 18 and 20, is the Canal Clipper. During the warm-weath-

er season, it gives visitors a taste of canal travel, with the help of rangers in period costume and a pair of mules. At Lock 20, which is the hike's 4-mile mark, step across a short wooden bridge spanning the canal to reach Great Falls Tavern. For much of the canal's lifetime, the building served as a lock house, hotel, or both. It now serves as a visitor center, and includes museum exhibits.

Head back down the towpath. Your first detour is down to the Great Falls Overlook and back. Located on a quarter-mile-long walkway the detour crosses narrow gorges often choked with flood debris, if not filled with roaring torrents. At the spray-flecked mid-river overlook, discover just how great the falls are—not so much from their height as from the awesome sense of brute force.

Continue down the towpath. At Lock 17, embark on your second detour by turning right onto a side trail that pitches steeply downhill. Two wooden steps from the bottom, take a narrow dirt trail to the right and clamber about 50 yards up to a rocky knoll that provides a splendid view down a narrow gorge.

Return to the narrow trail, turn right, and follow the undulating trail a couple of hundred yards to a lovely, off-the-beaten-trail spot featuring a rock-rimmed pool, a sand-and-shell beach, and—if it's off-season or a weekday—utter tranquility. Leaving the beach, stay to the right and take a narrow trail leading uphill. Turn right when you reach a retaining wall, and follow it until you find the low place where you can easily climb up and over. Turn right onto the towpath.

Just before reaching the stop gate, turn right at the sign for the blue-blazed Billy Goat Trail. The sign doesn't say so, but it's the trail's section A and your third detour. For most of its roughly 2 miles, section A follows the perimeter of Bear Island. It includes a rocky clifftop route along the Potomac's narrow, mile-long Mather Gorge.

The blue blazes lead through a wild and beautiful landscape dominated by steep rock and scraggy vegetation. Wend your way around huge boulders, over smaller ones, and past huge potholes and rockbound ponds (some with water lilies). After several chances to see the river below, perhaps you'll also gaze into the abyss to see if it gazes back. Eventually, after the trail curves left again, you'll reach the towpath, near the southern end of Widewater.

Continuing downstream on the towpath, ignore the various Billy Goat Trail signs (I prefer to skip section B) until you pass milepost 11. Then watch for a sign that puts you on the Billy Goat Trail's section C, your final detour, at the "West End." Section C takes you on a scenic 1.7-mile wood-land trek along the edge of a side channel and then the now-broad main channel. It has its ups and downs, but it's a lot easier than section A. Follow the blue blazes.

Eventually, the towpath appears again at the "East End," near the ruins of a swing bridge built in 1941. From there, head upstream for half a mile, passing milepost 10. Then, soon after crossing an overpass, turn left onto the inconspicuous woodland path, which began the hike, and return to the trailhead.

One way to shorten this hike is to omit detours. Rough estimates: omit section A to save almost 1 mile and 2 hours; omit section C to save almost 2 miles and 1.25 hours; omit the overlook to save 0.5 miles and 0.75 hours; and omit the rock pool detour to save 0.1 miles and 0.5 hours.

NEARBY/RELATED ACTIVITIES

Do the C&O Canal Association's spring-time Justice Douglas Annual Hike (the association started as a small group formed by Douglas on his 1954 save-the-canal hike). Contact the association, (301) 983-0825.

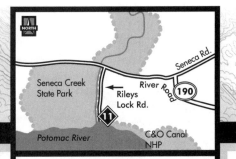

#11
C&O Canal Towpath: Rileys Lock to Swains Lock

IN BRIEF

This scenic C&O Canal towpath outing in Maryland features woodlands and wildflowers, a water-filled canal, an aqueduct, locks, and lock houses.

DIRECTIONS

Starting from American Legion (or Cabin John) Bridge, drive north on Capital Beltway (Interstate 495) for about 1.8 miles. Get off at Exit 39A and take the 0.7-mile exit ramp onto River Road (MD 190) heading west. Proceed for about 11.6 miles toward and through Potomac to reach stop sign where MD 190 ends. Then turn left to continue west on River Road for 0.7 miles, and turn left onto Rileys Lock Road. Go 0.7 miles to end of road at Rileys Lock parking lot.

DESCRIPTION

This 13.2-mile out-and-back hike in Montgomery County will acquaint you with the loveliest stretch of the C&O Canal towpath south of Monocacy.

The towpath stretch lies between Rileys Lock, 0.2 miles below milepost 23, and Swains Lock, 0.4 miles below milepost 17. The hike starts at Rileys. I like the novelty of doing the downriver part first. Also, Rileys has ample parking, but Swains's small lot can fill up quickly. Strangely, the towpath in between is almost always uncrowded.

Before or after the hike, explore the trailhead area, commonly called Seneca.

KEY AT-A-GLANCE INFORMATION

Length: 13.2 miles

Configuration: Out-and-back

Difficulty: Easy/moderate

Scenery: Woodlands, river/canal views

Exposure: Mostly open

Traffic: Light to moderate; heavier near trailhead, Swains Lock on warm-weather weekends, holidays

Trail surface: Chiefly hard-packed dirt or pebbly dirt; some grassy, sandy patches; muddy when wet

Hiking time: 5–6.5 hours

Access: Open daily, dawn to dusk

Maps: USGS Seneca, Vienna

Facilities: Toilets, water, phone at trailhead; toilets at Violettes Lock, Pennyfield Lock; toilets, water, phone, warm-season snack bar at Swains Lock

Special comments: For more information on the canal and hike route, contact the Great Falls visitor center (301) 299-3613, or the C&O Canal National Historical Park headquarters office in Sharpsburg, (301) 739-4200 or www.nps.gov/choh.

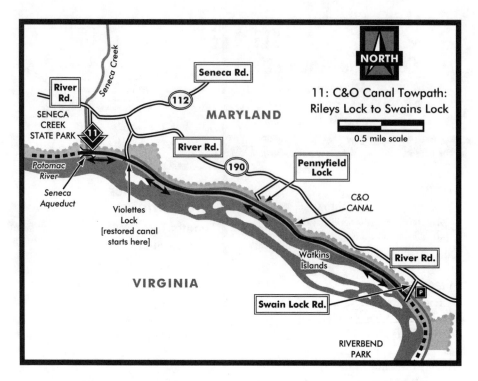

Seneca Creek

River Rd.

Seneca Rd.

112

MARYLAND

SENECA
CREEK
STATE PARK

11

River Rd.

190

Pennyfield
Lock

11: C&O Canal Towpath:
Rileys Lock to Swains Lock

0.5 mile scale

Potomac
River

Seneca
Aqueduct

Violettes
Lock
[restored canal
starts here]

C&O
CANAL

VIRGINIA

Watkins
Islands

River Rd.

Swain Lock Rd.

P

RIVERBEND
PARK

Adjoining Rileys Lock (Lock 24) is Seneca Aqueduct, a 126-foot-long structure that carried the canal across the mouth of Seneca Creek. Completed in 1833 as a single unit, the lock and aqueduct were built of red Seneca sandstone from nearby quarries. Next to the lock is the restored lock house once occupied by lockkeeper Riley and his family.

Originally, the aqueduct had three arches, but now has only two, thanks to a savage 1972 flood. For good views across the Potomac, walk over to the nearby flared wing wall of the aqueduct. Also note the stone pillar etched with a short line and a date. The line marks the height reached by floodwaters on June 2, 1889, the canal's second-to-last ruinous flood.

To get started, step onto the towpath, turn left, and head downriver. The woodland path is next to a dry and overgrown canal—but only for about three-quarters of a mile. After that, the scenery

changes to an open area close to the river dominated by two restored locks. Violettes Lock (Lock 23), on the left, was a regular move-the-boats-through lock. Look closely at the top of the downstream wing wall on the towpath side to see the grooves worn by straining towropes. The other lock, linked to the river, supplied the canal with water and enabled boats to enter and leave the canal.

Beyond the locks, follow a restored and water-filled canal under an open sky. About half a mile beyond milepost 22, is an area that is lovely, if not gorgeous. The canal winds along the foot of a line of cliffs, and the towpath faithfully follows its curves. In places, the canal and river are scarcely 30 feet apart. At milepost 21, turn right to start the first of four short and scenic off-the-beaten-trail detours. It's an out-and-back dirt side trail, leading about 150 yards to the river and a cluster of huge red maples.

The Seneca Aqueduct

Over the next 1.5 miles, the cliff walls subside into hilly woodlands as the canal pulls away from the river. After that is Pennyfield Lock (Lock 22), with its towrope-grooved wing wall.

The side trail adjoining the lock house is the start of detour no. 2. Follow the dirt trail to the water, turn left, and walk along the wooded shore. At a small clearing containing a large maple festooned with poison ivy, turn left. Then take a 10-yard trail to reach the towpath.

Back on the towpath, find yourself once more in a picturesque setting of cliffs rising above the canal and towpath, plus a low stone wall along the river's edge. You'll have a mile of this scenery, passing milepost 19 on the way.

Then, about half a mile beyond milepost 18 and just after passing under a concrete bridge, take a short passageway to your right—detour no. 3. Walk out onto an overlook atop a concrete water-intake structure for a view of the undiverted river tumbling through a narrow channel hemmed in by Watkins Island.

Three-quarters of a mile more down the towpath, past milepost 17, is Swains Lock, with its signature towrope grooves. A wooden bridge spans the lock. On the far side is the original lock house, now home to Fred Swain. His father lived there, as did his grandfather, who was the lockkeeper from 1907 until the canal closed in 1924. Fred Swain runs the canoe-and-bicycle concession, as well as the snack bar.

When you're ready, head back to Rileys. On the way, watch for milepost 20, and turn left there for detour no. 4. A short dirt-and-grass side trail leads about 200 yards to a riverbank wildlife sanctuary. In the summer and fall, the trail is a sea of yellow as it passes through a large patch of wingstem.

NEARBY/RELATED ACTIVITIES
Tour the lock house at Rileys. Tours are offered on weekend afternoons, March to November, by Girl Scouts in period costume.

#12
C&O Canal Towpath: Edwards Ferry to Whites Ferry

IN BRIEF

This all-Maryland C&O Canal towpath hike has few vistas or points of specific interest. But it gives hikers a chance to trek serenely along a lightly used trail.

DIRECTIONS

Starting from American Legion (or Cabin John) Bridge, drive north on Capital Beltway (Interstate 495) for about 1.8 miles. Get off at Exit 39A and take 0.7-mile exit ramp onto River Road (MD 190) heading west. Proceed for about 11.6 miles toward and through Potomac to reach stop sign where MD 190 ends. Then turn left to continue west on River Road for about 4.5 miles to where it passes West Willard Road. Proceed for 4.1 miles on narrow and partly unpaved River Road (although in places it seems to become Mount Nebo Road and then West Offut Road). Turn left onto paved Edwards Ferry Road and proceed for about 1 mile. Where road forks, turn left and drive about 200 yards to Edwards Ferry parking lot.

DESCRIPTION

This hike follows a large and shallow bend made by the Potomac River in a part of western Montgomery County where farmlands rather than subdivisions predominate. It's a 9.4-mile out-and-back hike on the milepost-dotted, ever-so-flat towpath between Edwards Ferry and Whites Ferry. For company, you'll

KEY AT-A-GLANCE INFORMATION

Length: 9.4 miles

Configuration: Out-and-back

Difficulty: Easy/moderate

Scenery: Woodlands, some river views, glimpses of farmlands

Exposure: Mostly shady, less so in winter

Traffic: Generally light; heavier in spring, when cyclists, birders emerge on evenings, weekends, holidays

Trail surface: Mostly hard-packed dirt; pebbly, grassy, muddy, rutted in places

Hiking time: 3.5–4.5 hours

Access: Open daily, dawn to dusk

Map: USGS Waterford

Facilities: None at trailhead (but toilet 0.3 miles downriver); toilet, water (if pump works) at upriver camping area; toilets, phones, warm-season store, snack bar at Whites Ferry

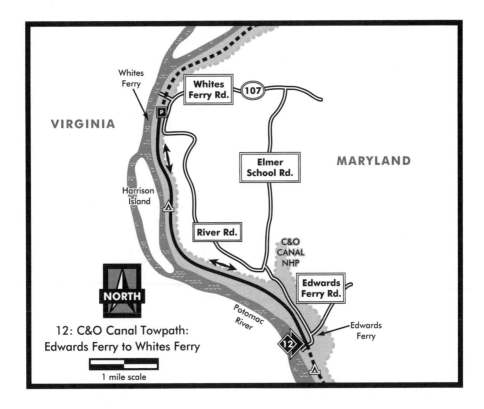

VIRGINIA

Whites Ferry

Whites Ferry Rd.

107

P

Harrison Island

MARYLAND

Elmer School Rd.

River Rd.

C&O CANAL NHP

Edwards Ferry Rd.

NORTH

12: C&O Canal Towpath:
Edwards Ferry to Whites Ferry

1 mile scale

Potomac River

12

Edwards Ferry

have the mostly-out-of-sight Potomac, the crumbling and overgrown remains of the C&O Canal bed, and woodlands galore. Keep in mind that there wasn't a single tree on the canal's towpath when the waterway was in operation.

Take a look around at Edwards Ferry before loping off up the towpath. The boat ramp at the end of the parking lot was the site of the dock from which a ferry service operated between the 1790s and the 1830s. Previously a fording place, it became one again after ferry service ceased. The ford saw military use during the Civil War, although Union forces built and used a pontoon bridge there during the Gettysburg campaign.

Union forces also took to the skies at Edwards Ferry during the war. Over several months in 1861–62, two manned balloons of the US Balloon Corps observed Confederate positions across

the river in Loudoun County. Tethered to the ground, the balloon observers used telegraph wires to send messages down to the ground.

At the towpath end of the parking lot are the remains of Lock 25, dating from the 1830s. Nearby is a brick lock house of the same vintage, boarded up but in good condition. The crumbling and overgrown brick shell is what's left of a large general store called Jarboe's.

While in the Edwards Ferry area in the spring, watch and listen for warblers and other migratory birds—and birders. It's one of the best birding spots along the towpath. Also watch for flocks of blue phlox along the towpath, and listen to the wind sighing through the sycamores.

To start the hike, step onto the towpath and head upstream, keeping the river on your left while passing milepost 31 after

0.2 miles. About 3.5 miles farther on, lies a small riverside camping area abreast of Harrison Island, one of the largest islands anywhere in the Potomac. It's worth tramping through the camping area to the water's edge, an off-the-beaten-trail spot with a good view.

Back on the towpath, you'll have scenery changes the last mile and a half leading into Whites Ferry. On the right, watch through the trees for acres of greensward, a reminder that these farmlands are the turf of the business people who help keep the metro area green. On the left, small cabins on stilts begin to appear, signs of a private "sportsman's club" in an area where the river floods.

Approaching Whites Ferry, half a mile beyond milepost 35, notice a pair of stone abutments supporting a skeletal iron structure. They're remnants of an 1870s bridge across the canal. They are also a reminder that crossing the canal in the old days was probably just as important as getting across the river. Nearby is a reminder of the canal's own importance—the overgrown remains of a huge granary. Canal boats would tie up there to take on chute-delivered local grain. Now the canal bed is a neatly mowed lawn area.

Walk a short distance along the road (staying on the shoulder) and toward the river to get to Whites Ferry and the ferryboat. There's been ferry service at this spot since well before the Civil War, when it was known as Conrads Ferry. It's now the last of the hundred or so regular ferry operations that once existed along the Potomac. Without a bridge across the 40-mile stretch of the Potomac between the American Legion Bridge and Point of Rocks, it's also an active enterprise. Sometimes on summer weekends, long lines of vehicles wait on both sides of the river. No wonder that metro area politicians are now debating the merits of an additional Potomac bridge. Check out the store and snack bar (if they're open), and then start back for Edwards Ferry.

Consider either shortening your hike by turning around before Whites Ferry, or lengthening it by going farther upriver. In either case, use the mileposts to gauge your distance and stamina.

For more information on the canal and towpath, contact the National Park Service's Great Falls visitor center, (301) 299-3613, or the C&O Canal National Historical Park headquarters office in Sharpsburg, (301) 739-4200 or www.nps.gov/choh.

NEARBY/RELATED ACTIVITIES

At Whites Ferry, take a short break from hiking by taking the ferry. The General Jubal A. Early, which runs back and forth on a tethered cable, takes just 3 to 4 minutes to reach Virginia, and always has room for pedestrians willing to pay the 50-cent fare. Take a longer break (or return by car) and rent a canoe or rowboat at the store. The river is usually smooth and tranquil in the Whites Ferry area.

#13
C&O Canal Towpath:
Monocacy River Aqueduct
to Calico Rocks

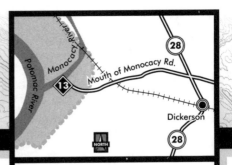

IN BRIEF

On the outermost of this book's C&O Canal hikes, there's more scenery and less trail traffic. After crossing a massive stone aqueduct, hikers can savor the pleasures of a riverside trek in rural Maryland.

DIRECTIONS

From junction of Capital Beltway (Interstate 495) and I-270, head northwest on I-270 for about 6 miles. Get off at Exit 6B in Rockville onto MD 28 heading generally northwest. Stay on MD 28 for about 30 miles as it undergoes several name changes. About 0.4 miles past Dickerson (still on MD 28), turn left onto Mouth of Monocacy Road. Go 1.3 miles to parking lot at end, turning left at fork en route.

DESCRIPTION

This 10.8-mile towpath hike in southern Frederick County follows the gloriously unspoiled Potomac River upriver from a point a couple of hundred yards past milepost 42 to half a mile beyond milepost 47—and back. It also follows the C&O Canal, of course, but in this area the old waterway is just a dry and overgrown trough.

The hike route is rich in woodlands year-round. It displays tree leaves and wildflowers galore during the warm-weather months and plays host to migratory birds in spring and fall.

KEY AT-A-GLANCE INFORMATION

Length: 10.8 miles

Configuration: Out-and-back

Difficulty: Easy/moderate

Scenery: Woodlands, river views

Exposure: Mostly shady; less so in winter

Traffic: Very light; slightly heavier on warm-weather weekends, holidays in trailhead, Nolands Ferry areas

Trail surface: Chiefly hard-packed dirt (muddy when wet); 560 feet of stone

Hiking time: 3.5–5 hours

Access: Open daily, dawn to dusk

Maps: USGS Poolesville, Point of Rocks

Facilities: Toilet at trailhead; toilets, water at pumps (if working) at Indian Flats, Nolands Ferry, Calico Rocks

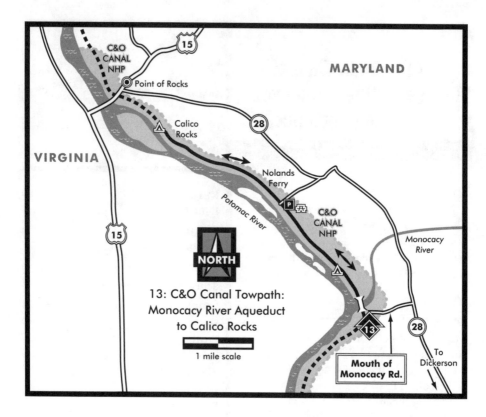

13: C&O Canal Towpath: Monocacy River Aqueduct to Calico Rocks

Its winter glory consists of almost constant views of the river, plus towering sycamores with their stark white upper trunks and branches. What's delightfully lacking year-round is a lot of human foot traffic. At times in the fall, I've encountered more deer than people.

At the trailhead, the most conspicuous sight is the huge aqueduct that carried the canal and its towpath across the Monocacy River. Built of locally quarried pinkish quartzite, the 560-foot-long aqueduct was an engineering marvel when completed in 1833. It's still impressive, even though it's been battered by Confederates (who tried to demolish it), storms, and age; it's now held together by metal supports.

To start the hike, step onto the towpath, turn right, and head for the aqueduct, with the Potomac on your left.

Crossing the aqueduct, be careful not to trip over the wooden covers covering the steel bindings. Halfway across, pause to take in the views up and down the Monocacy. Downstream it joins the Potomac. Upstream you may see a shallow waterway disappear into the woods, and some of the people who like to canoe and fish there. On the aqueduct itself, look for a faded stone plaque listing the contractors.

Stepping off the structure onto the familiar dirt-surfaced towpath, head into the woods and upriver. Pass the Indian Flats camping area (an old fording place) and then milepost 43. Another mile or so along the towpath and you'll find more river views and fewer trees, along with (if it isn't winter) myriad wildflowers in the canal bed. Then you'll get to Nolands Ferry, with its large picnic area and parking lot served by an access road that crosses the canal bed.

Like other Potomac riverbank locations surnamed "Ferry," Nolands had a long history as a crossing place. The ford there was used as part of a traditional Native American pathway between what came to be Maryland and the Carolinas—a route later adopted by colonists. Ferry service was started in the 1750s, and a small trading settlement developed. However, the building of the C&O Canal and of a bridge across the Potomac at Point of Rocks, a few miles upstream, led to the isolation and decline of Nolands. A bridge across the canal there in the 1850s proved economically futile. Today, all you'll see of the old community are the bridge's stone abutments on each side of the canal. Just beyond those relics, watch for what looks like an old stone house on the riverbank. It's actually a water intake that sends river water by pipeline to local communities.

Beyond milepost 46, you'll be on one of the most scenic stretches of the hike. There it's tempting to linger and watch the play of sunlight on the nearby river set against the looming backdrop framed by Catoctin Mountain. And if the season is right, the old canal to the right will look less like a canal bed than a wildflower garden. Near milepost 47, the color scheme is enhanced by multihued rock outcroppings along the canal's far side. The rock is variously referred to as Potomac marble, calico marble, or Potomac breccia. It's actually a conglomerate, or pudding stone, consisting of multicolored pebbles embedded in a limestone matrix. It looks its colorful best just after a light rain.

About half a mile beyond milepost 47 is the hike's halfway mark (5.4 miles) and your turnaround spot, the Calico Rocks camping area. There, on the outskirts of Point of Rocks, walk down to the riverbank and linger awhile. Then head back to Monocacy. Hiking downriver, perhaps, you'll notice things you hadn't been aware of before.

Consider shortening your hike by turning around sooner. Alternatively, lengthen it to include the little community of Point of Rocks, with its ugly but essential bridge. Use the mileposts to gauge your distance and stamina.

For more information on the park and towpath, visit or call NPS's Great Falls visitor center, (301) 299-3613, or contact the park's headquarters office in Sharpsburg, (301) 739-4200 or www.nps.gov/choh.

NEARBY/RELATED ACTIVITIES

On driving back from Monocacy in the warm-weather season, stop at Staub's Country Inn for an unusually good milk shake—made with fresh fruit instead of the usual flavored syrup. Reaching Beallsville on MD 28, turn right onto MD 109, and then immediately right again into Staub's parking lot. Head for the serving window on the side.

Continuing east on MD 28, stop at one of the roadside farms to buy or pick fruit and vegetables. Or, about 6 miles beyond Staub's, turn sharply right onto Whites Ferry Road (MD 107) and follow the signs to Homestead Farm, (301) 977-3761, a family-run farm with an unusually large variety of fruit, including gooseberries.

#14
C&O Canal Towpath: Washington to Sandy Hook

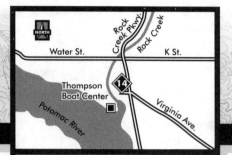

IN BRIEF

This hike is one response to the implied question, "Can I experience the C&O Canal towpath in springtime by taking one long hike instead of several short ones?"

DIRECTIONS

From Washington's Mall area, drive west on Constitution Avenue and turn right (north) on 23rd Street NW. Go several blocks and then turn left onto Virginia Avenue. Go several more blocks and cross Rock Creek Parkway to enter Thompson Boat Center parking lot, catty-corner from Watergate. *Note:* Parking at Thompson's is metered during day and forbidden overnight, but parking on nearby streets is permitted without fee or time limit on weekends. It's best, though, to get a ride to trailhead for this one-way hike.

DESCRIPTION

This hike is unlike any other in this book. It's much longer. It's more challenging. It's not one to do on your own. It's an organized event supported by trailside volunteers. It requires participants to register in advance. It happens only once a year. And I say it's worth trying.

The hike is 100 kilometers, or 62.14 miles, long, and event veterans call it the "the hundred K." It's a one-way hike on the C&O Canal towpath from Washington to Sandy Hook, Maryland, just short

KEY AT-A-GLANCE INFORMATION

Length: 62.1 miles

Configuration: One-way

Difficulty: Extremely difficult

Scenery: Colorful springtime woodlands, river views, endless towpath views, passing glimpses of communities and farmlands

Exposure: Mostly open; less so at night

Traffic: Light; less so near Chowstops

Trail surface: Mostly hard-packed dirt, with sandy, pebbly, rocky, grassy patches (very hard when dry, muddy then puddly when wet); pavement at start, end

Hiking time: 17–20 hours

Access: Advance registration required; registration fee

Maps: USGS Washington West, Falls Church, Seneca, Vienna, Waterford, Poolesville, Point of Rocks, Harpers Ferry; BSA booklet

Facilities: Toilets at trailhead, 16 towpath locations; phones at 6 locations; Chowstops at 6 locations; toilets, water, phone, at Sandy Hook; bike patrols, paramedics on towpath

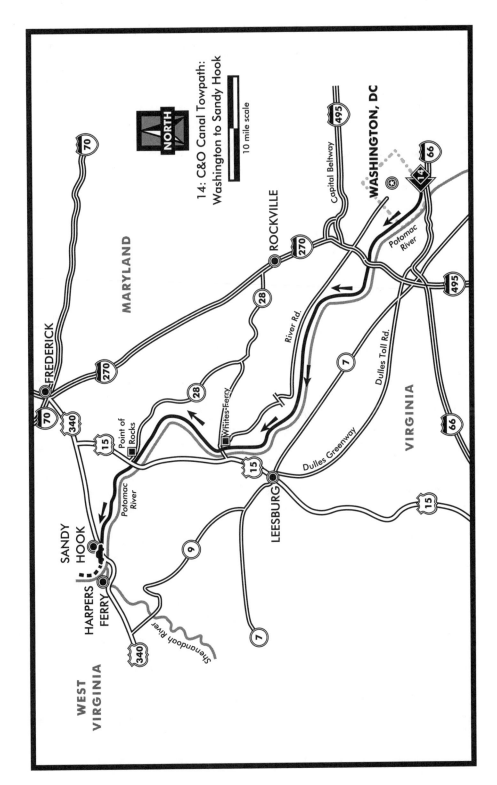

14: C&O Canal Towpath:
Washington to Sandy Hook

NORTH

10 mile scale

WASHINGTON, DC

MARYLAND

FREDERICK

ROCKVILLE

Capital Beltway

Potomac River

River Rd.

Whites Ferry

Point of Rocks

Dulles Toll Rd.

Dulles Greenway

VIRGINIA

LEESBURG

SANDY HOOK

HARPERS FERRY

Potomac River

Shenandoah River

WEST VIRGINIA

of Harpers Ferry and West Virginia. It's also a one-day hike, the day being the first Saturday in May (as it has been since 1974). The day is a very long one, starting at 3 a.m. and lasting into the evening for most participants.

Sponsored by the Sierra Club's Metropolitan Washington Regional Outings Program (MWROP), this mega-hike is organized and run by a special group of volunteers (including myself) who support the participants before and during the hike.

In the months prior to the hike, the organizers provide information and encouragement, field questions, and advocate training hikes for participants. Training hikes are essential for toughening the feet and getting the leg muscles used to the grueling repetitive motion involved in flatland hiking. That's why MWROP organizes local training hikes—including towpath outings—over the four months before the big day.

During the hike, MWROP operates six towpath checkpoints—known since 2001 as Chowstops in honor of retiring 100K veteran McLean Gary (who subsequently unretired). At each Chowstop, volunteers and paramedics track the hikers and dispense drink, food, and first aid (especially foot aid). Also, volunteer bike patrols roam the entire hike route.

The route is easy to follow, with the bulk of it on the milepost-studded towpath. But that's only 58 miles of the hike. The towpath portion is augmented front and back by short stretches on paved surfaces. The "back" one leads to the American Youth Hostel at Sandy Hook.

The dirt-surfaced towpath is mostly level, wide, and smooth. But it can be hard when dry, and soft and muddy when wet. It's also dark for the hike's first few hours—and again later, when most participants are still out there, under the wide and starry sky. That's

why flashlights are popular. (For this annual hike, the National Park Service (NPS) allows hikers to be on the towpath at night.)

Participants tackle the 100K differently. Some buddy up, some don't. Some talk, some don't. Some zone out, some use the mileposts to pull themselves along. Some cocoon themselves in headsets. Some (at least early on) take in the glorious spring scenery—if the weather cooperates.

The weather tends to be variable. Veterans reminisce about 90-degree scorchers, 50-degree chillers, all-day rain and mud, buffeting winds, and even the few glorious times we've had sunny, cool, and windless weather.

Each year's 100K attracts about a hundred people, give or take fifty. They vary in size, shape, sex, ethnicity, age, hair color, and hiking style. Anywhere between 40 and 80 percent of them get all the way to Sandy Hook, with weather often being a major factor in the success rate.

For some participants, the hike is shortened by exhaustion, dehydration, foot problems, or weather conditions. When that happens, the hiker in trouble either stops at one of the checkpoints or waits for help to arrive (bike patrollers and fellow hikers make that possible). No one has yet been lost or abandoned on this hike.

Tempted? Although the 100K is difficult, many people have done it. You can too, if you prepare properly. You'll have to get into really good physical and mental condition and put many training miles on your feet and leg muscles. On 100K day, you'll have to drink literally gallons of water, as well as average about 3 miles an hour to make the checkpoint cutoff times. At the end of the hike, though, you'll be welcomed with applause, camaraderie, drink, food

Towpath hikers enjoy the sunny spring weather.

(including the fabled chili of long-time event coordinator Alexandria Roger), and a place to sit down or collapse.

If the 100K seems too long, what about doing a 50K (31.07 miles) or an 80K (49.71 miles)? Starting in 2000, MWROP added the 50K, which starts at 10:30 a.m. in the Edwards Ferry area about halfway to Sandy Hook. And for 2002, the 80K is an option for the first time, starting in the Carderock area at 6 a.m.

For more information on the hike, visit the 100K web site (www.oneday-hike.org) or contact the MWROP, (202) 547-2326 or www.mwrop.org. For more information on the towpath, see the other towpath hikes in this book and contact the NPS office in Sharpsburg, (301) 739-4200 or www.nps.gov/choh.

NEARBY/RELATED ACTIVITIES

Before deciding to do the 100K—or 50K or 80K—get to know the towpath by trying other towpath hikes in this book (nos. 10–14), by going on organized hikes, or by exploring on your own.

After doing the annual Saturday hike, sleep at the hostel or a nearby motel (by pre-arrangement), and go home on Sunday. Or, sleep at home by having someone pick you up at the hostel. Or, return to Washington on Sunday by train (get a ride to the local station). If you stay over and can move well enough on Sunday morning, explore historic Harpers Ferry before going home. See hike no. 3, p. 7.

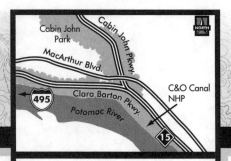

#15
Cabin John Creek
Parklands

IN BRIEF

Embedded in parklands, Cabin John Creek slips almost secretly through Maryland's suburbanized Montgomery County just west of Washington. A waterside trail enables hikers to take a long, close-in woodland trek.

DIRECTIONS

From Capital Beltway (Interstate 495) in Bethesda, take Exit 41 onto Clara Barton Parkway heading east (to do that if southbound on I-495, first go west on parkway for 0.9 miles, take overpass across parkway, and then go east). Proceed for about 2 miles to parking lot 7. Alternatively, from MacArthur Boulevard (and also from westbound parkway heading upriver from Chain Bridge and Washington), you can get onto eastbound parkway by using overpass at Glen Echo. *Note:* If parking lot 7 is full (there's room for only about 8 vehicles), start hike from Cabin John Park. To get there, continue eastward on parkway and Canal Road for roughly 3.5 miles; go left onto Arizona Avenue at traffic light, and then left again at next traffic light onto MacArthur Boulevard heading back westward; just after crossing Union Arch Bridge, turn right into Cabin John Park parking lot (and if that's full, continue on MacArthur for one long block and turn right to park on 75th Street NW, near community center).

KEY AT-A-GLANCE INFORMATION

Length: 14.3 miles

Configuration: Out-and-back

Difficulty: Quite difficult

Scenery: Woodlands along urban stream valley, historic bridge, towpath

Exposure: Mostly shady; less so in winter

Traffic: Very light to light; heavier on warm-weather evenings, weekends, holidays, especially on towpath and in nature center vicinity

Trail surface: Mostly dirt; some pavement, grass; rocky, rooty in places

Hiking time: 5.5–7.5 hours

Access: Open daily, dawn to dusk

Maps: USGS Falls Church, Rockville; PATC Map D

Facilities: None at trailhead; toilet off-trail at Cabin John Park; toilets, water at nature center, off-trail at community center (west of park)

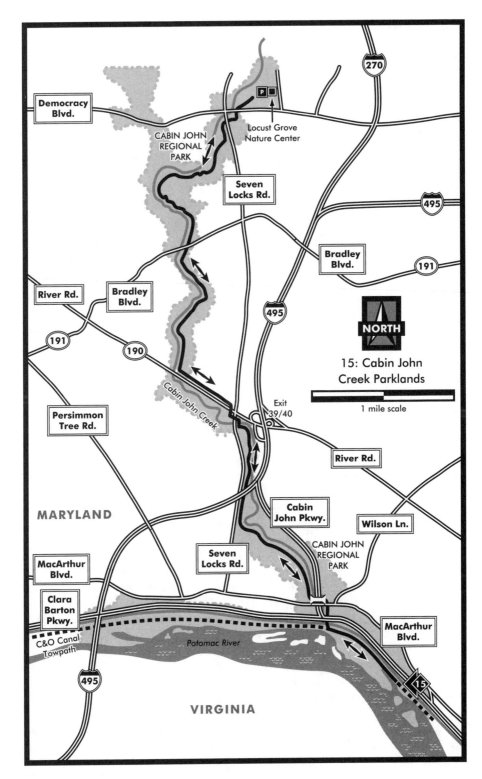

Democracy Blvd.

CABIN JOHN
REGIONAL
PARK

270

P

Locust Grove
Nature Center

Seven
Locks Rd.

495

Bradley
Blvd.

191

River Rd.

Bradley
Blvd.

NORTH

191

190

495

15: Cabin John
Creek Parklands

1 mile scale

Cabin John Creek

Exit
39/40

Persimmon
Tree Rd.

River Rd.

MARYLAND

Cabin
John Pkwy.

Wilson Ln.

CABIN JOHN
REGIONAL
PARK

Seven
Locks Rd.

MacArthur
Blvd.

Clara
Barton
Pkwy.

C&O Canal
Towpath

Potomac River

MacArthur
Blvd.

495

15

VIRGINIA

DESCRIPTION

Cabin John Creek flows south through the affluent suburbs of Montgomery County between Rockville and the Potomac River. Swathed in state-owned parkland, its well-wooded valley is a delightful hiking venue, thanks to the Cabin John Trail.

This out-and-back, 14.3-mile hike uses the lightly used lower part of the trail, between Cabin John Park and Locust Grove Nature Center. With the scouting help of Springfield Ray, I have also included a trail along the creek lying south of the park, plus a short stretch of the nearby C&O Canal towpath.

The hike, which accumulates 2,200 feet of elevation change, consists essentially of a series of woodland segments briefly interrupted by road crossings. Each segment has tempting side trails, so be sure to stay on the blue-blazed main trail (and thereby also avoid the poison ivy).

To get started from parking lot 7, head down the nearby dirt trail and curve left past the canal's first lock house. Opened in 1829, it was occupied for almost a century—until the canal itself was abandoned. However, look for evidence of occupancy; the National Park Service (NPS) is putting tenants in some of the old lock houses.

Take the short bridge across Lock 7, turn right onto the dirt-surfaced towpath, and hike upstream for about three-quarters of a scenic mile. To the left, trees and thickets will block views of the Potomac. On the right, thanks to a late-1930s restoration project, is a water-filled stretch of the canal.

At a wooden bridge spanning the canal, take it, turn right, and double back along the other side on a gravelly dirt trail. On reaching a vertical pipe topped with a mesh cap, swing left and head uphill alongside Cabin John Creek. Note where the creek disappears beneath both

the towpath and canal on its way to the Potomac. Enjoy views of the creek while ascending to MacArthur Boulevard. There, turn left and head for what a historical marker calls "Cabin-John Bridge and Cabin John Aqueduct." When completed in 1864, the stone bridge carried not only a roadway but also a major water-supply pipe, or conduit, that tapped the river upstream at Great Falls and ran beneath Conduit Road (later renamed MacArthur Boulevard).

Take the sidewalk across the renovated Union Arch Bridge (the name reflects the structure's original wartime name). Then continue on the grassy shoulder and cross the road—carefully—into Cabin John Park. Staying to the right on a paved path, follow the park's short access road until reaching stairs that lead down to a lawn, on the right. Cross the grass to the brown trail sign marking the south end of the Cabin John Trail, 1.3 miles into the hike.

Take a steep flight of steps downhill onto a narrow dirt trail to the left of the creek. Continuing northward, watch your step; the rooty trail twists and bucks up and down through the woods. About 1.4 miles after leaving MacArthur Boulevard, ascend a short rise to reach a road (it's Seven Locks Road). Turn right onto the sidewalk-cum-bike path. Proceed for almost a quarter-mile, passing beneath the beltway. At the end of the guardrail, leave the bike path and traverse a parking area, passing between wooden posts and then bearing left with an old chain-link fence to your right. Wind through the woods on a dirt trail for a half-mile. Heed Springfield Ray's warning that blue blazes may be a trifle sparse.

Returning to Seven Locks Road, turn right onto the bike path. Continue northward, crossing a bridge over the creek. Here, since this is an area of recent trail rerouting, Ray also suggests temporarily ignoring the blue blazes. On reaching a major intersection, first cross Seven Locks Road and then River Road—using the crosswalks, traffic lights, and pedestrian walk button (it helps). Then turn left onto a mostly gravel path that follows River Road northwestward for just over half a mile. It's noisy, but you'll have a safety barrier between you and the rushing vehicles.

Just before reaching a road bridge (beneath which is the creek), watch for a gate and a familiar brown Cabin John Trail sign. There, go right to pick up what becomes a hilly woodland trail. Within a hundred yards, the blue blazes will reappear.

To reach the next road crossing, follow the main trail for about 1.25 miles, staying close to the creek on your left. In many places, the rooty trail is right on the edge of the steep creek bank, so watch your step, especially when the ground is wet or leaf smothered. Also remember that the polluted creek is best not touched, accidentally or otherwise.

As the creek is subject to flooding, it's likely to be clogged in places with trunks and other tree parts, along with plastic junk. But the surrounding woods are generally attractive. They feature yellow poplars (tulip trees), oaks, maples, and mountain laurels.

After the trail turns away from creek and traffic becomes audible again, watch for a fork in the trail. Bear left and head downhill past an unusually large sycamore near where the creek passes beneath Bradley Boulevard.

There, a few wooden steps on the left lead to the water's edge. Then turn right and go up a few stone steps to the guardrail alongside the road. Cross the two-lane road very carefully and pick up the northbound trail on the far side at the usual brown trail sign.

For the next 1.3 miles, until the next road crossing, follow the blue blazes through hilly woods. Then cross Seven Locks Road again, with care, and slide back into the woods on the far side.

For the next half-mile, follow the blue blazes as the zigzag route pitches up and, using short stretches of both old road and present-day road. At a divided road (Democracy Boulevard), cross vigilantly, then walk along the road leading into Cabin John Regional Park. Go about 100 yards, turn right, and head across a footbridge to Locust Grove Nature Center, the hike's halfway and turnaround point. Visit the nature center if it's open and you're interested. Then return to the trailhead the way you came.

For more information on the Cabin John Trail, contact its maintenance organization, the Potomac Appalachian Trail Club, (703) 242-0693, or try Locust Grove Nature Center, (301) 299-1990. For more information on the towpath, contact NPS's Great Falls Tavern office, (301) 299-3613.

NEARBY/RELATED ACTIVITIES
Roam through nearby Glen Echo Park, amid the remnants of an old amusement park and ride the Dentzel carousel. It's now a federal cultural arts park. The park is on Oxford Road—off Mac-Arthur Boulevard a half-mile east of the Union Arch Bridge. You could detour there while hiking. For information, contact the park, (301) 492-6282 or www.nps.gov/glec.

Take a guided tour of the Clara Barton House. It was the last home of the remarkable woman who gained fame in the Civil War as the Angel of the Battlefield, and who later organized and headed the American Red Cross. For more information, contact the site, (301) 492-6245 or www.nps.gov/clba.

#16
Capital Crescent Trail

IN BRIEF

A former railroad line, the multi-use Capital Crescent Trail swings through Northwest Washington and nearby suburban Maryland. For hikers, its paved Georgetown-Bethesda portion provides a good workout and scenic outing in a parkland setting.

DIRECTIONS

From Georgetown end of Key Bridge, drive west on M Street NW/Canal Road for 0.5 miles. At third traffic light, turn left to stay on Canal Road. Go 1.6 miles to Fletcher's Boathouse, on left. If upper parking lot is full, use lower and larger one. To get to Fletcher's from Chain Bridge, go east on Canal Road for 0.4 miles and make extreme right turn into Fletcher's. *Note:* Canal Road is a weekday rush-hour route that's one-way inbound in morning and one-way outbound in afternoon.

Or use Metro to do hike. Take Metrobus along MacArthur Boulevard, get off at V Street, and walk down to Canal Road and Fletcher's. Alternatively, use Metro to start hike in Bethesda (see text). Contact Metro, (202) 637-7000 or www.wmata.com.

DESCRIPTION

The Capital Crescent Trail forms a large C-shaped arc that extends for 11 miles between Silver Spring and the District's Georgetown waterfront. It's one of the

KEY AT-A-GLANCE INFORMATION

Length: 10.2 miles

Configuration: Modified out-and-back

Difficulty: Moderate

Scenery: Woodlands, parklands, street scenes, river glimpses

Exposure: Mostly shady; less so in winter

Traffic: Mostly light to moderate; moderate to very heavy on warm-weather evenings, weekends, holidays

Trail surface: Pavement almost whole way

Hiking time: 4–5 hours

Access: Open daily, dawn to dusk

Maps: USGS Washington West; map in coalition brochure

Facilities: Toilets, water, phone, warm-season snack bar at trailhead; water along trail; off-trail amenities at River Road and near Bethesda turn-around location

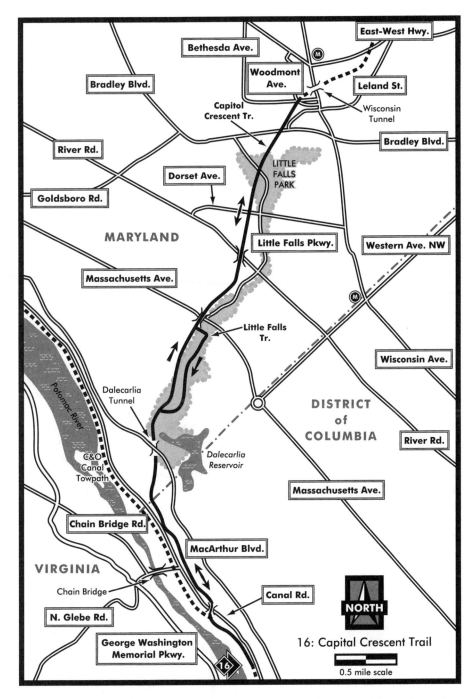

Bethesda Ave.

East-West Hwy.

Woodmont Ave.

Bradley Blvd.

Leland St.

Capitol Crescent Tr.

Wisconsin Tunnel

River Rd.

LITTLE FALLS PARK

Bradley Blvd.

Dorset Ave.

Goldsboro Rd.

MARYLAND

Little Falls Pkwy.

Western Ave. NW

Massachusetts Ave.

Little Falls Tr.

Wisconsin Ave.

Potomac River

Dalecarlia Tunnel

DISTRICT of COLUMBIA

River Rd.

C&O Canal Towpath

Dalecarlia Reservoir

Massachusetts Ave.

Chain Bridge Rd.

MacArthur Blvd.

VIRGINIA

Chain Bridge

Canal Rd.

NORTH

N. Glebe Rd.

George Washington Memorial Pkwy.

16

16: Capital Crescent Trail

0.5 mile scale

metro area's newest trails, with the first section having opened at the end of 1996. That section, consisting of 7 miles between Bethesda and Georgetown, is the most complete portion of the trail. Minus a couple of miles at the Georgetown end, it's the basis for the hike presented here.

The 10.2-mile hike starts at Fletcher's Boathouse and follows the paved trail very gradually uphill to Bethesda, flanked mostly by a ribbon of parklands. Then it's back to Fletcher's, largely on the main trail. For variety, though, most of the paved and parallel Little Falls Trail is included, plus a bit of the dirt-surfaced C&O Canal towpath.

It seems a bit odd that a new trail can go right through so many affluent subdivisions, as well as downtown Bethesda. The explanation: although the trail itself is new, the route is a century old and predates modern suburban expansion. For much of the twentieth century, it was a railroad spur line used to deliver coal and building supplies to the industry-cluttered Georgetown waterfront. That fact also explains the route's gentle grades, with only 600 feet of elevation change between Georgetown and Bethesda. When its last coal customer switched to truck delivery in 1985, the rail line was closed.

The following year, volunteers organized the Coalition for the Capital Crescent Trail (CCCT) to campaign for converting the right-of-way into a multi-use trail. With the help of assorted organizations, public agencies, individuals, and good luck, the effort succeeded. Today, the District portion of the trail is managed by the National Park Service as part of the C&O Canal National Historical Park. The Maryland portion is in, owned, and maintained by Montgomery County.

CCCT continues to press for completion of the 4-mile section between Bethesda and Silver Spring. That stretch is a key link to trails east of Rock Creek Park. Although now passable, it includes some unpleasant on-street detours and gravel surfaces. Completion remains complicated by various political and funding issues.

The Georgetown-Bethesda section is popular year-round, mostly as a neighborhood recreational trail. At least half of the users seem to be cyclists, with hikers, in-line skaters, joggers, strollers, and dog walkers, making up the balance; so be sure to stay alert and over to the right.

To get started from Fletcher's Boathouse, head upriver on the paved Capital Crescent Trail (rather than the adjoining dirt-surfaced C&O Canal towpath). Keep the Potomac River on your left, although you won't see much of it thanks to the thickly wooded floodplain. Watch for a distinctive brown sign bearing the number "8." It's one of the half-mileposts that count down the trail from Silver Spring.

About a half-mile from Fletcher's, the trail gently ascends uphill, then crosses the canal and Canal Road on a refurbished ex-railroad bridge. Beyond the bridge, it angles up the bluffs and, when the trees are bare, provides panoramic glimpses of the Potomac valley.

Climbing very gradually, the trail crosses into Maryland and then swings northward and away from the river. Soon after passing half-milepost 6.5, you'll cross a water treatment facility. Pass by, then go through Dalecarlia Tunnel. The high-vaulted tunnel was built in 1910 to carry the railroad line under both Conduit Road (now MacArthur Boulevard) and the pipes feeding river water to Dalecarlia Reservoir. It's dimly lit, but try to read the informative plaque on the tunnel wall.

Beyond the tunnel, on your right, is a small lobe of the large, tree-lined reservoir, still one of the District's chief water-storage units. Just after half-milepost 6, you'll start following Little Falls Branch Park all the way to Bethesda. Take bridges across heavily traveled Massachusetts Avenue and River Road. At Dorset Avenue, cross carefully. At

Little Falls Parkway, near the Bethesda Pool, cross even more carefully (traffic can be heavy and fast).

Continuing northward, cross Bradley Boulevard vigilantly, pass half-milepost 3.5, and then reach a halfmoon-shaped display area that has water and detailed information boards about the trail. About 100 yards farther on is the Bethesda Avenue sidewalk, next to a public parking lot. That's the turn-around spot. The trail itself continues eastward as the Georgetown Branch Trail (there's a signpost nearby). That's the interim name (derived from the old rail line's) for the extension to Silver Spring.

From the turn-around spot, glide back down south and downhill. At Massachusetts Avenue, though, after crossing the bridge, turn left onto a short dirt trail and go downhill. Turn right onto a paved trail, walk roughly 50 yards, and turn right onto the paved Little Falls Trail. The trail wiggles scenically through the well-wooded Montgomery County park, following a stream. Emerging wild-flowers, re-leafing trees, and flitting migratory birds can make this area a springtime delight. After a mile, swing right to rejoin the main trail at half-milepost 6.

Back in the District, after crossing the old railroad bridge, turn immediately right and take the stairway down to the towpath. Turn right, and return to Fletcher's by doing the final half-mile along the canal. But stay on the parallel Capital Crescent Trail if the weather or towpath is very wet.

If you prefer to start the hike at the Bethesda end, either use the metered public parking lot on Bethesda Avenue (it's free on weekends) or take Metrorail to the nearby Bethesda station (on the Red Line).

For more information on the trail, contact the Coalition for the Capital Crescent Trail (CCCT), (202) 234-4874 or www.cctrail.org. Also consider becoming a CCCT volunteer.

NEARBY/RELATED ACTIVITIES

If you're hiking on a day in late March or April, detour to see the glorious cherry blossoms of Bethesda's Kenwood area, an affluent neighborhood located between the trail and Kenwood Country Club to the west. At peak blossom time, it's likely to be very crowded, but mostly with cars, so you can walk around freely under the pink and white canopy. To get started, leave the trail at Dorset Avenue and circle west (that's left, if you're en route to Bethesda).

The hike's halfway point is close to many eateries, so consider breaking for lunch indoors—or make it dinner if you start at the Bethesda end. Either way, step off the trail, cross Bethesda Avenue, and pick a place as you head up restaurant-lined Woodmont Avenue. Or, as hiker Alexandria Ellen does, go a little farther to Napa Thai Cuisine, at 4924 St. Elmo Avenue, (301) 986-8590. The extra mile round-trip is worth it, except on Mondays, when the restaurant is closed.

If you do the hike in reverse, have a picnic lunch at Fletcher's riverside park. Make do with the snack bar there or stock up beforehand, just before the River Road bridge, at an upscale supermarket on the right.

#17
Catoctin Mountain Park and Cunningham Falls State Park

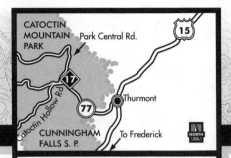

CATOCTIN MOUNTAIN PARK — Park Central Rd. — 15

17

Catoctin Hollow Rd. — 77 — Thurmont

CUNNINGHAM FALLS S. P. — To Frederick

NORTH

IN BRIEF

These two parks north of Frederick in Maryland's Blue Ridge region are endowed with a touch of wilderness, a sense of history, and exceptional vistas. They also enable hikers to practice three of the four principles of optimal day hiking, which are described in this hike.

DIRECTIONS

From junction of Capital Beltway (Interstate 495) and I-270, drive north-west on I-270 for about 32 miles to Frederick. There, access US 15 (Catoctin Mountain Highway) heading north and proceed for about 16 miles to Thur-mont. On reaching Thurmont, take MD 77 exit ramp, turn right at bottom of ramp, and proceed westward on MD 77 (Foxville Road) for about 3 miles. Turn right onto Park Central Road and into Catoctin Mountain Park. Then turn right into visitor center parking lot—or use overflow parking lot on left.

DESCRIPTION

Located scarcely 60 miles northwest of Washington, Catoctin Mountain Park and Cunningham Falls State Park let arriving visitors know immediately that they're far removed from the urban plains. The air is fresher and cooler, the sky is bigger, trees are everywhere, and the endless ridges rolling softly to the horizon evoke a sense of being in a mountain fastness.

KEY AT-A-GLANCE INFORMATION

Length: 11 miles

Configuration: Loop

Difficulty: Quite difficult

Scenery: Wooded uplands, water-fall, sweeping vistas from overlooks

Exposure: Mostly shady; less so in winter

Traffic: Very light to light; heavier on warm-weather weekends, holi-days; heaviest in beach, waterfall areas

Trail surface: Mostly rocky or sandy; some boardwalk, pavement, grass; quite rooty

Hiking time: 6–8 hours (including vista, siesta, and lake time)

Access: Open daily during daylight hours

Maps: USGS Blue Ridge Summit, Catoctin Furnace; PATC Map 5; ADC Frederick Co.; sketch maps in free park brochures

Facilities: Toilets, water, phone at visitor center, park headquarters; toilets, water at Hog Rock parking area

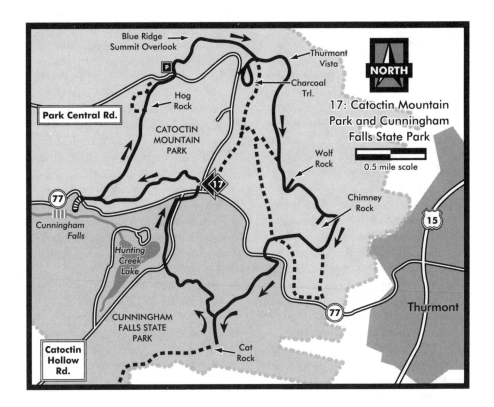

Such a place can be restorative, as I learned on a 1991 fall hike led by St. Marys Louise. Later, I expanded her route and also applied three of the four principles of optimal day hiking I deduced from hiking with Chicago Hugh. They are 1) enjoy mountain vistas, 2) sustain a good pace but break for a leisurely lunch and short siesta, and 3) end a summer hike at or in water.

As alluring as it is, the Catoctin/Cunningham area is still recovering from severe despoliation. During the nineteenth century, Catoctin Mountain—an outlier in the eastern part of the Blue Ridge region—was stripped of timber chiefly for making charcoal for local iron smelting furnaces. By 1900, much of the area near Thurmont, in Frederick County, consisted of logged-over woodlots and submarginal farmlands.

Three decades later, the federal government assembled over 10,500 acres of land as a demonstration project—one of about 50 nationally—for restoring the environment and creating recreation facilities. In 1945 the demo area was transferred to the National Park Service. Nine years later, it was divided very roughly in half, with Maryland getting the southern portion for a state park and NPS retaining the rest as Catoctin National Park.

This 11-mile clockwise loop through the heavily wooded parks has a cumulative elevation change of about 2,200 feet. Try the hike at any season. Remember that summer visitors flock to Cunningham's lake and lifeguarded beach, that hunters are allowed in Cunningham in the fall (except on Sundays), and that the wintertime closing of Catoctin's Park Central Road abets on-the-trail solitude.

Going around the rocky loop, pick up your feet, stay out of the poison ivy, and watch for snakes. Also, try to guess the general location of Camp David, the presidential hideaway that was initially Franklin D. Roosevelt's Shangri-La.

To get started from the visitor center, head west across Park Central Road and then across the overflow parking lot. Pick up the Falls Nature Trail at the far end of the lot, on the right, and disappear into the woods. After crossing a bridged stream and passing some large boulders, curve to the left and climb a short, rather steep slope.

Going moderately uphill for about a mile, you'll traverse an area decorated with huge boulders. Some are as big as a bus, others merely car sized. Look for the one found by Birmingham Bud when checking the hike's front end: "It's locked in a wrestling contest with a large tree that long ago found firm purchase in a stony fissure."

After the trail noses downhill to link up with a nameless trail, go left to take a detour of a few hundred yards into the state park. Start by heading downhill to MD 77, turning left, and walking about 70 yards along the road. Then cross carefully into a handicapped parking lot. At the lot's far end, walk on the boardwalk that follows Big Hunting Creek upstream to the base of one of Maryland's highest and loveliest waterfalls. Stay on the boardwalk both to protect the fragile riparian environment and to admire the stepped cascade easing 78 feet down the gorge. Then return along the boardwalk and unnamed trail and slip back into the national park. At the junction of choice, go straight through and uphill, toward Hog Rock.

On a northeasterly course, the trail gains some 600 feet in elevation while passing through areas of moss, grass, and rockiness. En route, watch on the right for a landmark tree—a tall and splendid sassafras. Note the species' odd habit of displaying three shapes of leaves, sometimes on the same branch. As Frederick Law Olmsted commented, sassafras is "very sportive in its form of foliage." In winter, you'll know it by its much-furrowed, old looking, red-brown bark.

The trail then passes by a large rock formation on the right, descends, crosses a small streambed by bridge, and nips uphill to Hog Rock. Look around there, on a high promontory, taking in the views. Then resume your journey and swing left. On reaching a fork, jog right and continue past a small boulder field.

Eventually, the trail smoothes out into level grassiness. At Park Central Road, cross carefully and head for a well-appointed parking area, complete with picnic tables, trash cans, water, and a toilet that looks, said Birmingham Bud, like "an elegant miniature Swiss chalet." This is about 3 miles into the hike.

Leave the parking area, going past two ordinary toilets on the left, then follow the trail as it descends through maples and oaks, and rises toward the next viewpoint, the Blue Ridge Summit Overlook. As the trail turns left and runs along a squat, rock ridge, you'll reach a plateau. Shortly thereafter, turn left onto a short side trail and see what the overlook looks over, including Pennsylvania.

Back on the main trail, turn left, and press on through the woods for about a mile as the path undulates and starts curving to the right, or south. At a four-way intersection, turn right to take a side trip on the Charcoal Trail. It's a self-guiding, half-mile loop trail that explains the area's ruinous former industry. To get there from the main trail, head for a nearby parking area, some picnic tables, and a dumpster. Just past an interpretive sign about morels, turn left to hike the Charcoal Trail.

Then return to the intersection, and go straight, heading east and south toward the next overlook, Thurmont Vista. At a fork, bear right to reach the vista and perch at the hike's 5-mile mark. Consider taking a Chicago Hugh–style lunch break.

Continuing south for about three-quarters of a mile, follow a wooded ridgeline that's initially level but then descends. At a junction, stay to the left. At the next junction, turn left onto a short side trail leading to Wolf Rock. There, look at far-off places and also at your feet, which may well be close to deep crevices.

Back on the main trail, head for the next overlook, Chimney Rock, a half-mile to the southeast. A right turn onto a short and rocky side trail leads to Chimney Rock along with its big boulders, deep crevices, and glorious views.

Returning to the main trail, stay and curve to the right and west as the trail pitches sharply downhill through an understory of mountain laurel. At a four-way intersection, go straight, continuing to descend, and reach MD 77 near the park headquarters, 7 miles into the hike.

Cross the road to return again to the state park and to pick up the trail leading to the sixth and final overlook, Cat Rock. It's a somewhat strenuous haul of about a mile horizontally and about 600 feet vertically, on a shaded and yellow-blazed trail that swings west and south. Halfway up, notice but don't take an orange-blazed trail on the right. At the top, head for the main overlook, a noble rock formation to the right of the trail—and also where Chicago Hugh first showed me his technique for a post-lunch cat nap. Take in the view, but don't take the trail past Cat Rock. Instead,

head back down the way you came. Then go left onto the orange-blazed trail. Follow it across the wooded slopes for just over a mile and steeply downhill to the Hunting Creek Lake area. If it's summer, note the inviting, man-made, 43-acre lake—and see my first posthike suggestion below.

At Catoctin Hollow Road, cross carefully, turn right, and proceed for just over half a mile to MD 77, staying on the left shoulder and facing traffic. Cross MD 77 even more carefully. Then turn right, and walk along the shoulder for a few hundred yards to the trailhead.

For further information, contact Catoctin Mountain Park, (301) 663-9388 or www.nps.gov/cato, and Cunningham Falls State Park, (301) 271-7574 or www.dnr.state.md.us/publiclands/western/cunninghamfalls.html.

NEARBY/RELATED ACTIVITIES

If it's summer and you've taken a long lunch and short nap at an overlook and completed the full hike, you're obliged to cool off in the lake before heading home.

Attend the Catoctin Colorfest, Thurmont's big and popular mid-October craft fair; call (800) 999-3613, (301) 663-8687, or www.colorfest.org.

Homeward bound through Frederick, make a dinner stop at the Bentz Street Raw Bar, (301) 694-9134, just off Market Street. There, you can belatedly honor Chicago Hugh's fourth principle: The ideal coda for a hot summer hike is a cool microbrew. Then go shop for used books at Wonder Book & Video, open until 10 p.m., except on Saturdays when it's closed, (301) 694-5955.

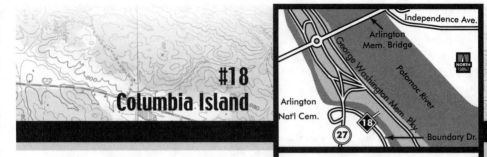

#18
Columbia Island

IN BRIEF

Columbia Island is one of Washington's best-kept secrets. Hidden in plain sight, it lies in the Potomac River across from the Lincoln Memorial. Often mistaken for part of Virginia, it's a novel and view-rich hiking locale.

DIRECTIONS

From Washington's Mall area, head west across Arlington Memorial Bridge. Swing right, past (not around) traffic circle. Take first left, and follow road as it curves left. On reaching fork, 0.5 miles after circle, stay right. Then take next right, at sign for Lyndon Baines Johnson Memorial Grove. Go 0.4 miles and turn left at stop sign into grove's parking lot (note 3-hour limit). Or use no-parking-limit Columbia Island marina as trailhead. To get there, follow above route to fork, but go left at fork, then south for 0.7 miles, and turn right into marina. *Note:* Beware LBJ grove signs along George Washington Memorial Parkway that confusingly lead to *marina* parking lot.

You can use Metro to access the hike starting at traffic circle. Take Blue Line train to Arlington Cemetery station, and then walk 0.2 miles east along Memorial Drive to circle. Contact Metro, (202) 637-7000 or www.wmata.com.

DESCRIPTION

Columbia Island came into being in 1916, when the Potomac River was dredged and the spoils piled up on the

KEY AT-A-GLANCE INFORMATION

Length: 3.9 miles

Configuration: Modified loop

Difficulty: Very easy

Scenery: Waterside parklands, cross-Potomac views of mainland Washington

Exposure: Mostly open

Traffic: Generally light; moderate on Mount Vernon Trail on warm-weather evenings, weekends, holidays

Trail surface: Mostly pavement; some grass, dirt

Hiking time: 1.5–2 hours

Access: No restrictions other than Mount Vernon Trail closes at dark

Map: USGS Washington West

Facilities: None at trailhead; toilets, water, phones, cafe at marina; water at LBJ grove

Special comments: Be very careful when crossing roads

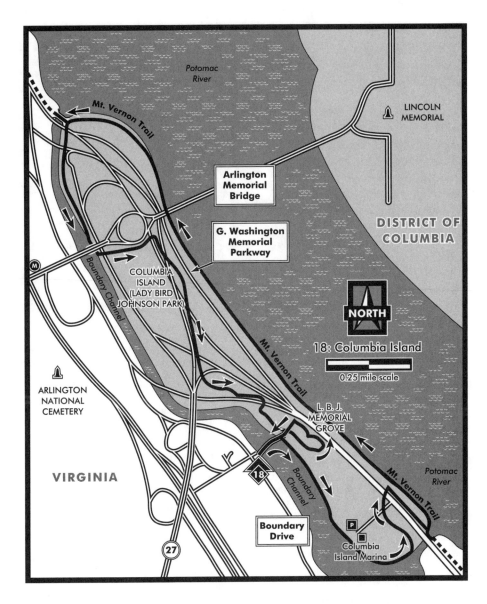

Potomac
River

LINCOLN
MEMORIAL

Mt. Vernon Trail

**Arlington
Memorial
Bridge**

DISTRICT OF
COLUMBIA

**G. Washington
Memorial
Parkway**

Boundary Channel

COLUMBIA
ISLAND
(LADY BIRD
JOHNSON PARK)

Mt. Vernon Trail

NORTH

18: Columbia Island

0.25 mile scale

L. B. J.
MEMORIAL
GROVE

ARLINGTON
NATIONAL
CEMETERY

Mt. Vernon Trail

Potomac
River

VIRGINIA

18

Boundary
Channel

27

**Boundary
Drive**

P

Columbia
Island Marina

Virginia shore. Because the new land formed an island, it automatically became part of Washington, thanks to an ancient law that denies Virginia even part-ownership of the Potomac. But that didn't prevent Virginia from protesting. The matter was settled in the 1930s, when the District received the island and Virginia received reclaimed land later developed as National Airport.

That same decade the island became a key link in the metro area's growing road network. The George Washington Memorial Parkway and Arlington Memorial Bridge were created, along with many connecting roads. The island was also landscaped, but its chief purpose was to carry motor traffic.

In 1968 the National Park Service (NPS) designated the island as Lady Bird

63

The Navy and Marine Memorial graces the southern end of Columbia Island.

Johnson Park in honor of the then first lady's efforts to beautify the country. The Lyndon Baines Johnson Memorial Grove was added in 1974, the year after the ex-president died. The island now has many dogwoods, pines, and flowering bushes, as well as literally a million daffodils and some fine views of mainland Washington and the river.

This hike is a 3.9-mile counterclockwise loop that follows much of the perimeter of the mostly flat island. It crosses heavily-traveled and high-speed roadways, so be vigilant and patient. Remember that traffic is lightest on weekend and holiday mornings, and plan to watch your watch en route; the parking lot has a 3-hour time limit.

To get started, take the footbridge across the Boundary Channel, which separates the island from Virginia. Then, turn immediately right onto a dirt trail. Follow it to a paved path that, if you turn right, leads to the marina parking lot. In the parking lot, locate and access a waterfront dirt trail. When the trail ends,

swing counterclockwise around the cafe building, then head across the grass to follow the entrance road to the parkway. Cross the road to the nearby crosswalk spanning the parkway—cross carefully. Turn right and follow a narrow paved trail along the parkway for several hundred yards.

At a fork, swing left and climb some shallow steps to get close to seven aluminum seagulls skimming the crest of a large aluminum wave breaking across a granite base. That's the Navy and Marine Memorial, created by Ernest Bagni del Piatti. The graceful work was erected in 1934 (Congress decreed that it be located on public grounds in the District). Circle it, and read the eloquent inscription. A few days after the deadly terrorist attack on the USS Cole in Yemen, in mid-October 2000, I noticed a simple spray of flowers lying at the base of the wave.

Look around and you'll see that you're on a landscaped knoll bordered by willows and maples at the island's southern end. Head down the steps toward the river. Halfway down, go left a few yards to scrutinize a large sign. Dated 1990, it's the memorial's inscription translated into contemporary bureaucratese.

Then, on the paved Mount Vernon Trail, head upriver 1.5 miles along the manicured and tree-dotted riverbank to the northern end of the island. Take the opportunity to walk briskly and make the most of the splendid views of Potomac Park and the familiar skyline. Be sure to stay to the right at the fork just before Memorial Bridge.

A small concrete bridge with gray metal railings is just past the hike's halfway mark; stop immediately or you'll overshoot the island. Turn left, clamber up the short steep slope (use the culvert), and very carefully cross the northbound parkway lanes (traffic coming from your left). Proceed across a grassy area and make a safe crossing of the southbound parkway lanes (traffic coming from your right).

Swing right along the grassy edge of a landscaped area, passing between a conifer nursery on the left and a tangle of maples and underbrush on the right. Soon, just yards away from the Boundary Channel, the tangle will thin. Walk to the water's edge to savor an off-the-beaten-trail spot, where the channel burbles through the woods like a country stream.

Continuing, squeeze to the right on a narrow shoulder as the southbound parkway lanes slide beneath Memorial Drive (the boulevard between Memorial Bridge and Arlington National Cemetery). Then turn left and very alertly cross the lanes (eyes left). Climb the grassy slope. At the top, head for a paved path that circles the traffic circle at the western end of the bridge. Swing right onto the path, follow it to a nearby

crosswalk, and cross very carefully (eyes right). Then, turn right and south on a paved path. But first, detour a few yards to the left to read a plaque explaining the island's connection to the L. B. Johnsons. After that, head south on the paved path. Staying on the path, carefully cross an exit ramp, go right at a fork, and cross two more ramps the same way.

Swing left off the path and down a grassy embankment; cross an open area alongside a parkway feeder road; head for the far curve in the road; and carefully cross there (eyes right). Locate a dirt trail that'll take you into the 15-acre LBJ grove area, then swing right onto a paved path and follow it to the footbridge leading back to the trailhead. But don't take the bridge. Rather, turn left onto a paving-stone path and follow it to the end as it spirals leftward to the heart of the memorial grove. There, set on a circular paving-stone plaza rimmed with white pines, is a simple, rough-hewn 19-foot-high slab of Texas granite. From there, you'll also have a lovely view of the Washington Monument.

To see more of the grove, step toward the view and swing left across the grass and under the pines. Turn right onto a paved path. Follow it through two left turns and a right turn to get back on the paving-stone path. Then recross the footbridge and, for a surprise, press the "Listen" button on the far wall.

If you prefer to start the hike from an alternative trailhead, tap into the described route at the marina or traffic circle (see under Directions). In either case, be sure to walk over the Boundary Channel footbridge—to savor the view, press the "Listen" button, and not lose any precious mileage.

Contact the NPS's George Washington Memorial Parkway, (703) 289-2500 or www.nps.gov/gwmp.

#19
Cosca Regional Park

IN BRIEF

For hikers, multi-use Cosca Regional Park serves as a delightful, trail-laced nature preserve tucked away in suburban Maryland just southeast of Washington.

DIRECTIONS

From Capital Beltway (Interstate 495 and I-95), take Exit 7 and drive south on Branch Avenue (MD 5), heading toward Waldorf. After about 3.5 miles, turn right onto 0.4-mile exit ramp leading to Woodyard Road (MD 223). Turn right onto Woodyard. Go 0.8 miles and turn left onto Brandywine Road. Go 0.9 miles and turn right onto Thrift Road. Go 2 miles and turn right at "Clearwater Nature Center" sign. Follow park entrance road for 0.2 miles to parking lot nearest nature center.

DESCRIPTION

Cosca Regional Park lies near Clinton, in suburbanized southern Prince George's County. Opened in 1967, it's best known for its playing fields, lake, nature center, and other amenities. But the 700-acre park consists mostly of rolling woodlands where savvy hikers can enjoy nature, exercise, and solitude year-round.

The woods are deciduous, with a scattering of pines and hollies. Wildflowers dapple the woods with color over three seasons. Migratory songbirds do the same in spring. Butterflies follow suit in

KEY AT-A-GLANCE INFORMATION

Length: 5.5 miles

Configuration: Modified loop

Difficulty: Easy

Scenery: Rolling woodlands, lake views, stream valleys

Exposure: Mostly shady; less so in winter

Traffic: Usually light or very light; heavier close to nature center, lake, picnic areas, and on warm-weather weekends, holidays

Trail surface: Mostly dirt; some pavement, grass

Hiking time: 2.5–3 hours

Access: Open daily, 7:30 a.m.–dusk

Map: USGS Piscataway

Facilities: Toilets, water inside nature center; warm-season-only-toilets, snack bar at boathouse, toilets at pavilion, water at picnic area

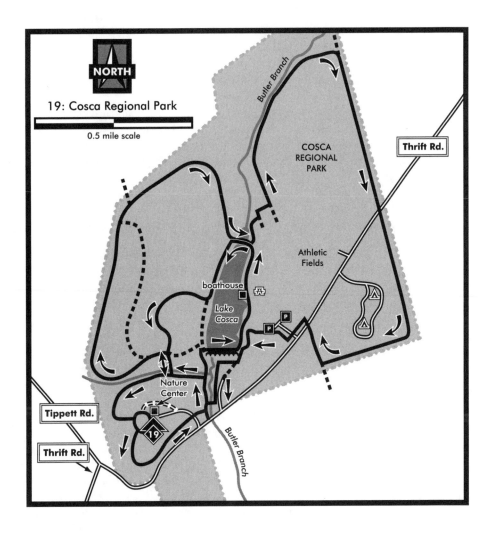

19: Cosca Regional Park

0.5 mile scale

NORTH

Butler Branch

COSCA REGIONAL PARK

Thrift Rd.

Athletic Fields

boathouse

Lake Cosca

P

P

Nature Center

Tippett Rd.

Thrift Rd.

19

Butler Branch

a special garden in summer. Oaks, hickories, beeches, maples, yellow poplars (tulip trees), and gums add to the park's palette in the fall. Deer and squirrels are the most frequently seen four-footed creatures, but others are also present, as beaver-chewed trees attest.

This hike is an easy 5.5-mile loop with only 700 feet of elevation change, which uses of most of the park's trails. Except in warm weather and around the nature center, lake, and picnic areas, there are few visitors. The trails are well maintained, but not well marked or

signposted. So be alert, and stay on the trail and out of the poison ivy.

To get started from the parking-lot trailhead, head uphill on a service road that goes past the nature center. At a circular paved path, go either way around until you see a lopped-off beech tree. There, turn onto a dirt trail. Follow it downhill through the woods to a paved road (the entrance road). Cross and pick up the trail on the far side, next to a "butterfly garden" sign. At a streambank junction, turn right and proceed to the Prince George's Butterfly Garden. With

67

its labeled wildflowers and domesticated plants, the oak-rimmed garden is charmingly colorful in spring—and doubly so in summer, when butterflies abound. Return to the streambank junction.

From here, walk alongside the stream and stay on the trail as it crosses an intersection next to a footbridge and turns sharply left to follow a tributary. At the next intersection, turn right, cross the culverted tributary, and proceed to what I call the "Five Trails intersection." There, take the left-hand-most trail, which goes uphill past several graffiti-ridden beeches. At the first fork, turn left and head downhill. The trail levels off near the tributary stream, on the left. It then climbs and curls to the right. As it levels off again, ignore a side trail on the right and then another on the left. Proceed past a "I Still Love Cindy" beech and an orange trail marker. Continue on a mostly level trail close to the edge of the woods.

Then the trail angles downhill and curves to the right. When you reach a fork, take the main trail to the right, which leads to a T-junction at the north end of man-made Lake Cosca. Turn left and follow the trail across two bridges, pausing to take in the view. If you're there on a warm-season weekend or holiday, you'll probably see boaters and other visitors, as well as ducks and geese (which, alas, expect and get handouts).

Continuing, turn left at the next T-junction to start the hike route's most scenic portion, a half-mile-plus section mostly along Butler Branch, the lake's chief feeder. Follow the stream out from under the trees and across a power-line right-of-way, turning left at a junction. Then cross a small tributary, turn right, and reenter the woods.

Twenty yards farther on, at a T-junction marked by yet another defaced beech, turn left onto a trail that goes uphill. The path then levels off to become a winding trail that stays mostly close to Butler Branch. Stay left at a T-junction marked by an old and signless signpost.

The trail swings right, leaving the stream, proceeds uphill, and then crosses a mini-plateau to reach another T-junction. There, turn right onto a broad and undulating dirt trail—a utility right-of-way dotted with orange markers. Follow the markers for over a mile along the park's eastern boundary. En route, cross another trail and also Thrift Road (the hike's halfway point). At a fence, abandon the markers, turn sharply right along the park's southern boundary and a line of backyards, and head downhill.

After crossing another trail, you'll eventually reach another part of the power-line right-of-way. Out in the open, cross to the far side to reach a T-junction. There, turn right onto a broad dirt-and-grass road and head uphill.

At a paved road (Thrift Road again), turn left and walk along the shoulder for about 100 yards, then cross carefully and head down a paved entrance road. At the bottom, turn left and walk along the road to the second parking lot. Then turn right and walk toward the red-and-white sign at the far end of the lot. There, enter the woods again and step onto a paved path. Take the next left-hand fork, which goes uphill and then curves right and swings gently downhill through the picnic areas. At the end of the pavement, turn left. Then turn right to descend some steps to an intersection close to the dam.

At the bottom, turn left and take a paved path downhill. As it levels off, notice a group pavilion on the left. Just after that, turn sharply right onto a grassy trail leading to the base of the dam. Then turn left to walk along the base to reach Butler Branch, reborn as the lake's outlet.

Turn left to walk along the grassy stream bank and continue on a narrow trail that hugs the shore. When you reach some steps, ascend them to a trail that goes straight, away from the stream, and toward a parking lot. At the lot, turn right and follow a paved road to a foot-bridge spanning the stream. Cross, and then go up the steps to the streambank intersection near the butterfly garden.

There, turn right onto the streambank trail. But at the spot where the trail turns sharply left to follow the tributary, turn right instead and go around a downed tree trunk to reach the water's edge. Step across the tributary and walk upstream along the bank for about 30 yards to the foot of some steps. Ascend and swing left to follow the trail very gently uphill to a T-junction. There, turn right and walk 40 yards to emerge from the woods into a meadow.

Stay to the right on the grass and fol-low the edge of the woods to the dam. Turn right, cross the path-topped dam, and then turn left onto the paved and gravel path along the lake's east bank. Pass the boathouse; note the anti-beaver wire mesh on trees; and swing around the lake's north end, which you visited earlier. Then head south on the dirt trail on the lake's west bank.

Across from the boathouse, turn right onto a hilly woodland trail (the second side trail after a green bench). Follow it to the Five Trails intersection. There, avoid the two trails on your left and the one on the right. Instead, go straight, cross the culverted tributary again, and turn right. From there, a dirt trail follows the stream, then curves to the left and uphill. The trail reaches the circular paved path near the nature center, not far from the trailhead. Remember that the entrance gates close at dusk.

For more information, contact the park, (301) 868-1397, or its nature cen-ter, (301) 297-4575.

NEARBY/RELATED ACTIVITIES

Explore the nature center. Outside, visit the herb garden and the caged hawks, owls, and eagle guarding it (they're maimed birds that couldn't survive in the wild). Go inside to see nature exhibits and live creatures, including Tumbleweed the black-tailed prairie dog. Ask about the center's programs and events.

#20
Fraser Preserve

IN BRIEF
Fraser Preserve is a private nature sanctuary in the northwestern corner of Virginia's Fairfax County close to the Potomac River. It's open to the public and a delightful place to hike.

DIRECTIONS
From Capital Beltway (Interstate 495) in McLean, Virginia, take Exit 44 onto Georgetown Pike (VA 193) heading roughly west. Pass through Great Falls (the community) at 6-mile mark. Proceed on VA 193 for almost 2 miles and turn right at traffic light onto Springvale Road (VA 674). Proceed for 2.3 miles to Beach Mill Road intersection. There, at yellow arrow, take a sharp left, continue about 25 yards, and take first right to stay on Springvale (which becomes VA 755). Continue for about 0.5 miles and turn left onto Allenwood Lane. Park on shoulder on south side of Allenwood close to Springvale.

DESCRIPTION
Fraser Preserve is a 220-acre tract of mature woodlands and floodplain some 14 miles northwest of Washington. Formerly a Washington family's summer refuge, the property was bequeathed to the Nature Conservancy in 1975. A Washington church uses a small inholding as a children's summer camp and church retreat. A single-lane paved road links the preserve's gated entrance to a

KEY AT-A-GLANCE INFORMATION
Length: 6 miles

Configuration: Modified loop

Difficulty: Easy/moderate

Scenery: Woodlands, riverbank views, remnants of 200-year-old canal

Exposure: Mostly shady; less so in winter

Traffic: Very light to light; occasionally heavier when summer camp in session

Trail surface: Chiefly dirt; rooty, gravelly in places; muddy when wet along river

Hiking time: 2.5–3.5 hours (including look-around time at old canal)

Access: No restrictions, but call preserve manager before visiting

Map: USGS Seneca

Facilities: None

Special comments: Observe regulations, posted at entrance; don't drive into preserve, even if gate is open

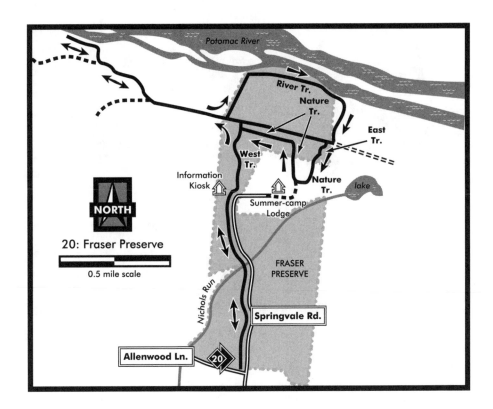

20: Fraser Preserve

0.5 mile scale

cleared area containing the camp's lodge and a caretaker's cottage.

The preserve is slowly reverting to an untamed woodland state, in keeping with the conservancy's emphasis on eco-preservation. Mature deciduous trees dominate the hillsides, with a sprinkling of pines, hollies, and spicebushes providing wintertime color. Alder thickets thrive on the floodplain, and come alive with birds—and bugs—during the warm-weather months. Maples and sycamores lean out over the river. Wildflowers flourish, and resident animals range from deer to salamanders.

This hike is a 6-mile modified loop on well-marked trails with about 1,200 feet of elevation change. It's "modified" for including an out-and-back, history-oriented excursion into undeveloped land owned by the Northern Virginia Regional Park Authority.

The Arlington-based preserve manager asks that hikers call him before entering the preserve (see p. 73).

To get started from the roadside trailhead, return to Springvale Road, turn left, and walk down a narrow paved road about 100 yards to the preserve's entrance. Head north into the preserve, where the road goes up and down for about half a mile before crossing a stream (Nichols Run).

At the end of the road, turn left onto the blue-blazed West Trail. Pause first at an information kiosk. Then head downhill for about a third of a mile. At the bottom, turn left onto a level, unpaved road that follows a sewer-line right-of-way. Stay on the road as it crosses a grassy expanse marking another right-of-way (a buried oil pipeline, at right angles to the sewer line). Continue along the gravelly road, which gradually

This wall formed part of a former canal along the Potomac River.

becomes more of a woodland trail. Stay to the right whenever a side trail tempts you to veer left (I'm not being political).

After about a mile on the road/trail, you'll see the Potomac River on the right. Turn onto a short side trail leading down to the water. At the riverbank, pick up a narrow angler's trail that wriggles upstream for about 100 yards, roughly paralleling a narrow channel between the bank and a small island. Don't stray off the trail; poison ivy thrives in this area.

Watch for the remains of stone walls on both sides of the channel. A little farther on, past the island, you'll find yourself atop a massive piece of old wall that ends at an inlet. The stone work is a remnant of one of several short eighteenth-century canals built by the Potowmack Company as part of its fitful effort to make the Potomac commercially navigable (the small island is still called Potowmack Island). In the 1820s the insolvent company handed over its remaining assets to the Chesapeake and Ohio Company.

Retrace your steps to the main road/trail, and head back to the preserve. At the pipeline right-of-way, turn left onto a dirt trail leading down to the river. The river's edge marks the hike's halfway point 3 miles from the trailhead. If the Potomac seems narrow, remember that you're looking at wooded islands, not the far shore.

Turn right onto the River Trail and head downstream about half a mile on a dirt trail. Rain makes it muddy; horses' hooves make it even muddier. Also watch for nettles and poison ivy close by the trail. Follow the trail inland, go right at a fork, and head upstream alongside Nichols Run. Turn right onto the sewer-line road, go about 15 yards past a gate, and then turn left and head uphill on the blue-blazed East Trail.

Along this trail are the only visible private dwellings beyond the preserve. Some of them are perched above a dam-impounded lake that interrupts Nichols Run on its way to the Potomac. Puff up the trail for several hundred yards and watch for a short metal post splashed with orange and red paint. There, turn right onto the orange-blazed Nature Trail, which snakes across the preserve to the West Trail. The trail itself is faint (and invisible when the leaves are down), so be sure to follow the blazes. On reaching the West Trail, turn left and uphill to return to the information kiosk. From there, head back to the trailhead.

For more information on the preserve, contact National Conservancy's web site (nature.org) or its Virginia chapter, in Charlottesville, (804) 295-6106. You can reach preserve manager Joe Keiger at (703) 528-4952 and caretaker John Thayer at (703) 757-0288.

RELATED/NEARBY ACTIVITIES

After doing the hike once (so you know the route), do it again as a moonlight hike. Return on the same day to try for birdsong at morning and starshine at night. Pick a clear-sky evening when the moon is full. Take along good company, a flashlight, and insect repellent if necessary. Listen for owls, too. Skip the Nature Trail, which is difficult to follow at night. Instead, after hiking the River Trail, take the sewer-line road over to the West Trail and return that way to the trailhead.

Also consider becoming a preserve volunteer. Contact the conservancy's Virginia chapter or Joe Keiger.

#21
Glover–Archbold and other Northwest Trails

IN BRIEF
Using a network of parkland trails, hikers can semicircle semi-secretly through upscale neighborhoods of Northwest Washington, closing the loop along the riverfront.

DIRECTIONS
From Georgetown end of Key Bridge in Northwest Washington, drive west on M Street NW/Canal Road for 0.5 miles. At third traffic light, turn left to stay on Canal Road. Go 1.6 miles to Fletcher's Boathouse, on left. If upper parking lot is full, use lower and larger one. To get to Fletcher's from Chain Bridge, go east on Canal Road for 0.4 miles and make extreme right turn into Fletcher's. *Note:* Canal Road is a weekday rush–hour route that's one–way inbound in morning and one–way outbound in afternoon.

Or use Metro to do hike. Take Metrobus along MacArthur Boulevard, get off at V Street, and walk down to Canal Road and Fletcher's. Alternatively, take Metrobus along Reservoir Road to tap into hike route at 44th Street. Contact Metro, (202) 637-7000 or www.wmata.com.

DESCRIPTION
Ribbons of National Park Service (NPS) parkland carry this diversified, pleasant, and mostly off-street hike through well-to-do Northwest Washington

KEY AT-A-GLANCE INFORMATION
Length: 8 miles

Configuration: Loop

Difficulty: Easy/moderate

Scenery: Woodlands, river views, street scenes

Exposure: Mostly shady; less so in winter

Traffic: Generally light; moderate to heavy along river on warm-weather evenings, weekends, holidays

Trail surface: Mostly dirt; some pavement

Hiking time: 3–4 hours

Access: Trails open daily, dawn to dusk

Maps: USGS Washington West; PATC Map N; map in free NPS Rock Creek Park brochure

Facilities: Toilets, water, phone, warm-weather snack bar at Fletcher's; toilets, water inside recreation center; emergency phone at canal tunnel

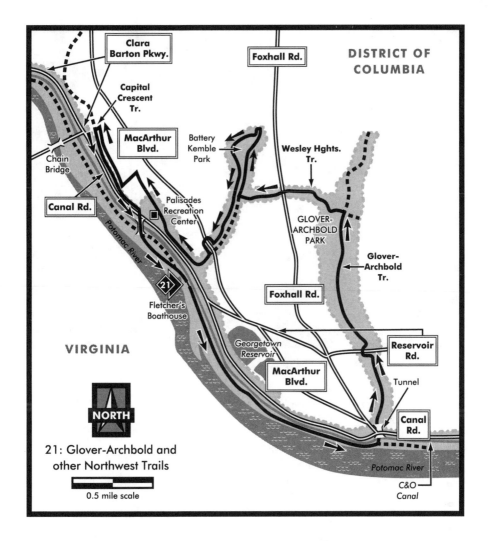

21: Glover-Archbold and other Northwest Trails

0.5 mile scale

neighborhoods. It's an 8-mile counter-clockwise loop that starts and ends on level trails along the Potomac River. The trails in between provide about 1,400 feet of elevation change on a moderately hilly inland excursion.

From the trailhead at Fletcher's Boathouse, head downriver on the unpaved towpath, between the watered C&O Canal and the Potomac. After about a mile, pause to read a plaque about the inclined-plane system used in 1876–89 to transfer boats between the canal and river. Then descend past the

granite and iron remnants of the inclined plane to reach the nearby Capital Crescent Trail (CCT).

Turn left onto the paved, multi-use CCT, and continue downriver for about three-quarters of a mile. Then swing right onto a curving concrete bridge that provides views of both the river and the canal's overflow streams. At the end of the bridge, take a short dirt trail back to the towpath. Then turn right onto another dirt trail and follow it for 40 yards to an off-the-beaten-trail viewing spot on the riverbank.

In summer, the Glover-Archbold Trail spreads a leafy canopy over passing hikers.

Go back to and cross both the CCT and towpath. Follow a lighted tunnel under the canal and Canal Road. Emerging, ascend some stone steps onto a dirt trail (or reach it by taking a sign-posted detour if repairs aren't finished). Then walk under an old trestle (part of the trolley line that once served the Glen Echo amusement park) onto the Glover-Archbold Trail.

The blue-blazed, mostly dirt path follows the wooded Foundry Branch valley gently uphill and northward. After about half a mile, it emerges onto open parkland leading uphill to a busy street (Reservoir Road). Swing left to cross Reservoir carefully (the traffic doesn't have to stop) at 44th Street.

Continuing, follow the trail downhill and through woodlands dominated by mature yellow poplars (tulip trees). At a stream and T-junction, cross on the stepping stones and turn left. Proceed on the mostly dirt trail, even when the surface becomes a large-diameter sewer pipe. Stay on the main trail and ignore the side trails.

At a four-way intersection, turn left onto the yellow-blazed Wesley Heights Trail and head west through the woods. Crisscross a small stream three times, then turn right at the next junction. Follow the trail gently uphill to 44th Street (no street sign there), cross, and turn right onto the sidewalk. Go about 50 yards, then turn left to descend some wooden steps back to the trail at a yellow-blazed post. The trail pitches uphill to reach Foxhall Road at Edmunds Street—the hike's halfway point.

Cross Foxhall carefully, descend some wooden steps, and keep going, generally downhill. Cross 49th Street (no street sign there) and then a short wooden bridge to enter Battery Kemble Park. At the end of the bridge, turn right and head uphill, into the open, and across a popular dog run. Continue to the summit, once occupied by a Civil War gun battery.

Descend 30 yards from the summit and turn right onto a narrow dirt trail. Follow it downhill and across the park's access road. Go left at a fork and then swing right to continue through the woods. You'll emerge at MacArthur Boulevard (no street sign visible), opposite an old schoolhouse. Turn right onto the sidewalk and walk to the corner of Nebraska Avenue to cross MacArthur carefully (the traffic doesn't have to stop). Follow the far sidewalk to the schoolhouse.

Just beyond the building, turn right onto a narrow dirt trail going downhill along Battery Kemble Run's wooded ravine. Near the bottom, stay to the right and on the trail as it curves away from the stream. Go left at a fork. Stay on the trail as it follows the broad, level, and somewhat overgrown former trolley line right-of-way for 1.5 miles. You'll pass a lot of backyards and the Palisades Recreation Center.

Cross Arizona Avenue on a concrete, plant-festooned footbridge, then keep going straight until you reach Galena

Place. Turn left at the sidewalk and go three blocks to where Galena ends at Potomac Avenue (no street sign visible). Cross Potomac and turn right onto the grassy and open shoulder. Stay on it for the next three blocks.

Just after passing Manning Street, take a wooden stairway on the left (across from a speed-limit sign) down to the CCT. Turn left, walk along the trail for half a mile to cross the bridge spanning the canal and Canal Road. Then descend some steps, turn right, and do a final towpath half-mile back to Fletcher's.

For more information on the hike-related parks and trails, contact Rock Creek Park, (202) 282-1063 or www.nps.gov/rocr, and the C&O Canal National Historical Park's headquarters office in Sharpsburg, (301) 739-4200 or www.nps.gov/choh.

NEARBY/RELATED ACTIVITIES
Explore the river or canal in a Fletcher's rental boat (available during warm-weather months). Picnic at Fletcher's riverside park. Or try tiny, eclectic, and inexpensive Bistro Bernoise, (202) 686-3939, located at 5120 MacArthur Boulevard.

#22
Greenbelt Park

IN BRIEF

Secreted in Prince George's County, well-wooded Greenbelt Park is a great place to get fresh air and exercise, look for seasonal color, discover mini-vistas, walk with friends, and contemplate life.

DIRECTIONS

From Capital Beltway (Interstate 495 and I-95), take Exit 23 and head south for 0.5 miles on Kenilworth Avenue (MD 201). Turn left onto Greenbelt Road (MD 193), head east for about 0.3 miles and turn right into park. Alternatively, from Baltimore-Washington Parkway, head west on Greenbelt Road for about 1 mile and turn left into park. Within park, follow winding entrance road for 200 yards and turn right onto Park Central Road (park's chief artery). Follow it for 1.6 miles around Sweetgum picnic area and south through park. Just before the end of that road, turn right onto paved side road (leading to campground) and park at ranger station about 100 yards ahead on right.

Or use Metro to do hike starting near park entrance. Take Green Line train to Greenbelt station, Metrobus C2 along Greenbelt Road, and 100-yard walk into park. Contact Metro, (202) 637-7000 or www.wmata.com.

DESCRIPTION

Located a dozen miles northeast of the White House, Greenbelt Park ranks as

KEY AT-A-GLANCE INFORMATION

Length: 6 miles

Configuration: Loop

Difficulty: Easy

Scenery: Woodlands, stream valleys

Exposure: Lots of shade; less in winter

Traffic: Usually very light to light; heavier near picnic areas, especially on weekends, holidays

Trail surface: Basically hard-packed dirt; rocky, rooty, or grassy in some places; boardwalked in wet places

Hiking time: 2.5–3 hours

Access: No restrictions

Maps: USGS Beltsville; ADC Prince George's Co.; sketch map in free, park brochure

Facilities: Toilets, water, phones near trailhead; toilets at Sweetgum picnic area near park entrance

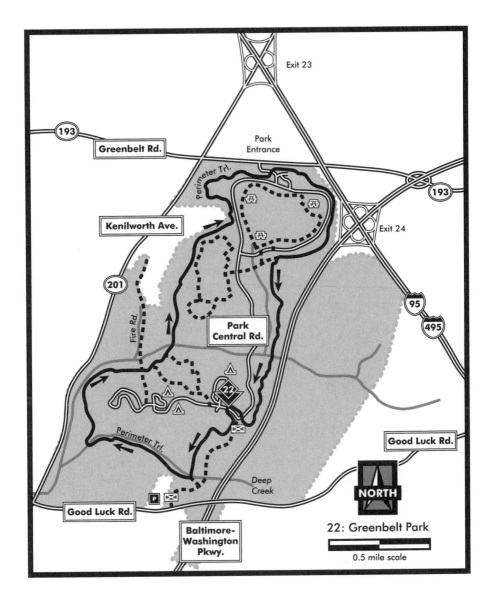

Exit 23

193

Greenbelt Rd.

Park
Entrance

Perimeter Trl.

193

Kenilworth Ave.

Exit 24

201

Fire Rd.

**Park
Central Rd.**

95

495

22

Perimeter Trl.

Good Luck Rd.

Good Luck Rd.

P

Deep
Creek

NORTH

22: Greenbelt Park

0.5 mile scale

**Baltimore-
Washington
Pkwy.**

the second largest nature preserve (after Rock Creek Park) within the Capital Beltway. Covering 1,100 acres, it nestles amid a grid of major highways and suburban streets. Most of it remains undeveloped, with picnic areas and a campground being its major attractions. But it's also an attractive—if little used—hiking locale.

The park is not a wilderness that has thwarted developers. Rather, the park stems from an ambitious federal attempt at large-scale social engineering in the 1930s. Inspired by the international "garden city" movement, the Roosevelt administration bought up marginal and abandoned tobacco fields in Prince George's County. It planned to create an experimental community shielded from Washington by a green belt of open land. But the plan was modified.

The city of Greenbelt was duly built. Most of the open space, though, was incorporated into a sprawling US Department of Agriculture research center. That left Greenbelt Park—formally taken over by the National Park Service in 1950—as the chief buffer zone. The park remains a work in progress. Over six-plus decades, the hemmed-in but well-protected tract has gradually transformed itself into a thriving woodland area that is rich in plant life. It also serves as a haven for such four-footers such as deer, foxes, groundhogs (although I've not seen anything larger than a squirrel), and scores of bird species.

The hike described here is an easy 6-mile loop through the woods, with little elevation change. Each season offers an array of phenomena to observe and experience. Only in a few places does the outside world intrude and that's mostly in the form of traffic noise near the park boundaries.

The hike begins at the ranger station (open every day except Christmas). Remind yourself to stay on the trail and avoid the poison ivy. Then, start the first leg by walking along the side road to Park Central Road. Turn right onto that road and go around the vehicle barrier that protects the bike trail beyond.

Take the dirt trail to the right and then quickly turn left onto the yellow-blazed Perimeter Trail. You'll be on it for the rest of the hike, following the yellow blazes around the park in a clockwise direction. (Most of the park's major trails are color coded and well marked.)

Head south to a boardwalk spanning a marshy area along a shallow stream called Deep Creek. At the next intersection, turn right and stay on the trail as it curves westward close to the same stream. At the next intersection, leave Deep Creek and embark on the second leg by following the Perimeter Trail to the right and north, close to the park's western flanks. Anytime you reach an intersection, take the yellow-blazed option. After crossing a fire road and another stream, Still Creek (which lives up to its name about as much as Deep Creek does), you'll have covered about 2 miles, or a third of the hike.

The hike's third leg is a 2-mile segment that curves past a residential area and turns east across the park's northernmost boundary. There it intersects the entrance road. Cross carefully, then swing past the aptly named Holly and (Mountain) Laurel picnic areas. After that, on the fourth leg, follow the yellow blazes south, cross Still Creek again, and hike roughly parallel to the Baltimore-Washington Parkway. Eventually the trail curves to the right and away from the parkway. At Park Central Road, take the side road back to the ranger station.

For more information, contact the park's on-site headquarters office, (301) 344-3948, or visit www.nps.gov/gree.

NEARBY/RELATED ACTIVITIES

Attend some of the park's annual events held in the fall and also in the spring on Earth Day. Explore the park's birth twin—the nearby city of Greenbelt—and see what's left of the 1930s experimental community, including the Greenbelt Museum, (301) 474-1936), housed in one of the community's original buildings on Crescent Road.

#23
Greenbrier State Park

IN BRIEF

Western Maryland's Greenbrier State Park, is a multi-use facility known for its mountain lake and lakeside amenities. It's also a tranquil and pleasing hiking venue.

DIRECTIONS

From intersection of Capital Beltway (Interstate 495) and I-270, drive northwest on I-270 for about 32 miles to Frederick. Access I-70 and continue northwest for about 15 miles. Leave I-70 at Exit 42 in Myersville and turn right onto MD 17 (Wolfsville Road). Go 1.3 miles and turn left onto US 40. Proceed for about 3.5 miles, crossing I-70 at 3-mile mark. Turn left into park. Drive 0.75 miles to parking lot near visitor center. *Note:* If that lot and others are full, as can happen on summer weekends and holidays, use perimeter parking areas (ask at park for directions).

DESCRIPTION

Greenbrier State Park is a popular facility within the South Mountain Recreation Area. Located in the Blue Ridge region on the mountain's western flanks roughly 60 miles northwest of Washington, the park consists of about 1,300 acres of rolling woodlands surrounding a 42-acre man-made lake. In summer, visitors flock to the lake and its sandy beach mostly to swim, boat, fish, sunbathe, and picnic. Others camp or bike. Strangely, though, hikers are absent.

KEY AT-A-GLANCE INFORMATION

Length: 6.4 miles

Configuration: Loop

Difficulty: Moderate

Scenery: Mountain woodlands, lake views

Exposure: Mostly shady; less so in winter

Traffic: Usually light or very light

Trail surface: Mostly dirt or rocky, with rooty or grassy patches; some pavement

Hiking time: 3–4 hours

Access: Open daily from 8 a.m.–sunset; entrance fee

Maps: USGS Myersville, Funkstown; sketch map in free park pamphlet

Facilities: Toilets, water, phone, warm-season snack bar in trailhead area

Special comments: Stay away during hunting season or take advantage of Maryland's ban on Sunday hunting (see text)

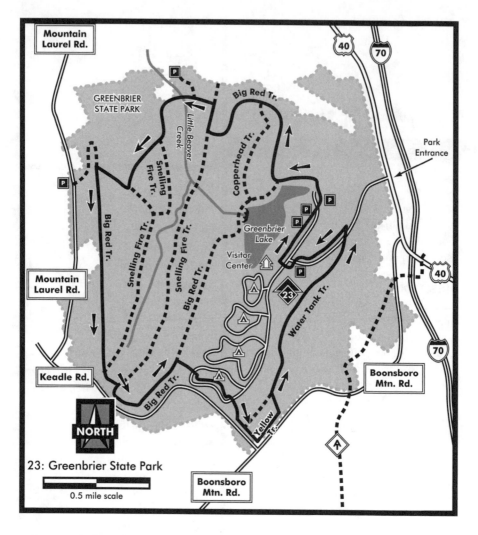

Mountain Laurel Rd.

GREENBRIER STATE PARK

Big Red Tr.

Little Beaver Creek

Snelling Fire Tr.

Copperhead Tr.

Park Entrance

Big Red Tr.

Snelling Fire Tr.

Snelling Fire Tr.

Greenbrier Lake

Visitor Center

Big Red Tr.

Mountain Laurel Rd.

Water Tank Tr.

Keadle Rd.

Big Red Tr.

Boonsboro Mtn. Rd.

NORTH

Yellow Tr.

23: Greenbrier State Park

0.5 mile scale

Boonsboro Mtn. Rd.

Even so, the heavily wooded park, four decades old, is a fine hiking venue. Its deciduous trees mark the change of seasons. Its pines, hollies, and mountain laurels give winter some green. It has wildflowers and birds that add color and flash in the other seasons. It has greenbrier, a thorny vine that not only gives the park its name but also provides deer with browse.

The park's main trails—all lightly used—are named, color coded, blazed, and well maintained—another plus for hikers. Although rather rocky, says

College Park Scott, who recently checked out the hike route, they're smooth, well drained, and quite easy to walk on. Map boards are posted at most major intersections.

In the fall, hunters are allowed to roam the park's western third, which also covers about half of the hike route. Hikers should either stay away in the fall or limit their hiking to Sundays, when hunting is banned statewide.

This hike is a 6.4-mile loop with about 2,000 feet of elevation change. To get started from the visitor center, take either of the paved paths that lead toward the north end of the lake. Pass the boat launching area and follow the lakeshore. At the red-blazed Big Red Trail, turn right to follow it northward into the woods and downhill. You'll be on Big Red for over half of the hike, so think red at trail junctions for the next 3 miles. After the trail swings to the west (left) and is joined by the black-blazed Copperhead Trail, begin the first sustained uphill climb.

At the next junction, where the blue-blazed Royal Oak Fire Trail goes left, stay on Big Red by turning right. At the junction after that, stay on Big Red by turning left rather than going straight on an unblazed trail. Then, after passing another unblazed side trail on your right, you'll arrive at Little Beaver Creek, one of the park's chief streams. Find your way across, with dry or wet feet. On the far side, continue on Big Red.

At the next trail junction, despite the lack of red blazes, stay on Big Red as you pass the white-blazed Snelling Fire Trail on the left. At the junction after that, go right. Ignore any white blazes you encounter and stay on Big Red.

As Big Red's gradient tapers off, look back to see the wooded upper slopes of South Mountain to the east. Continuing, watch for Big Red to turn sharply to the left and level off. Ignore the unblazed trail to the right.

From there, trek southward for almost a mile on an old dirt road that's mostly level, straight, and flanked for half the way by an old stone wall. Big Red follows the crest of aptly named Hickory Ridge, but the tree mix includes conifers that partially block the view.

Continuing, you'll pass the other end of the Snelling Fire Trail on your left. Just after a double-blaze sign (signaling a junction), turn right, proceed for about 10 yards, and then turn left. Still on Big Red, you'll be just past the hike's halfway point in an area of mountain laurel, where wildflowers pop up in attendance in the spring.

At the next junction (to the left is the other end of the blue-blazed fire trail), Big Red jogs sharply to the right. It then curves leftward and heads uphill. About a third of a mile later, after passing through a ruined stone wall, you'll finally part company with Big Red. Turn right onto a short, unblazed trail leading to the Dogwood campground.

That trail, another old dirt road, traverses an impressive pine grove before reaching a clearing. There, leave the campground trail and turn right onto an overgrown dirt road paralleling a stone wall. Follow that road for roughly 200 yards. Then, turn left onto Keadle Road, which cuts through the park.

Starting uphill, watch for Boonsboro Mountain Road and turn left onto it. Continuing uphill, the next turning point, on your left, will be the yellow-blazed Yellow Trail. It'll take you quickly downhill to an intersection. There, turn right onto the silver-blazed Water Tank Trail. Follow it for three-quarters of a mile as it eases gently downhill to the park's entrance road. At the road, turn left and follow it for a third of a mile back to the visitor center.

For more information about the park, contact South Mountain Recreation Area office in Boonsboro, (301) 791-4767.

NEARBY/RELATED ACTIVITIES

In summer, after hiking, cool off at, in, or on the lake. At any season, explore nearby Boonsboro (see p. 16).

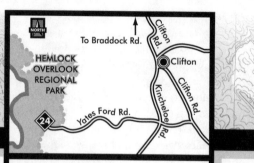

#24
Hemlock Overlook
Regional Park

IN BRIEF

Hemlock Overlook Regional Park borders scenic Bull Run, in southwestern Fairfax County, Virginia. It provides a short and lovely woodland outing for busy or short-winded hikers.

DIRECTIONS

From intersection of Capital Beltway (Interstate 495) and Braddock Road (VA 620) at beltway Exit 54A in Annandale, drive west on Braddock for about 11 miles. Turn left onto Clifton Road (VA 645) and drive south for 5 miles to town of Clifton. Cross railroad tracks, and continue straight on Kincheloe Road at stop sign. At next four-way stop, turn right onto Yates Ford Road (VA 615). Proceed westward for 1.5 miles, almost to end of road. Use parking area on right, shortly before entrance gate to education center's buildings.

DESCRIPTION

Hemlock Overlook Regional Park is one of several multi-use parks lining Bull Run some 25 miles southwest of Washington. Like the others, it's full of hilly scenery. But it covers a mere 400 acres and lacks such amenities as campgrounds and picnic areas. So it's both an attractive and uncrowded hiking locale.

Like the other parks, Hemlock is managed by the Northern Virginia Regional Park Authority. However, it also doubles as George Mason University's Hemlock

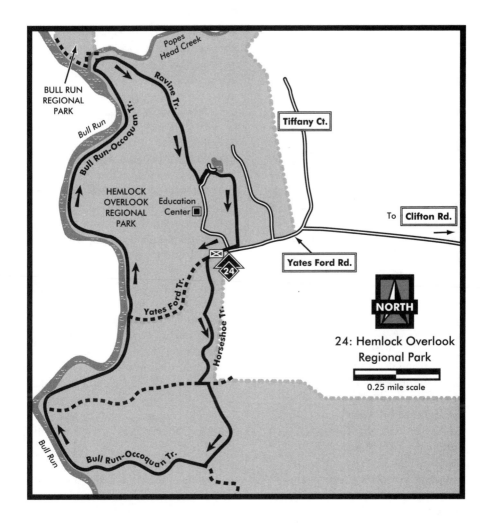

24: Hemlock Overlook Regional Park

0.25 mile scale

Overlook Center for Outdoor Education. The center occupies a small cluster of buildings near the park entrance. Its year-round programs, which also involve the park's grounds, are open to the public by reservation. Hikers should stay on the trails and away from the buildings.

This hike is a short and easy clockwise loop that starts and ends in wooded uplands, accumulating 1,000 feet of elevation change along the way. Be prepared for water, mud, and poison ivy along Bull Run.

To get started from the parking-area trailhead, head west along Yates Ford

Road. Close to the entrance gate, look for a posted trail map and a vehicle barrier. Walk past the barrier and follow the heavily eroded old roadbed downhill between deepening banks.

Watch for the Horseshoe Trail on the left, then climb up and over the bank and head south with the yellow blazes—and an occasional nailed-up horseshoe. After crossing a steep gully and stream go left at a T-junction, where the Horseshoe Trail goes right. Stay on an old road for about 50 yards, then turn right onto a dirt trail and meander through the woods. Ignore the red-triangle plaques;

they're part of the center's orienteering course.

Just over a mile into the hike, as the trail heads steadily downhill, watch for a junction and turn right onto a blue-blazed trail. That's the Bull Run-Occoquan Trail, also called the Blue Trail, which extends along the stream valley. The double-sided mileposts tell hikers—and equestrians—how far they are from the trail's northern terminus (Bull Run Regional Park) and southern terminus (Fountainhead Regional Park).

Follow the blue blazes and Bull Run for almost 2 miles along the stream's floodplain. Take in the fine views; watch for Virginia bluebells and other wildflowers; watch your step in areas that are rocky or rooty; and don't lose the trail when it detours to cross a tributary creek.

Continuing upstream, pass a smallish rock cliff and reach a fork. There, and elsewhere on the floodplain, follow Birmingham Bud's dictum of going right wherever the trail splits (excluding formal side trails). As he says, "You'll get better views of Bull Run and a smoother walk."

After passing through an open area and beneath some power lines, look for the ruins of Virginia's first hydroelectric power plant. Built after the Civil War, it supplied electricity for Clifton. Staying with the blue blazes, climb over some cement steps and continue through a grassy, gladelike area.

At milepost 7/11, watch for the park's namesake overlook and a great stand of eastern hemlocks. Some are two centuries old and seem very tall for growing on a bluff. Take in their soft, sweeping lines and graceful beauty. See if you agree with the long-ago writer who described the hemlock as "music in the form of a tree." If the sunlight is right,

look for the distinctive blue highlights thrown off by hemlock needles.

About 3 miles into the hike, you'll get to Popes Head Creek's mouth on Bull Run. Follow the trail to the right, and walk 50 yards to a trail junction. There, quit the blue-blazed trail, which goes left, and turn right onto the unblazed Ravine Trail. It drops a short way into the creek's ravine, and then climbs a moderately steep ridge. Pause to scan the ravine below. After gaining about 400 feet in elevation, the trail levels off and swings south, away from the ravine.

Just beyond some downed pine trees, emerge onto a large field with man-made blocks used in GMU's onsite programs. Cross the field, ignoring all side trails, and duck back beneath the trees. Proceed along a broad path, ignoring all side paths. At a fork, go left and head for a truly enormous yellow poplar (tulip tree), then keep going, past some cedars.

At a gated paved road, turn left and go downhill on it until you reach a small pond. Look for a boardwalk heading off to the right. Take it, walking alongside the pond on your left. Then watch for a trail going to the right. Take it and head south until a power-line right-of-way appears. Follow that out to Yates Ford Road, then turn right to get back to the trailhead. Contact the park for more information, (703) 993-4354 or hemlock.gmu.edu.

NEARBY/RELATED ACTIVITIES

Sample the activities described in hike no. 8 (Bull Run-Occoquan Trail, p. 26). Homeward bound, stop to explore picturesque Clifton, as Birmingham Bud recommends. The town grew up around an 1868 railroad depot. Today, it remains much as it was a century ago, retaining much of its original architecture.

DORA KELLY
NATURE
PARK

Chambliss

Fillmore Ave.

Beauregard St. N.

Seminary Rd.

Exit 4

395

IN BRIEF

Parklands along Holmes Run enable hikers to traverse western Alexandria on a mostly off-street route that's even somewhat scenic.

DIRECTIONS

Access Shirley Memorial Highway (Interstate 395) heading southwest out of Washington. Get off at Exit 4, about 5.4 miles beyond 14th Street Bridge. There, turn right onto Seminary Road and drive northwest for 0.6 miles. Turn left onto Fillmore Avenue and go 0.5 miles. Bear left onto Chambliss Street North and drive 150 yards to tennis courts on left, near Grimsby Avenue. Park on street or next to courts.

DESCRIPTION

On this easy/moderate and hill-less hike, you'll mostly follow the Holmes Run valley across Alexandria's nontouristy western section. Along the way, you'll encounter city-owned parklands, a healthy marsh, both scenic and scruffy views, an oak older than Alexandria, a colorful off-trail spot—and but a single significant street crossing.

The hike route has no blazes and few signs, so follow the directions carefully. And before starting, check for flooding as follows: From I-395 at Exit 3, drive east on Duke Street, north (left) on Van Dorn Street, and then east (right)—just a

KEY AT-A-GLANCE INFORMATION

Length: 8 miles

Configuration: Modified out-and-back

Difficulty: Easy/moderate

Scenery: Parklands, stream valleys, suburban buildings

Exposure: Mostly shady; less so in winter

Traffic: Usually light; heavier on greenway, especially on warm-weather evenings, weekends, holidays

Trail surface: Mostly pavement

Hiking time: 3–4 hours

Access: Open daily during daylight; until 10 p.m. below Beauregard Street

Maps: USGS Alexandria, Linconia; ADC Northern Virginia

Facilities: None at trailhead; toilets, water, phones at nature center (off trail), along Duke Street, in Ben Brenman Park; toilet on greenway

Special comments: Beware of flooding (see text)

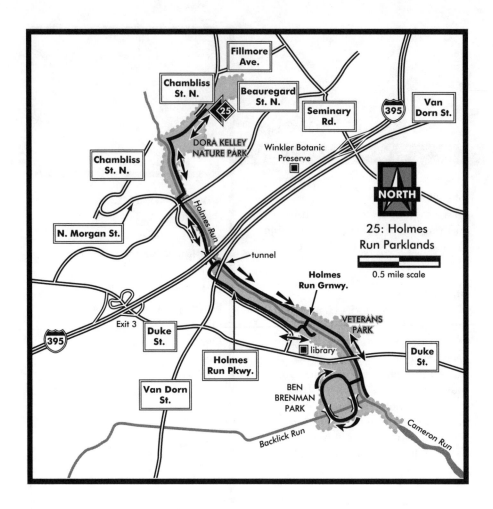

few yards—on Holmes Run Parkway. Park and make sure the causeway is dry.

To get started on the 8-mile out-and-back hike, walk to the end of Chambliss Street North and step onto a paved and downhill woodland trail. At a sidewalkless street, continue on the shoulder. At the bottom of the hill, turn left into heavily wooded Dora Kelley Nature Park (near where Holmes Run also enters).

At the first intersection, turn left and go gently uphill on a fine-gravel trail, passing several numbered nature-trail markers. Just past marker no. 17, turn right, descend some steps, and walk onto a dirt trail bordering a small and flourishing marsh.

Continuing, watch for a paved path. Turn left onto it and proceed, with Holmes Run on your right. At a bulletin board on the left, about 0.75 miles into the hike, detour up the steps (if you want) to visit the nearby Jerome Ford Nature Center (closed Sundays). It has toilets, as well as booklets keyed to trail markers.

At a fork in the main trail, swing right to cross Holmes Run and contemplate the bucolic view upstream. A short incline will take you to North Morgan

Street. There, turn left, follow the side-walk to the nearby traffic light, and cross Beauregard Street North at the hike's only major street crossing.

The tree-shaded path on the far side winds through garden-apartment-fringed woods for half a mile and then passes beneath I-395 in a dimly lit tunnel. Next, it joins Holmes Run (which has its own tunnel) as a concrete walkway that passes beneath Van Dorn Street. After emerging into the open, you'll reach a causeway where the stream continues and the walkway turns left to cross to the far side atop the structure.

After you cross, turn right (past a toilet) onto a paved path that forms the spine of a manicured stretch of parkland known as the Holmes Run Greenway. It's the hike's most popular trail segment.

Just over a mile long, the greenway is bordered on the right by Holmes Run, against a backdrop of big-box condo buildings. On the left are single-family houses that soon give way to woods. Note the huge tree surrounded by a wooden fence. It's a willow oak that's about three centuries old, older than Alexandria. It's still fecund, judging by the nearby seedlings.

A few hundred yards beyond the oak, the trail splits. The left fork leads a few yards to a Duke Street strip mall, the Shops of Foxchase. Detour if you must, but then take the right fork and follow an underpass beneath the busy street to emerge behind a large apartment complex. Staying on the shadeless paved path, take a sharp right at the playground. Walk past a metal footbridge over Holmes Run and then a small waterfall. Continue for 100 yards to where Holmes Run is joined by Backlick Run to form an ugly channelized stream, Cameron Run. But pause to listen to the birds and winds and streams.

Water levels fluctuate on Holmes Run.

Then turn around, having done 3.2 miles, and start the 4.8-mile return trip. At the metal footbridge, again, cross the stream to take a mile-long circuit through Ben Brenman Park. It's mostly a landscaped open space around a central lake. The park occupies part of a former military facility (Cameron Station) that's now covered with condos.

Once across the bridge, take a sharp left onto a perimeter path, then take the next left to cross Backlick Run by bridge. Turn right, follow the stream bank, and then recross the waterway. Swing right onto a side road, cross to the sidewalk, and then watch for a trail on your left. Follow it clockwise around the lake (and its water birds), then return to the metal footbridge and head back to the greenway.

At the first intersection after the old oak, cross Holmes Run on a concrete footbridge and turn left into James Marx All Veterans Park. Follow the winding paved path to the end, continue on a short gravel path, and then pick your way down the overgrown streambank to a lovely, off-the-beaten-trail spot. In summer, you'll find Virginia dayflowers and other plants in bloom—and dragonflies, goldfinches, and chimney swifts in colorful motion.

Retrace your steps to the concrete footbridge, but don't cross. Instead, take the unpaved trail that continues upstream in a narrow strip of parkland between the stream and Holmes Run Parkway. The trail provides good views of the stream and of a large community garden where exotic plants abound in summer. Beyond the garden, the trail is paved and ends at steps leading down to the causeway. That's where you should descend and then turn left and make your way back to the trailhead.

NEARBY/RELATED ACTIVITIES

Explore the nature trail, booklet in hand. Linger at the Shops of Foxchase to eat or visit the city's surviving independent movie theater. Visit the Winkler Botanic Preserve (see hike no. 60, p. 215). Look over Alexandria's central library; bold and geometric outside and spacious inside, it was designed by Michael Graves, who clad the Washington Monument in blue fabric for its restoration year.

#26
Huntley Meadows Park

IN BRIEF

Huntley Meadows Park is a huge nature preserve located in southern Fairfax County, Virginia. It's a great place to take a short hike and a lot of time observing wildlife, especially birds.

DIRECTIONS

From Capital Beltway (Interstate 495 and I-95) in Alexandria, Virginia, take Exit 177A onto Richmond Highway (US 1) heading roughly southwest. After 3 miles, turn right onto Lockheed Boulevard. Go 0.7 miles west to end of Lockheed at Harrison Lane. There, turn left into park's main entrance and go 0.2 miles to visitor center parking lot. If lot is full, park along Harrison and walk in.

DESCRIPTION

Covering 1,424 acres just south of Alexandria, Huntley Meadows Park ranks as one of the metro area's largest close-in parks. Its centerpiece is a 500-acre freshwater marsh—the area's largest—surrounded by mostly deciduous woodlands. The result is a protected natural habitat with a remarkable array of plants and animals.

Huntley is an attractive year-round hiking venue, especially for people keen on natural history. But it has only a few maintained trails. Consequently, Huntley hikes tend to be short in distance, although not always so in time.

KEY AT-A-GLANCE INFORMATION

Length: 4 miles

Configuration: Modified out-and-back

Difficulty: Very easy

Scenery: Wetlands, woodlands

Exposure: Mostly shady; much less so in winter

Traffic: Usually light; crowds of birders, school groups on spring mornings

Trail surface: Mostly fine gravel on main land trails; boardwalk across marsh; dirt on side trail—muddy when wet

Hiking time: 2–4 hours (including time spent looking, listening, inhaling)

Access: Open daily, dawn to dusk

Maps: USGS Alexandria, Mount Vernon

Facilities: Toilets (inside), water, phone at visitor center

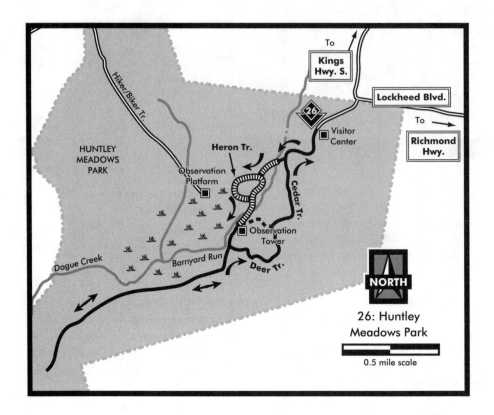

NORTH

26: Huntley Meadows Park

0.5 mile scale

This very easy, 4-mile, and hill-less outing makes maximum use of the trails, which are in good condition, even if sparingly signposted. While hiking, look for well-prepared information boards. In addition, the visitor center stocks seasonal trail guides keyed to trailside markers, as well as flora and fauna checklists. If you're out early in the morning, you're likely to encounter friendly and expert birders.

Be sure to stay on the trail to avoid both poison ivy and ticks, as well as to avoid getting lost (visitors sometimes do go astray). Carry insect repellent during the warm-weather months; Huntley is bug-rich and unsprayed. Also, take along binoculars and maybe a pocket reference book or two.

To get started from the parking lot, take the short paved trail toward the visitor center. Step inside, or return later (it's closed on Tuesdays). At least pick up a seasonal trail guide from the outside dispensing box. Then, walk onto a broad, level, and fine-gravel trail—the Cedar Trail—that heads away from the center and into the woods. With trail guide in hand, watch for the numbered trail markers. At the first trail intersection, go right onto the Heron Trail. Just after that, and past marker 5, is the edge of the marsh. There, a wooden boardwalk crosses almost half a mile across the wetlands to an observation tower with instructive information boards and great views.

See, hear, read, and even smell what the marsh has to offer. In spring, for example, look and listen for migrating songbirds and mating frogs. In summer, watch for water birds and dragonflies galore (sometimes they look like moving

The marsh's beaver lodges are most visible in winter.

blossoms on the duckweed-carpeted water) and maybe catch the scent of a common white-plumed plant called lizard's tail. In the fall, watch for migrating raptors, warblers, and water birds. In winter, ducks hang around if the marsh doesn't ice over.

At any time of the year, look for beaver lodges and dams—and maybe the builders as well. After the former farmland became federal property in 1941, it was used by a succession of agencies. But beavers got a clawhold in some unused areas, and their construction efforts went unchecked when the low-lying land was converted into a county park in 1975.

Leaving the observation tower, step off the end of the boardwalk, walk about 15 yards and turn right onto a dirt side trail. At a broad woodland trail, turn right and hike for about a mile, perhaps picking up the pace along this stretch.

The trail dead-ends at a larger dirt road, your turn-around point and the hike's halfway mark. Heading back, go past the side trail on the left that initially put you on the trail and swing left at the next intersection. Turn right onto a gravel trail (the Deer Trail). At trail marker 12, turn right again to access the Cedar Trail, and head back to the visitor center's parking lot. To learn more, contact the park, (703) 768-2525.

NEARBY/RELATED ACTIVITIES

Explore Huntley's thoughtful visitor center. Check out its nature exhibits and the photo-rich display about the park's history. Scan the visitor logbook for the latest bird finds and peek through the observation window at the outside bird feeder. Ply the friendly staff with questions. For instance, ask about the emu mentioned on the bird checklist. Take advantage of the park's naturalist-led tours and other year-round programs. Try the volunteer-led Monday morning bird walk.

#27
Kenilworth Aquatic Gardens and Park

IN BRIEF

Kenilworth Aquatic Gardens and Park, in Washington's gritty eastern section, is an alluring botanical gem, a too-well-kept secret, and a hiking locale worth visiting in any season.

DIRECTIONS

From downtown Washington, access New York Avenue NE (US 50) heading out of town (northeastward). After passing Bladensburg Road intersection and US National Arboretum, go about 2 miles and turn right onto Kenilworth Avenue (DC 201). Head south for 0.4 miles toward Interstate 295 and then take first right (watch for sign for Addison Road and Eastern Avenue) onto Kenilworth Avenue frontage road. Follow large brown "Aquatic Gardens" signs. Go straight at Eastern Avenue T-junction, proceed for two blocks, and turn right onto Douglas Street. Go 0.3 miles to end of Douglas and turn right onto Anacostia Avenue. Then go left through large gate into visitor parking lot—the trailhead. *Note:* Leaving park can be somewhat tricky. One option is to return to Kenilworth Avenue frontage road and Douglas Street, turn right onto one-way frontage road, go 1.5 miles, turn right onto Benning Road, go right onto 17th Street, and, at Bladensburg Road, go either right toward New York Avenue or left toward Capitol Hill area.

KEY AT-A-GLANCE INFORMATION

Length: 2.5 miles

Configuration: Two out-and-backs separated by a figure eight

Difficulty: Very easy

Scenery: Water-lily ponds, marshlands, woodlands

Exposure: Two-thirds shady; less when leaves are down

Traffic: Very light; heaviest during Founders Day celebration (fourth Sunday in July)

Trail surface: Mostly hard-packed, pebbly dirt; some gravel, grass, boardwalk

Hiking time: 2–2.5 hours (allowing for both birding and water-lilying)

Access: Open daily, 7 a.m.–4 p.m. (but closed on Thanksgiving Day, December 25, January 1)

Map: USGS Washington East

Facilities: Toilets, water, phones at visitor center; water at parking lot

Special comments: Be sure to leave park by 4 p.m., when outer entrance gate is closed

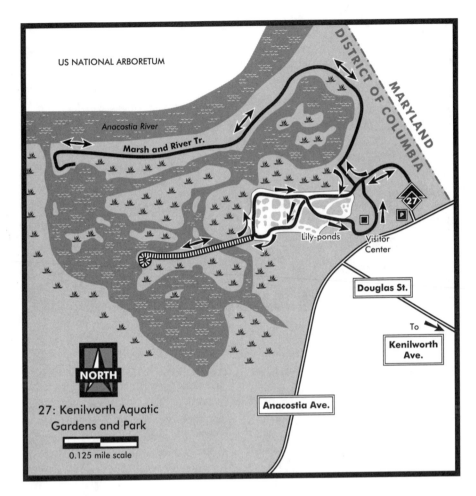

US NATIONAL ARBORETUM

DISTRICT OF COLUMBIA

MARYLAND

Anacostia River

Marsh and River Tr.

Lily-ponds

Visitor Center

27

P

Douglas St.

To Kenilworth Ave.

Anacostia Ave.

NORTH

27: Kenilworth Aquatic Gardens and Park

0.125 mile scale

DESCRIPTION

For a short and exotic urban hike that's wonderfully non-urban, visit Kenilworth Aquatic Gardens and Park, on the Anacostia River near the Prince George's County line. There you'll find gorgeous water-lily ponds, a plant-and-wildlife-rich tidal marsh, wildflower-infested woodlands, and a lovely air of serenity.

As the only National Park Service (NPS) unit devoted to aquatic plants, the park is an intriguing blend of garden and mini-wilderness. Water lilies from several continents fill a 12-acre area of diked ponds (the garden part). Cattails, sedges, American lotus, wild rice and other mostly native plants flourish in the 50-acre marsh and adjoining woods (the wilderness area).

This 2.5-mile hike covers both the gardens and woods. The first leg is a brisk out-and-back excursion of 1.5 miles on a woodland trail. The second leg is a stroll through about half of the lily-pond area. The third is an out-and-back trip on a boardwalk that goes deep into the marsh (take binoculars). The fourth covers the rest of the pond area.

In planning a trip to Kenilworth, remember that the water-lily blooming season lasts from May until September, with color lingering into November.

Fragrant yellow flowers in one of Kenilworth's lotus ponds

The hardy lilies, which stay outside year-round, have blooms that open during the day and are at their peak in June and July. The lotuses and other tropical lilies, which winter in greenhouses, are at their flowering best in July and August. They include both day bloomers and night bloomers. On a morning visit, you'll see—and smell—the day bloomers as they open and the night bloomers before they close.

Remember, too, that the park can be glorious at just about any time of year. I especially recommend using an early morning in winter to watch the sun rise over the marsh and its waterfowl.

To get started from the visitor parking lot, head catty-corner from the entrance gate onto an unpaved service road. It follows the perimeter fence and curves left. The greenhouses beyond the fence produce fresh flowers for the White House. After about 300 yards, turn right onto the signposted Marsh & River Trail. A large information board tells

about the marsh, including its decline and subsequent recent restoration. Both processes involved the US Army Corps of Engineers.

The dirt-surfaced Marsh & River Trail follows a man-made spit rimming the Anacostia River (to your right, although summer foliage hides it). Winding through young and mostly deciduous woods for three-quarters of a mile, it's nicely flanked by wildflowers, shrubs, and poison ivy. You'll get glimpses of the marsh and waterfowl, and perhaps a muskrat or beaver.

The trail hooks to the left along the bank of a narrow channel linking the Anacostia River proper to the marsh and then peters out at the water's edge. Check out the view, note the distant boardwalk, and then return to the information board. From there, swing right at a bamboo clump, and enter the pond area. (Although a figure-eight route is plotted here through the area, you may want to just wander around freely.)

The ponds date from the late nine-teenth century, when a government clerk named Walter Shaw planted some Maine lilies in an old farm pond. His hobby soon became a business. New ponds were dug, exotic species were imported and cultivated, and Shaw's water gardens became both a thriving enterprise and tourist attraction. In the late 1930s, though, the gardens seemed doomed when the US Army Corps of Engineers embarked on dredging the Anacostia and reclaiming the marsh. But the Department of the Interior stepped in and bought the gardens—for $12,000—and made them the core of a new NPS park.

Proceed along the broad gravel perimeter path, passing hardy water lilies and other aquatic plants on your left. Then take the first left (where a white ash holds a large branch over the path) onto one of the many grassy dikes that separate the ponds. Go right at the Y-intersection, past lotuses on your left and hardy lilies on your right; stay left at the next intersection and walk straight through at the one after that. Then, turn right to rejoin the perimeter path. Next, turn left across a small bridge and circle clockwise around a cluster of lotus ponds to reach the boardwalk.

Extending almost a quarter of a mile into the marsh, the boardwalk—and its information boards—introduce visitors to the ecology of a freshwater tidal marsh. Where the boardwalk ends, it's possible to see herons and egrets fishing, ducks bobbing, or an osprey or bald eagle flapping by. Contemplate, or even marvel at, the existence of such a place within the city limits, then retrace your steps to dry land.

Leaving the boardwalk, continue straight on a gravel path and return to the figure-eight pattern by swinging left onto the perimeter path past hardy lilies on your right. The marshlands to the left of the path are a last remnant of the area's original wetlands.

Next are the ponds' spectacular South American tropical lilies called *Victoria amazonica,* with their huge floating pads and night blooming, football-sized flow-ers. Gawk for a moment, and then con-tinue on the perimeter path as it curves to the right, past more hardy lilies. In this area, watch for wet trails that cross the path; they're made by beavers that like to slip into the ponds to munch on water-lily roots.

Turn right at the overhanging white-ash branch (oddly, this seems to be the only tree in the park that's labeled). Swing left at the Y-junction, and head for the rear of the visitor center. There, you'll see specimens of East Indian lotus descended from a couple of centuries-old seeds discovered in Manchuria in 1951. Nearby is a spectacular aquatic plant called *Thalia divaricata,* a native to the Americas. It has rhubarb-colored flower stems up to ten feet in length and two-foot-long spearhead-shaped green leaves. (These plants spend the winter in the greenhouses.)

Finally, head for and pass a large conifer, cross a small parking lot, and then turn right onto a narrow gravel trail that leads through a gate and out to the visitor parking lot. For more infor-mation about the park, contact National Capital Parks—East/KAG, (202) 426-6905 or www.nps.gov/nace/keaq.

NEARBY/RELATED ACTIVITIES

There's much to do at Kenilworth. Tour the visitor center. Take a ranger-guided morning tour of the ponds (daily from Memorial Day through Labor Day; by appointment at other times).

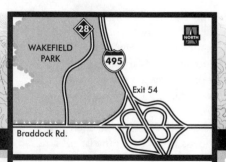

WAKEFIELD PARK
28
495
Exit 54
Braddock Rd.
NORTH

#28
Lake Accotink Park

IN BRIEF

On this woodland outing in the Virginia suburbs just beyond the Capital Beltway's southwestern curve, hikers follow a tree-lined creek, circle an unspoiled lake, and pass a trailside carousel.

DIRECTIONS

From Exit 54 on Capital Beltway (Interstate 495), near Annandale, drive west on Braddock Road (VA 620). At first traffic light, about 100 yards beyond beltway ramp coming in from right, turn right into Wakefield Park. Proceed on park's main road for about 0.5 miles, pass first parking lot, turn left into second parking lot, and park near tennis courts. Alternatively, reach park by using Metrobus service on Braddock Road, and then walk to trailhead. Contact Metro, (202) 637-7000 or www.wmata.com.

DESCRIPTION

Lake Accotink Park is a neighborhood park in the Springfield area of south-central Fairfax County. Most of its 480 acres are covered by deciduous woods that serve as a nature preserve. In warm weather, visitors head for the park's namesake lake to boat, fish, picnic, wander around, loaf, or enjoy the nearby playground and carousel. Year-round, some local cyclists, joggers, and even a few hikers circle the 70-acre lake on a scenic woodland trail. The smart ones stay out of the poison ivy.

KEY AT-A-GLANCE INFORMATION

Length: 6.4 miles

Configuration: Modified loop

Difficulty: Easy

Scenery: Woodlands, lake views

Exposure: Mostly shady; less so in winter

Traffic: Usually light to moderate; heavier on warm-weather evenings, weekends, holidays, and in marina area

Trail surface: Chiefly dirt or crushed gravel; some pavement

Hiking time: 2.5–3.5 hours

Access: Open daily, dawn to dusk

Maps: USGS Annandale; posted trail map around lake

Facilities: Toilets, water, warm-season snack bar, phones near trailhead, at marina

Special comments: Watch for bikers speeding on blind curves

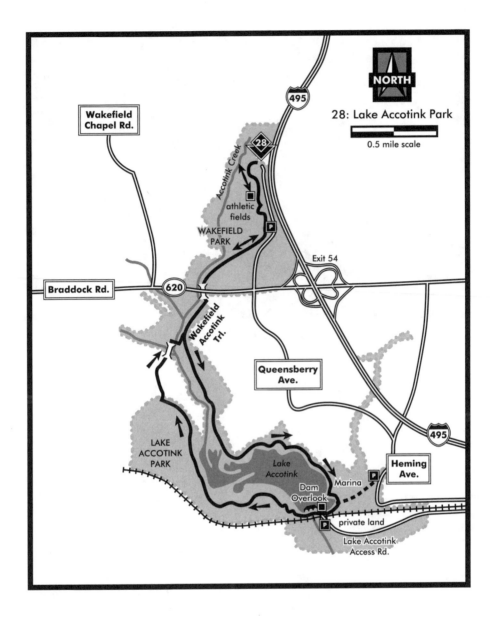

The lakeshore trail makes up much of the 6.4-mile route described below. Although it's no aerobic challenge, it's hilly enough to provide lake views and a modest workout. The rest of the route consists of a level spur trail that follows Accotink Creek downstream from nearby Wakefield Park. The two trails provide an easy and pleasing hike through a seasonally changing landscape in which nature is evident but suburbia rarely absent.

To get started from the Wakefield Park trailhead, head toward the nearby power lines. Take the paved trail that goes downhill past the basketball courts and then swings to the left. Follow it through and past playing fields and a snack bar to

Canada Geese on the beach near the Accotink marina

a sidewalk alongside a parking lot. Then, head for the sign that reads "Wakefield Accotink Trail" and take the crushed-gravel trail that disappears into the woods through an underpass beneath Braddock Road. As other trail signs indicate, this local trail partially coincides with the north-south Cross Country Trail. Continue for about 0.75 miles, following the creek to a trail junction. There, go straight as directed by the "Lake Accotink Marina" sign. Note the trail on the right; you'll take it later after the lake loop. Keep going, though, watching for the lake off to the right as the trail gets a bit hilly, and follow the to-the-marina signs. About 3 miles into the hike is the marina. If you have time, walk out on the spit of land partially enclosing a sandy beach for a panoramic and quite lovely view of the lake.

Resuming the hike, take note of or visit the nearby and colorful carousel. Then continue along the shore toward the dam. The dam dates from the 1930s, when the creek was impounded to provide a water supply for Fort Belvoir. The resultant lake and the surrounding area remained U. S. Army property until the 1960s, when it was transformed into a Fairfax County park. Below the dam, the creek still wanders south to Accotink Bay, accompanied by the Cross County Trail.

Swing right onto the unpaved path that leads to the dam overlook. Take in the view, including the railroad trestle high overhead. Then take the steps down to the paved path that skirts the popular-with-anglers pool at the foot of the dam. Walk past a concrete post marked "Accotink Tr.," then clamber up the steep but short path on the far side (the hike's severest uphill). After that, the trail is fairly level as it follows the long-abandoned bed of a railroad that was the focus of several Civil War skirmishes (the trestle is part of the line that later replaced it). The trail then leaves the lakeshore.

Continuing, watch for a row of houses on your right and then a stumpy marker engraved with "1.5" (that's miles from the marina). Soon thereafter, turn right at the big "Lake Accotink Park Trail" sign and walk downhill into a quiet residential area.

Cross a traffic circle, get on the right-hand sidewalk, and follow undulating Danbury Forest Road for 0.3 miles, past an elementary school. Then, just after crossing Loisdale Road, turn right onto the Accotink Trail (there's another engraved concrete post there). Descend a steep flight of steps, and go 100 yards on a flat dirt trail, then turn right to cross a footbridge spanning Accotink Creek. In another hundred yards or so, turn left onto the spur trail that leads to the Wakefield trailhead. For more information on both parks, contact Fairfax County Park Authority, (703) 324-8700 or www.co.fairfax.va.us/parks.

NEARBY/RELATED ACTIVITIES

During or after your hike, explore the lake by rental canoe (a warm-season amenity). There are some intriguing islands and channels at the lake's western end. For an easier excursion, rent a paddleboat or take a scheduled naturalist-led cruise aboard an electric-powered tour boat.

#29

#29
Lake Artemesia Park and
Northeast Branch Trail

IN BRIEF

This hike is a refreshing excursion through suburban Maryland just north-east of Washington. It features land-scaped parklands, a man-made lake, and a streamside trail.

DIRECTIONS

From Capital Beltway (Interstate 495 and I-95), take Exit 23 and head south for 0.5 miles on Kenilworth Avenue (MD 201). Turn right onto Greenbelt Road (MD 193) and head west for about 0.7 miles. At traffic light, turn right onto Branchville Road. Follow it for 0.7 miles as it traverses industrial park, U-turns under Greenbelt Road, and crosses Berwyn Road to become Bellew Road. Once on Bellew, turn left into parking lot.

Or use Metro to do hike. Take Green Line trail to Greenbelt station, Metrobus C2 along Greenbelt Road to Branchville Road, and then shank's mare for about 0.7 miles to trailhead. Contact Metro, (202) 637-7000 or www.wmata.com.

DESCRIPTION

A hole is to dig, as Ruth Krauss explained in a book so titled. Once dug, it's also a fine thing to use for a lake, especially one that's to be the center-piece of a park.

That's the story of Lake Artemesia, located in Prince George's County near College Park. The Washington

KEY AT-A-GLANCE
INFORMATION

Length: 10 miles

Configuration: Modified out-and-back

Difficulty: Easy/moderate

Scenery: Parklands, water views, glimpses of suburbia

Exposure: Mostly open; more so in winter

Traffic: Usually very light to light; heavier on warm-weather week-ends, holidays

Trail surface: Mostly pavement; some dirt

Hiking time: 4.5–5.5 hours

Access: Open daily during daylight hours

Maps: USGS Washington East, Beltsville

Facilities: Phone at trailhead; toi-lets, water, phone at lakeside build-ing; warm-season-only toilet in Riverdale Park; toilets in other trail-side parks

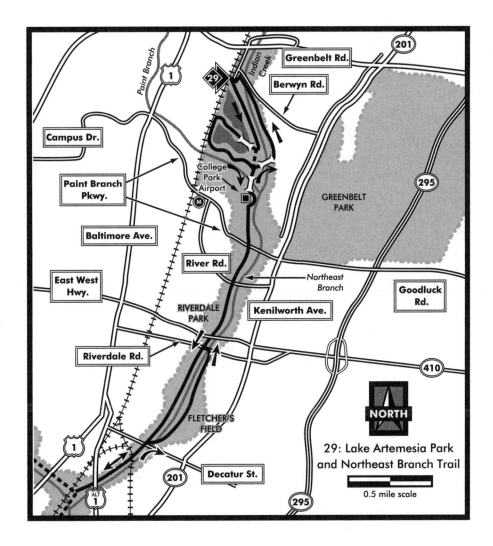

29: Lake Artemesia Park and Northeast Branch Trail

0.5 mile scale

Metropolitan Area Transit Authority needed sand and gravel to build a nearby section of Metrorail's Green Line. So it dug a huge hole in some county land. It then paid to have the hole and environs transformed into a park, complete with a 38-acre lake.

Opened in 1992, the park has a healthy animal population. Residents include beavers, muskrats, deer, and birds. In warm weather, amphibians add to the ambient buzz, as do approximately one zillion insects.

The park is also popular with locals, especially on warm-weather weekends and holidays. The park's paved trails are part of an evolving multi-use trail network known grandly as the Anacostia Tributary Trail System. This modified out-and-back hike of 10 miles extends along the system's Northeast Branch Trail.

From the parking-lot trailhead, head south on the paved trail that parallels Bellew Avenue to quickly reach the park's gated entrance. Walk to a nearby bulletin board. There, bear left and take the paved trail along the shoreline, keeping the water on your right.

The nearby trees are willows, which turn yellow-green in spring. Warm weather also brings color to the lake in the form of blossoming irises and water lilies. When the wind kicks up in the fall, the willows sway and water laps with low sounds by the shore. In winter, a glaze of lake ice and a dusting of snow can eerily bleach the lakescape.

At a five-way intersection, turn right and cross a rustic bridge spanning the narrow channel between the lake's two lobes. Turn right to follow the trail along the curving shoreline. Continuing, swing left and away from the lake. Then turn right just before reaching the park's lakeside building (toilets inside). At the next intersection, turn left.

Stay to the left and follow the lakeshore until just before reaching the rustic bridge. Then turn right and disappear into the woods. Bear right at the next junction, about 1.75 miles into the hike. Thereafter, the trail heads generally south on the mostly flat Northeast Branch Trail for just over 3.5 miles.

The first bridge you'll cross, in a lovely wooded glen, spans Paint Branch. When water reappears, it'll be where Paint Branch joins Indian Creek to form Northeast Branch. The trail then curls around the runway of College Park Airport, the world's oldest continuously used airport.

Passing under a highway (Paint Branch Parkway), reach a junction near the Denis Wolf Rest Stop (really just a sheltered bench). Go straight, across a wooden bridge, and continue. Then take another highway underpass (River Road), leave the woods, and reach Riverdale Park, the first of several well-used community parks you'll traverse.

The next underpass shelters the trail from the East-West Highway (MD 410).

After that, some houses and a few small apartment buildings begin to appear, along with Northeast Branch, a channelized stream in a sunken bed flanked by mowed-in-season grass. At the next and underpass-less road (Riverdale Road), be careful as you cross. After passing through Riverside Park, do the same at the next road (Decatur Street).

After passing under a railroad bridge, you'll be at the hike's 5-mile, or halfway, point. But keep going. Pass under yet another highway (Alternate US 1) and reach the junction of the Northeast Branch Trail and Northwest Branch Trail, the turn-around point. Nearby is the stream junction, where the two branches merge to form the Anacostia River, which flows to the Potomac River.

Heading back northward, recross Decatur Street, but then turn right to take the sidewalk to the far side of Northeast Branch. Turn left onto a dirt trail that follows the stream and passes through a community park called Fletcher's Field. A mile long, it's the hike's only unpaved portion. When the trail reaches a paved access road, continue on the grassy shoulder. At Riverdale Road, turn left, recross the stream, and turn right back onto the Northeast Branch Trail. Remember to turn right near the Denis Wolf Rest Stop.

At the lake area, forget the rustic-bridge intersection. Instead, stay to the right, and watch for a bridge spanning another stream. Cross it and then turn left onto the Indian Creek Trail. Follow that northward for about half a mile. At a paved road (Berwyn Road), turn left onto the sidewalk and keep going, for about 200 yards, to the parking-lot trailhead. For more information on the hike route, contact the Mount Rainier Nature Center, (301) 927-2163, or Prince George's County Department of Parks and Recreation, (301) 445-4500.

#30
Leesylvania State Park

IN BRIEF

While locomoting through Leesylvania State Park, in southeastern Prince William County, hikers can commune with nature and visit sites associated with Virginia's celebrated Lee family.

DIRECTIONS

From Capital Beltway (Interstate 495 and I-95), take Exit 57A onto I-95 heading southwest toward Richmond. If you start from Washington, head southwest on Shirley Memorial Highway (I-395) to automatically be on I-95 when you cross beltway. After going about 13 miles, you'll see next-exit signs for Leesylvania Park. At Exit 156, get into exit lane, and take left fork when it splits, following VA 784. Go east on VA 784 for 0.8 miles to its intersection with US 1. Turn right, go south for 1 mile, and turn left onto Neabsco Road. Go east for 1.5 miles to park entrance. Turn right onto park's access road, and go about 0.5 miles to fee-collection kiosk. Then continue to trailhead at first gravel parking lot on right. If lot is full, continue on access road and use another lot as alternative trailhead.

DESCRIPTION

Leesylvania State Park lies on a small peninsula poking into the Potomac River about 25 miles southwest of Washington. Its landscape features wooded uplands, wetlands, coastal bluffs,

KEY AT-A-GLANCE INFORMATION

Length: 7.6 miles

Configuration: Modified out-and-back

Difficulty: Easy/moderate

Scenery: Wooded uplands, wetlands, river and beach views

Exposure: Mostly shady; less so in winter

Traffic: On riverfront, mostly heavy on warm-weather weekends, holidays, much lighter at other times; elsewhere, very light to light

Trail surface: Mostly dirt; also some boardwalk, pavement, gravel, pebbles, sand

Hiking time: 3–4 hours

Access: Open daily, sunrise to dusk; entrance fee

Maps: USGS Quantico, Indian Head; sketch map in free park flyer; posted park map

Facilities: Toilets, water near trailhead; toilets, water, phone, warm-season food store on riverfront; water at Freestone Point

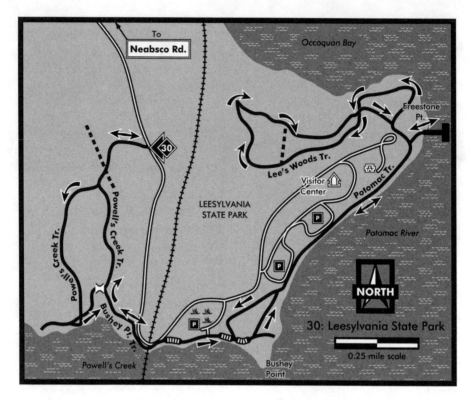

To **Neabsco Rd.**

Occoquan Bay

Freestone Pt.

30

Lee's Woods Tr.

Powell's Creek Tr.

Visitor Center

Potomac Tr.

LEESYLVANIA STATE PARK

Powell's Creek Tr.

P

Potomac River

P

Bushey Pt. Tr.

P

NORTH

30: Leesylvania State Park

0.25 mile scale

Powell's Creek

Bushey Point

a sandy beach, and hiking trails. Trees and wildflowers flourish, as do deer, beavers, and other four-footed creatures. Fauna watchers, though, mostly prize its eagles, ospreys, ducks, cormorants, and herons.

The park's origins date to the 1750s, when Henry Lee II developed a plantation called Leesylvania. One of the children born and reared there was Henry Lee III, the Light-Horse Harry of Revolutionary War fame. The property stayed in the family's hands until 1825. But the Lee link was revived during the Civil War, when a son of Light-Horse Harry's, General Robert E. Lee, had a gun battery installed to help blockade Washington. For a century thereafter, the area was used by assorted tobacco farmers, loggers, fishermen, traders, squatters, hunters, and gambling-ship operators. In the late 1970s, philanthropist Daniel

Ludwig acquired and donated much of the area to the state of Virginia. The park was opened in 1992.

The 508-acre park is a very popular warm-season destination for boaters and beachgoers. The riverfront gets crowded, and the boat engines roar. As hike scouter Birmingham Bud advises, "This bedlam mars the middle section of the hike, so schedule your visit carefully." Of course, the park's at its colorful best in the spring and fall, and some winter days there can be starkly beautiful.

This 7.6-mile hike includes several short trails and other paths. Some are named, color coded, and blazed, but some are not, so follow the directions diligently. The hills will give you only about 1,000 feet of elevation change.

To get started from the parking-lot trailhead, head for an interpretive kiosk to pick up a self-guiding booklet keyed to numbered trailside posts. Then hike south on a wide, gently rising trail. The trail levels off and passes a fire road on the right. At the information kiosk (where several trails intersect), go right and follow the "Powell's Creek Trail" sign.

At a trail fork, turn right to follow the western side of the nominally blue-blazed Powell's Creek Trail loop. You'll quickly lose some elevation and tree cover as you near Powell's Creek. At a set of stairs, detour some 50 feet to view the creek, and then descend the stairs.

The trail curves left at the bottom as it follows a gully filled with various aquatic plants. Stay with the trail as it takes you across a bridge and up a moderately steep hill to another set of stairs. At the top, just over a mile into the hike, are a bench and trail junction. Continue straight on the green-blazed Bushey Point Trail (to the left is the Powell's Creek Trail's return loop).

As the trail descends, enter a ravine, pass a marshy area, and cross a bridge. Then, walk up a short incline and some steps to reach the park's access road. Turn right to walk along the road berm. When an obvious path appears along the road, hop aboard to continue along the shore and beneath a railroad trestle on the Washington–Richmond main line. The path soon leaves the road, crosses, and traverses some marshy areas. There, in summer, watch for lizard's tail, a tall herb bearing tiny white flowers on drooping spikes. In winter, watch for eagle groupies and their prey, which roost around Bushey Point.

At the next trail junction, take the tree-shaded narrow path that runs along the water. Cross a bridge and parking lot, pass a maintenance building on the left, and cross another bridge to reach a trail junction. There, go straight, but note

the left-hand trail, which is the one you'll return on.

At the next junction, stay to the left and pass through a tunnel of pawpaws beneath towering yellow poplars (tulip trees). Soon after the trail merges with another (on the left), it ends, about 2.5 miles into the hike.

Then you'll need to negotiate a trail-less area to reach the Potomac Trail. To do so, leave the trees, head slightly to the right and follow a parking lot to a boardwalk just past the first boat ramp (the well-stocked park store will be off to your left). Stay on the boardwalk until it ends at a second boat ramp. Then walk straight ahead to where the trees resume and the Potomac Trail begins.

The half-mile yellow-blazed trail consists of a wide and flat gravel path running between the river on the right and the popular-with-families-in-summer beach and picnic area (the park's no-swimming rule minimizes your risk of tripping over kiddies). Toward the trail's end, as it begins curving left, you'll reach Freestone Point and draw abreast of a fishing pier to the right. Detour to visit the pier, which provides fine river expansive views. Also take a short walk on the beach, where sandstone blocks are reminders of a long-ago quarrying operation.

Return to the main path and turn right, pass through a gate, and continue to a sign for the "Lee's Woods Trail," and an interpretive kiosk featuring a park map. From the kiosk, get started on the 2-mile, red-blazed trail by walking straight and taking a pebble pathway that curves to the right and uphill. Note the amphitheater on your right, built on the ruins of a 1920s hunting club.

Continue up the hill until it flattens out at the Civil War fortification. The path winds around it, passes a replica cannon, and continues straight, affording views of Occoquan Bay to the right. Go through a fence into an open glade and then turn right, following a sign that points to stops no. 3 and no. 4 (consult your booklet). Just past no. 3, go straight on a short spur leading to a fenced area offering more views of the bay. If it's winter, watch for eagles, which roost in that area.

Return to the main trail and swing right and downhill. At the junction at the bottom, turn right onto a wider and stonier trail and immediately begin to ascend. As the trail curves to the right and flattens out, look for the ruins of the house built in 1825 by Henry Fairfax, Leesylvania's first post-Lee owner. The building burned down a century later.

Ascending once more, stay on the main trail and ignore the side roads as you proceed toward stop no. 8, the site of the original Lee mansion, destroyed by fire in the 1790s. There, take a sharp turn to the right and continue upward to an open glade. Then it'll be downhill yet again, initially on stairs. Reaching a trail fork, turn right and keeping going. At the next junction, just continue, Birmingham Bud suggests, rather than detour right to the Escaped Gardens where, he says, "You can see common trees you have already encountered on the hike."

The trail climbs another hill, and at the top is a gated enclosure around the Lee-Fairfax family cemetery (Henry Lee II is there). Follow the trail to the right, toward stop no. 11. It meanders through the woods, past a fire road and an above-ground sewer pipe, to reach an intersection where you should turn left and

initially head downhill. Stay on the main trail as it curves to the right and undulates back to the kiosk near the amphitheater. By then, you'll have completed about 5.4 miles.

The hike's remaining 2.2 miles mostly retrace the route back to the trailhead, but covers some new-to-you stretches of trail. Just after getting back on the Bushey Point Trail, turn right at the fork onto a new-to-you stretch of trail. At the following junction, turn left onto a gravel path. At the one after that, turn right to rejoin the main trail. Then work your way back to the railroad trestle and ravine to reach a junction. There, turn right onto the new-to-you eastern part of the Powell's Creek Trail.

At the next junction, turn right to do the final short leg back to the trailhead. Follow the signs, and don't be led astray by the fire roads. Contact the park for more information, (703) 670-0372 or www.dcr.state.va.us/parks /leesylva.htm.

NEARBY/RELATED ACTIVITIES
Visit the visitor center (summer only) to see its history and science exhibits. Attend the annual Leesylvania Natural Heritage Day, held on the riverfront in May. Contact the park for details.

Birmingham Bud suggests visiting the Julie J. Metz Wetlands Mitigation Bank to view its 200 acres of wetlands along Neabsco Creek. It's on Neabsco Road 1 mile west of the park entrance. Visit the Bug Box, an unusual insect zoo/museum in nearby Woodbridge. Call for details and directions, (703) 551-0071.

#31
Lincoln Memorial to Lincoln Park

IN BRIEF
Roaming the Mall and Capitol Hill on foot serves as a wonderful introduction to hiking in the nation's capital—and to the city's heritage and treasures.

DIRECTIONS
Head for Mall area. Park near trail-head—Smithsonian Metro station entrance within Mall (near Independence Avenue and 12th Street SW). Arrive early on crowded warm-weather weekends and holidays, beware local parking regulations. Or use Metro: Smithsonian station is on Orange, Blue Lines; Metrobuses operate on nearby streets. Contact Metro, (202) 637-7000 or www.wmata.com.

DESCRIPTION
Each Fourth of July, half a million folks crowd onto Washington's Mall for a special birthday celebration. Between one Fourth and the next, they and others frequent the Mall's museums, monuments, and memorials and gather to play, picnic, stroll, jog, bike, relax, protest, march, and sightsee. The Mall, in effect, serves as the nation's front yard, town square, commons, pulpit, soapbox, park, and memorial garden. It's also a great hiking venue where one can take self-propelled voyages of discovery and rediscovery. And it's small enough to cover on foot, but big enough for a person to get some serious exercise—and avoid the crowds.

KEY AT-A-GLANCE INFORMATION

Length: 8.6 miles

Configuration: Loop

Difficulty: Easy/moderate

Scenery: Parklands, public buildings, memorials, street scenes

Exposure: Mostly open

Traffic: Light to moderate; much heavier, in tourist season, especially on Mall, weekends, holidays

Trail surface: Mostly pavement; some gravel, grass

Hiking time: 4-5 hours (excluding impromptu detours)

Access: No restrictions

Maps: USGS Washington West; ADC Metro Washington; free map on Mall area display boards and other locations in and around the Mall

Facilities: None at trailhead; toilets, water, phones in museums,and other locations in and around the Mall

Special comments: Finish hike by dusk

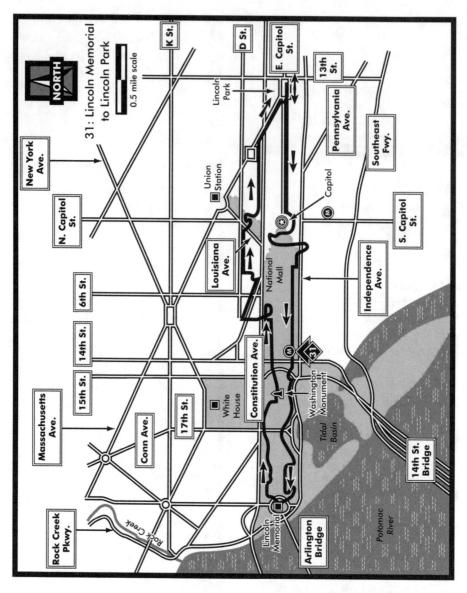

K St.

D St.

E. Capitol St.

13th St.

Lincoln Park

New York Ave.

N. Capitol St.

Pennsylvania Ave.

Southeast Fwy.

Union Station

Capitol

Louisiana Ave.

6th St.

National Mall

S. Capitol St.

Independence Ave.

14th St.

15th St.

17th St.

Constitution Ave.

White House

Washington Monument

14th St. Bridge

Massachusetts Ave.

Conn Ave.

Tidal Basin

Rock Creek Pkwy.

Rock Creek

Lincoln Memorial

Arlington Bridge

Potomac River

This 8.6-mile, clockwise loop ranges fully across the Mall. It also goes further, and encompasses other areas and aspects of the city. It's planned as a daytime hike, though, so it stays outdoors (except for a peek at the biggest Lincoln). Detour if you want to, but do maintain a good pace between stops, be careful crossing streets, and use the paths and sidewalks. Many people take "the Mall" to mean the

2.2-mile stretch between the Lincoln Memorial and the Capitol. Officially, though, the Mall—or National Mall—is only the part east of 14th Street, and the memorial is in West Potomac Park. But worry not. The entire area is under National Park Service jurisdiction.

To get started from the Smithsonian Metro station on the Mall, head south (toward Independence Avenue) for about

20 yards. Turn right onto a broad paved path alongside Jefferson Drive. Follow the path across 14th and 15th Streets NW, then turn left and almost immediately turn right onto a short, narrow, paved, and downhill path. At the bottom, turn left onto another paved path. Follow it west alongside Independence Avenue and past the Sylvan Theater.

At 17th Street, cross at the traffic light. Look or jog left to see the hike's first war-related memorial, on a traffic island. Erected in 1912, it depicts American Revolution naval hero (and later Russian admiral) John Paul Jones ("I have not yet begun to fight"), but supplies visitors with no details.

Continue on the path along Independence, detouring as needed around the fenced World War II Memorial construction area. Turn right to visit a circular bandstand, built in 1931 as a memorial to the District residents who served and died in World War I. Keep going, to reach and turn left onto a service road. Pass some yellow-topped bollards and continue on a paved path to a four-way intersection. There, turn left and tour the Korean War Veterans Memorial. Dedicated in 1995, it depicts a squad of soldiers on patrol in Korea. Made of stainless steel, the grim figures are reflected in a polished black granite wall on which hundreds of faces are faintly etched.

Return to the intersection, head for the nearby Lincoln Memorial, and climb the 56 steps (Lincoln died at age 56). Enter the great chamber to face the seated marble figure that's four and a half times life size. Notice Lincoln's fingers, bent to form "A" and "L" in sign language (Lincoln supported education for the deaf; sculptor Daniel French had a deaf son). An inscription above Lincoln's head celebrates his having saved the Union, but ignores his role in ending

slavery. As the writer later explained, the memorial—opened in 1922—was meant to help heal the North/South rift, so it was best to "avoid the rubbing of old sores." But architect Henry Bacon had the chamber walls inscribed with the Gettysburg Address and the second inaugural address, which make clear Lincoln's views.

Before leaving, look eastward along the Mall from the top of the steps. Note the World War II Memorial under construction beyond the Reflecting Pool. See if you think it will compromise the view. Then descend the steps, swing left, and head for the Vietnam Veterans Memorial.

After passing an information kiosk, stop near a flagpole to see a three-guys-with-guns sculpture. Then take the paved path along the base of a sunken black granite wall carrying the names of the Vietnam War dead and missing. When dedicated in 1982, the memorial designed by Maya Lin consisted solely of the engraved wall. As she later wrote, "I did not want to civilize war by glorifying it or by forgetting the sacrifices involved." But her design provoked controversy. That led to Three Servicemen being added near the flagpole in 1984. The Vietnam Women's Memorial, showing three nurses aiding a fallen soldier, was added in 1993. To see it, turn right at the far end of the wall and then right again at the next junction.

From there, retrace your steps to the last junction and walk straight (east) on a paved path through Constitution Gardens. At a small lake, swing left and follow the paved waterside path to an elevated plaza. Cross it, staying left, and swing left onto a diagonal paved path leading to 17th Street. Circle the nearby boarded-up stone house. An 1835 canal lock house, it's both the Mall's oldest building and a reminder that a canal once ran along what are now Constitution Avenue and 17th Street. The canal was paved over in the 1870s, but the area west of 17th was a mosquito-infested marsh until the 1920s.

Cross 17th and swing right onto a diagonal paved path. At the end of the path, cut right, across the grass, toward a broad paved path leading to the sublimely abstract Washington Monument. When finished in 1884, the shaft topped out at about 555.5 feet. It's still the city's tallest masonry structure. But it's sinking at a rate of 5.64 inches a century and will disappear by the year 118,900.

Circle to the left around the monument and take the paved path leading down to the ticket kiosk on 15th Street. Cross that street and 14th Street, and head east on the Madison Drive sidewalk for five blocks, past the American history and natural history museums. Then turn left to walk through a butterfly garden that's colorful in the spring and summer, even without butterflies.

At Constitution Avenue, turn right to cross 9th Street. Then turn right to circle through the 6-acre National Sculpture Garden. Opened in 1999, it's part of the nearby National Gallery of Art (the Mall's only non-Smithsonian museum). It features serious and whimsical modern sculptures set around what doubles as a summer fountain and winter ice skating rink.

From there, cross Constitution and walk north on 9th Street. At Pennsylvania Avenue, turn right onto the avenue. On that corner, next to the National Archives, note the memorial to Franklin D. Roosevelt that FDR himself had requested; it's desk-sized, unlike the 1997 FDR memorial at the Tidal Basin. Proceed along the avenue, cross to the other side at 6th Street, and proceed to the Embassy of Canada. Walk up the steps,

stand in the small rotunda, sing, and liste. to the acoustic effects incorporated into the striking 1989 building. Roam the open courtyard, with its hanging garden and Bill Reid's beguiling bronze sculpture, *The Spirit of Haida Gwaii*. Then cross a brick driveway to enter John Marshall Park. Cross to the far side to check on a playful 1988 chess game between two men seated on a low wall. Head uphill through the park, past a statue of Marshall (the country's fourth chief justice) and across two streets to view a thin and austere Lincoln, at the hike's halfway point. Carved by Lot Flannery, who had known his subject, the 1868 granite statue was funded by citizen donations as the first public monument to Lincoln.

Turn right to head east on D Street. Pause to inspect *Guns into Plowshares,* an arresting 1997 sculpture by Esther and Michael Augsburger. Continue for four blocks. Then cross and turn right alongside New Jersey Avenue. At the next corner, turn left onto Louisiana Avenue and then left again into the Japanese American Memorial to Patriotism during World War II.

Opened in 2001, the memorial, or Mahnmal, recognizes the unjust wartime internment of over 120,000 Japanese-Americans. It's the only memorial I know that's an apology, as affirmed by Ronald Reagan's inscribed words: "Here we admit a wrong." It also honors the Japanese-Americans who served in the armed forces. Designed by Davis Buckley, it includes powerful symbols; a sculpture of two cranes ensnared in barbed wire, a reflecting pool resembling a Zen garden, and a remarkable bell that, when sounded, emits a low and vibrant tone.

Leaving the memorial, turn left, walk to the corner of D Street, and cross Louisiana Avenue. Then take a paved path on the right to head south past a pool and a fountain. This is Union Station Plaza, atop a huge government garage. Continue walking through the lovely parklike area toward the Capitol. At Constitution Avenue, turn left and follow the avenue eastward.

At the corner of 2nd Street NE, take a look at the Sewall-Belmont House and its historical plaques. Since 1929, it's been the Women's National Party headquarters. In 1814, it was the only private building torched by the British invaders—after snipers in the house annoyed the British general by shooting his horse.

After crossing 2nd Street and Maryland Avenue to stay on Constitution, you'll be in a Capitol Hill area of tree-lined streets and well-kept row houses. Proceed for about five blocks and then swing right onto Massachusetts Avenue and follow it to 11th Street. Then turn right, walk one short block to East Capitol Street, and turn left to enter Lincoln Park.

Follow a paved path to *Emancipation,* a bronze monument paid for by emancipated blacks but designed by whites that depicts a magisterial Lincoln standing next to a crouching African-American man. At the 1876 dedication, the keynote speaker, abolitionist and local resident Frederick Douglass, chided sculptor Thomas Ball for the croucher's subservient posture.

Continue along the path to see the Mary McLeod Bethune Monument and what difference a century can make. Created by Robert Berks in 1974, almost two decades after Bethune's death, the twice-life-size monument shows the educator, civil-rights leader, and National Council of Negro Women founder handing a young boy and girl a rolled document. Composed the year

she died and as inscribed on the pedestal, it's her 68-word "Legacy": "I leave you love. I leave you hope. I leave you the challenge of developing confidence in one another. I leave you a thirst for education. I leave you a respect for the use of power. I leave you faith. I leave you racial dignity. I leave you also a desire to live harmoniously with your fellow man. I leave you finally a responsibility to our young people." When the monument was finished, *Emancipation* was turned to face it.

Walk back through the park and head west for ten blocks on boulevard-like East Capitol Street. As the Capitol looms ahead, you'll pass the Folger Shakespeare Library, the Library of Congress, and the Supreme Court building. Proceed directly to the Capitol and then turn left to walk around the south end to reach the vista-rich terrace on the west front—if you can.

You may have to detour if the terrace remains closed for post-9/11 security reasons and also if work has begun on a huge underground visitor center (the largest addition since Lincoln pushed wartime completion of the remodeled Capitol). If so, swing left and downhill and turn right onto a curving path leading past the base of the west terrace.

Continuing, turn right at a fork next to a stumpy tower (a Capitol ventilation shaft) to reach a roofless brick structure half-hidden in a small grove. It was designed as a summer retreat for members of Congress by Frederick Law Olmsted when he landscaped the Capitol grounds in the 1870s. Peer into its tiny and charming grotto if it isn't locked).

Then return to the fork next to the tower. There, turn right and follow a curving path (Olmsted didn't like straight lines) to 1st Street NW. Crossing it, note the so-called Peace Monument, erected in honor of the Union seamen who died in Civil War. Head for the nearby reflecting pool, and then turn left onto a promenade between the pool and a huge memorial to Ulysses S. Grant. Finished in 1922, the memorial depicts soldiers caught up in the frenzy of war, as well as a brooding Grant on horseback. It's realistic, but doesn't glorify war. Note the fallen trooper. The face is that of sculptor Henry Merwin Shrady, who labored on the memorial for over 21 years and died just before it was dedicated. This memorial is the most tersely labeled one I know. It bears just one word: GRANT.

Return to 1st Street and proceed southward, passing an 1887 statue of President James Garfield and then the US Botanic Garden's renovated and dazzling conservatory. At Independence Avenue, cross to explore a small garden packed with assorted and labeled plants set around a large fountain.

Recross Independence, turn left, and head west, past the conservatory and the site of the future National Garden. Turn right onto 3rd Street, cross Maryland Avenue, and turn left onto Jefferson Drive, across from the future National Museum of the American Indian.

Continue westward on Jefferson, past the Air and Space Museum and across 7th Street. Abreast of the doughnut-like Hirshhorn Museum, swing right to wander through its sunken and well-filled sculpture garden. Emerging on the inner Mall, follow a broad gravel path west to the trailhead. Along the way, your pass the Smithsonian Castle and more Smithsonian museums, as well as a working antique carousel.

For more information about the Mall area, contact National Capital Parks, (202) 619-7222 or www.nps.gov/nacc.

Nearby/Related Activities
During or after the hike, explore the buildings along the route. If you don't mind crowds, repeat the hike during the Mall's annual Smithsonian Folklife Festival or Fourth of July festivities—and allow yourself extra time.

#32
Little Bennett Regional Park

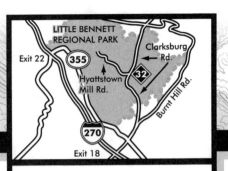

IN BRIEF

Little Bennett Regional Park, in northern Montgomery County, is a hiker's delight. Its secluded wooded hills offer such treats as a magnificent upland meadow and splendid grove of yellow poplars.

DIRECTIONS

From junction of Capital Beltway (Interstate 495) and I-270, head northwest on I-270 (toward Frederick) for about 18 miles. Get off at Exit 18 and turn right onto Clarksburg Road (MD 121). Drive east on Clarksburg for 2.3 miles. Then, after reaching bottom of hill on straight road, take first right—at gravel-road intersection—into small parking lot. *Note:* While on Clarksburg, ignore sign indicating that park is on Frederick Road (MD 355); that's just park office.

DESCRIPTION

Located about 23 miles northwest of Washington, Little Bennett Regional Park is a superlative hiking venue. It's Montgomery County's largest park, covering almost 3,650 acres (a small piece also juts into Frederick County). A park since 1975, it has the county's largest expanse of continuous woodland, splendid scenery, much wildlife, a trail network, and few human users.

This hike is a challenging 12.6-mile grand tour, with about 4,000 feet of

KEY AT-A-GLANCE INFORMATION

Length: 12.6 miles

Configuration: Modified loop

Difficulty: Difficult

Scenery: Wooded hills, meadow vistas, stream valleys

Exposure: Mostly shady; less so in winter

Traffic: Usually very light; light at its heaviest

Trail surface: Mostly dirt, plus some gravel, grass, pine needles; rocky, rooty, muddy in places

Hiking time: 7–8.5 hours

Access: Open daily during daylight hours

Maps: USGS Germantown, Urbana

Facilities: None at trailhead; phone at Hawks Reach Activity Center; roadside toilets, water, phone near camping area's loop C; toilets on Purdum Trail

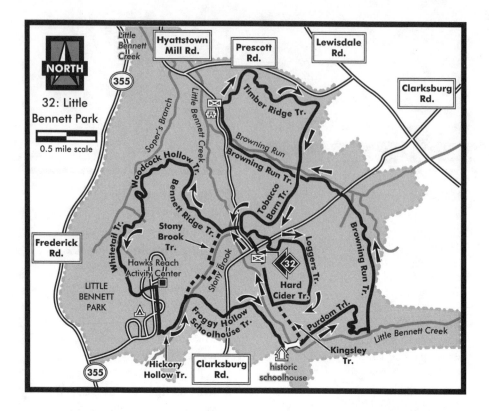

NORTH

355

32: Little
Bennett Park

0.5 mile scale

Little
Bennett
Creek

Hyattstown
Mill Rd.

Prescott
Rd.

Lewisdale
Rd.

Clarksburg
Rd.

Timber Ridge Tr.

Browning Run

Browning Run Tr.

Little Bennett Creek

Soper's Branch

Woodcock Hollow Tr.

Bennett Ridge Tr.

Tobacco Barn Tr.

Loggers Tr.

Browning Run Tr.

Whitetail Tr.

Stony
Brook
Tr.

Stony Brook

Hawks Reach
Activity Center

Frederick
Rd.

LITTLE
BENNETT
PARK

Hard
Cider Tr.

32

Froggy Hollow
Schoolhouse Tr.

Purdom Trl.

Little Bennett Creek

Kingsley
Tr.

355

Hickory
Hollow Tr.

Clarksburg
Rd.

historic
schoolhouse

elevation change. The mostly dirt trails are unblazed. Those west of Little Bennett Creek are quite well signposted and in good shape. They're also off-limits to bikers and horse riders. Those in the more rugged eastern area are twice as hilly (says my altimeter) and not as well signposted. And they're muddy, thanks to equine hooves. But don't be deterred. Mud washes off, and my irreverent eye sees a purpose in liquidity: fewer whizzing bikers. Yes, good can come of brook water and mud.

The major meadow trails are mowed periodically, but the grass grows rapidly. So, use common sense plus long pants or insect repellent where the trail is overgrown and ticks may abound. Stick to the trail anyway, in that poison ivy lurks.

The hike starts with a 5-mile counterclockwise loop through the area west of

Little Bennett Creek. To get started from the parking lot, return to and carefully cross Clarksburg Road. Follow gravelly Hyattstown Mill Road for about 300 yards. Then turn sharp left onto the mostly open Beaver Valley Trail. After crossing Little Bennett Creek, turn left, and follow the trail as it swings right and away from the stream, and heads gently uphill. At the next major intersection, turn right onto the Mound Builder Trail—named for the local Allegheny mound-building ants.

Continuing, turn right at a T-junction onto the Bennett Ridge Trail. At an open hilltop meadow, turn left onto the Woodcock Hollow Trail and enjoy an especially scenic half-mile of hiking. Also watch and listen for courting woodcocks. Ease on uphill a bit, then turn right at the next junction onto the

Whitetail Trail. It undulates through the woods for a mile and a half. Be sure to bypass the Antler Ridge Trail, cross two small streams, and follow a lovely fern-lined third stream uphill.

At the next junction, ignore the "Nature Trail" sign and turn left; also stay left at the next "Nature Trail" sign. Reach and cross carefully a road, one of several in the park's camping area. Keep going up the trail to emerge from the woods at another road—the area's main access road. Cross it alertly to reach Hawks Reach Activity Center, 3 miles into the hike. Formerly a nature center, the building is now used only for special events.

Continuing, follow the road very gently uphill for almost half a mile. Where it curves right, watch on your left for the aptly named Hickory Hollow Trail. Take it, and head downhill on a steep and rocky path. Then turn left onto the Stony Brook Trail. After about 300 yards, turn right onto Froggy Hollow School House Trail, cross the brook, and start climbing.

Emerge from the woods onto a level, grassy trail. Stay to the right as you pass a white house that usually barks. At a road (Clarksburg Road again), cross watchfully, jog left, and return to the trail. For the next half-mile follow a woodland trail. Watch for the one-room schoolhouse, well preserved, boarded up, and fenced in. It served the local community from the 1890s until the 1930s, when the Great Depression finished off the area's already meager economy. Turn left at the schoolhouse and take the nearby bridge over the creek. Access the nearby gravel road and head uphill to embark on the hike's second, longer, and tougher segment—a 7.6-mile embellished figure-eight through the eastern part of the park.

The mostly open road is part of the Purdum Trail (but ignore the trail sign pointing to an off-road trail). It provides the hike's steepest uphill stretch before leveling off, crossing a primitive camp-ground, and becoming a dirt trail in the woods. At a four-way intersection, turn right onto an unnamed trail (opposite what the signpost calls the Loggers Trail). However, if there's snow on the ground, stay on the Purdum Trail (see below). Faintly marked, the unnamed trail wriggles downhill to a small and sometimes muddy floodplain, and then glides left to follow a small creek upstream (Little Bennett Creek again).

At a white pole—the hike's halfway mark—turn right and walk about 50 yards to look at the quite lovely creek. Then turn around and follow the white poles uphill on a gas-pipeline right-of-way, which crosses the Purdum Trail to become the Browning Run Trail. At a fork, bear left into the woods, staying on the Browning Run Trail. Proceed gently downhill on the horse-churned trail. Emerging in a meadow, cross a small stream, pass through a T-junction (Pine Knob Trail goes to the left), and reach a road (Clarksburg yet again). Cross safely and continue.

Back in the woods, go either way at a fork. Where the paths reunite, cross a small stream and continue to another meadow, then walk straight through the trail's intersection with the Tobacco Barn Trail. Then return to the woods, dodge the mud, and reach a road (Hyattstown Mill Road). Turn right and follow it to Earl's Picnic Area. There, head for a near-by vehicle barrier and turn right onto the Pine Grove Trail.

For half a mile, you'll ascend through the pines on a winding trail that's nee-dle-soft underfoot. At a T-junction in a clearing, turn right onto the Timber Ridge Trail. Stay on it for half a mile as it snakes through the woods. At an unmarked fork, go either way; both paths veer left and reunite.

Soon after passing a sign warning of a private residence that you'll never see, pitch downhill into a serene and majestic grove of yellow poplars (tulip trees). The only such grove I know, it's stunning, both for its expanse and for the towering species with its tulip-shaped leaves and yellow-green-orange flowers.

After crossing a small stream and starting to climb out of the grove, turn right at a junction and head uphill to break out of the woods. Then step onto the Tobacco Barn Trail—and into an expanse of grass-covered slopes fringed with woods beneath the open sky. It's one of the metro area's finest upland meadow areas. Pause to look at the nearby ruins of a very old tobacco drying barn, then take the curving and signposted mowed path downhill. At the bottom, follow the trail into the woods to its intersection with the Browning Run Trail. Stay on the Tobacco Barn Trail as it skirts a meadow, which often features summertime aerial displays by butterflies, bluebirds, and dragonflies.

Reenter the woods for a mostly downhill trek on a narrow, rocky, rooty, and muddy trail section. Go right at the first fork (the sign promises the "Loggers Trail"). When you reach a road (Hyattstown Mill Road), turn left and proceed for a few hundred yards. Then turn left onto the Loggers Trail, just past where the Beaver Valley Trail goes right.

Do another hill climb, contend with a bit more mud, bear right at the first fork, and continue until a road appears (Clarksburg Road again). Cross at an uphill angle of 45 degrees to find the trail. Ascend to reach an unmarked T-junction, walk right, and proceed downhill. At the next junction, turn left, toward what the signpost promises will be the Hard Cider Trail.

After more climbing, turn right at a T-junction onto a sometimes mucky but level old farm road—the Loggers Trail continued (but there's no signpost). Finally, reach a fork and the promised Hard Cider Trail (to the right). It's the hike's longest downhill stretch, extending more than half a mile. It's also rocky and muddy. At a level gravel road, turn right and follow what's called the Kingsley Trail a third of a mile to the trailhead.

For more information on the park, contact the park manager, (301) 972-6581.

NEARBY/RELATED ACTIVITIES

Heading home, visit Kings Park, a small county park on Clarksburg Road. It's on the left, 2.1 miles from this hike's trailhead. Amble around and imagine being in a Currier & Ives lithograph.

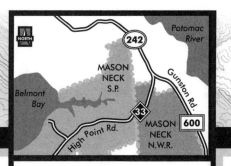

#33
Mason Neck National Wildlife Refuge

IN BRIEF
Trails in Mason Neck National Wildlife Refuge, in southeastern Fairfax County, Virginia, give hikers access to a splendid, eagle-inhabited wetland wilderness.

DIRECTIONS
From Capital Beltway (Interstate 495) in Springfield, Virginia, take Exit 57A onto I-95 heading southwest toward Richmond. Or take Shirley Memorial Highway (I-395) heading southwest out of Washington; on crossing beltway, you'll be on I-95. Drive about 6.5 miles south on I-95 and take Exit 163 to Lorton Road. Drive left onto Lorton Road and head east for 1.3 miles. Turn right onto Armistead Road, drive several hundred yards, and then turn right onto Richmond Highway (US 1). Drive 0.8 miles and turn left onto Gunston Road. Proceed generally southeast for 4.6 miles. Turn right onto High Point Road and proceed for 0.7 miles. Turn left into Woodmarsh Trail parking lot.

DESCRIPTION
Mason Neck, a secluded Potomac River peninsula roughly 25 miles south of Washington, is a huge nature preserve that supports a thriving population of bald eagles and other wildlife. For lucky hikers who know of its few trails, it's a rewarding hike venue rich in scenery and solitude.

KEY AT-A-GLANCE INFORMATION

Length: 4.6 miles or less, in two segments

Configuration: Modified out-and-back

Difficulty: Very easy

Scenery: Woodlands, marshlands

Exposure: Mostly shady; less so in winter

Traffic: Usually very light to light

Trail surface: Wood Marsh: mostly dirt, with some roots, mud in places; Great Marsh: dirt, gravel

Hiking time: 2.5–3.5 hours (including marsh gazing)

Access: Open daily during daylight hours

Maps: USGS Fort Belvoir, Indian Head; sketch map in free brochure for each segment

Facilities: Toilets at both trailheads, display shelter

Special comments: Do not enter any closed area

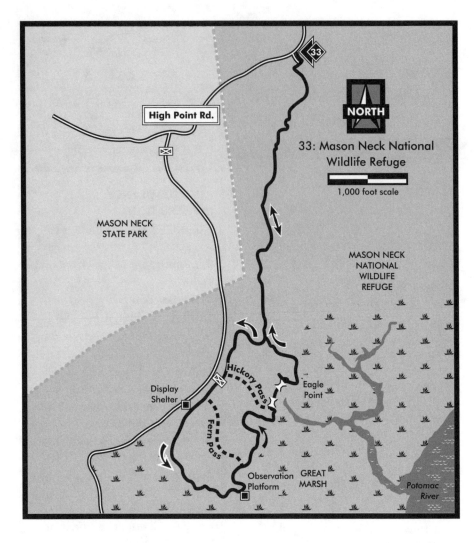

High Point Rd.

NORTH

33: Mason Neck National Wildlife Refuge

1,000 foot scale

MASON NECK STATE PARK

MASON NECK NATIONAL WILDLIFE REFUGE

Hickory Pass

Fern pass

Display Shelter

Eagle Point

Observation Platform

GREAT MARSH

Potomac River

Around 1960, though, the eagles seemed headed for extinction thanks to habitat loss and pesticide use, and the peninsula seemed headed for suburbia. But a public/private coalition launched in the mid-1960s helped reverse the situation. Today, most of the 9,000-acre peninsula consists of protected public lands, including the Mason Neck National Wildlife Refuge and adjoining Mason Neck State Park.

Established in 1969 as the country's first federal sanctuary for bald eagles, the refuge covers 2,277 acres. At its heart lies the Great Marsh, a large wetland wilderness spread across more than 250 acres.

This hike consists of two out-and-back segments on separate trails that angle through the woods to the marsh. One is a 3.2-mile jaunt on the somewhat hilly Woodmarsh Trail. The other is a 1.5-mile outing on the level Great Marsh Trail (also favored by local dog walkers). In both cases, you'll have a chance to savor what Thoreau called "the tonic of wilderness."

The marsh is a year-round faunal delight. Ducks, geese, and swans pass through in the spring and fall, with some wintering there. In summer, swallows and other insect eaters cruise the wetland, and herons and egrets dot the marsh like blossoms. The woods shelter migratory songbirds, as well as resident birds, deer, and other creatures.

As for the eagles, there's a winter population of perhaps 60, including both migrants (from the far north) and residents, and a summer population of roughly 20. The birds nest and roost in tall trees in the wood, and roam the local waterways. Starting in November or December, they take six months or more to raise their young. That's why trail sections are sometimes closed.

The refuge trails are well marked and generally well maintained. Take along binoculars and a reference book, plus bug repellent in summer. Pick up a trail brochure at each trailhead. Leafless winter is the best time to see eagles.

To get started from the Woodmarsh Trail parking lot, take the gravel road leading deeper into the refuge. After about 50 yards, turn right onto a blue-blazed dirt trail that wiggles gently downhill through the woods. At about 0.8 miles, you'll reach a signposted T-junction. There, turn right to begin a loop segment that passes a display shelter (the left-hand trail goes to Eagle Point). The trail swings generally to the left.

After several hundred yards, pause at another T-junction and a fence across the main trail. If the fence is open, continue on the trail, but if it's closed due to eagle nesting (as a large sign will explain), pause for two more paragraphs.

Continuing on the main trail, stop at the display shelter, where you can learn about eagles. After that, follow the trail as its swings left and down to the edge of the marsh. There, about halfway into the hike, linger at an observation platform.

After that, swing left and take the marsh-edge trail to Eagle Point. Watch for a beaver lodge along the way (a plume of steam on a winter day is hibernating beaver's breath). After passing Hickory Pass coming in from the left, reach a semi-marshy area spanned by what should be a new bridge.

But if you've been stopped by the closed fence at the T-junction, turn left there and take Hickory Pass downhill on what is, in effect, a shorter-by-0.8-miles alternative route to the bridge area. Along the way, if you know your hickories, watch for four different species.

Then cross the new bridge—or bushwhack around its closed predecessor if necessary. After that is a second bridge, which is rickety but safe. If it's winter, stand in various places and look high in the nearby trees for an active eagle's nest. Finish crossing the bridge, turn right, and proceed to the trail's end at Eagle Point. There, look again for the treetop nest. Also scan the endless marsh for a chance to see the way of an eagle in the air.

Leaving Eagle Point, retrace your steps to the second bridge. Don't turn left to cross it. Rather, just continue up the trail, which leads to the signposted T-junction where the loop started. There, turn right and head back to the parking lot.

To see more, drive to the Great Marsh Trail. Take High Point Road toward Gunston Road, turn right onto Gunston, and proceed for 1.5 miles, then turn right into the parking lot. There, pick up the dirt-and-gravel trail at the back of the lot. Follow it through the woods for almost three-quarters of a mile to an observation platform at the edge of the marsh. Linger a while, and then return to the parking lot.

For more information on the refuge, con-tact the refuge office in Wood-bridge, (703) 490-4979.

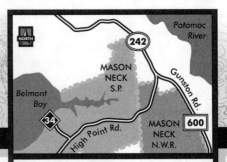

#34
Mason Neck State Park

IN BRIEF
Virginia's out-of-the-way Mason Neck State Park, in southeastern Fairfax County, provides protected habitat for wildlife and some fine beach and woodland trails for hikers.

DIRECTIONS
From Capital Beltway (Interstate 495) in Springfield, Virginia, take Exit 57A onto I-95 heading southwest, toward Richmond. Or take Shirley Memorial Highway (I-395) heading southwest out of Washington; on crossing beltway, you'll be on I-95. Drive about 6.5 miles south on I-95 and take Exit 163 to Lorton Road. Go left onto Lorton Road and head east for 1.3 miles. Turn right onto Armistead Road, drive several hundred yards, and then turn right onto Richmond Highway (US 1). Drive 0.8 miles and turn left onto Gunston Road. Proceed generally southeast for 4.6 miles. Turn right onto High Point Road. Proceed for 1 mile to fee-collection kiosk. Continue for 2 miles to parking lot at visitor center. Go early on warm-weather weekends and holidays; if main lot and nearby picnic-area lot are full, walk back along entrance road to parking lot on Wilson Spring Trail. Make that your alternative trailhead (see map).

DESCRIPTION
Opened in 1985, Mason Neck State Park has played a major role in keeping

KEY AT-A-GLANCE INFORMATION
Length: 3.6 miles

Configuration: Loop

Difficulty: Very easy

Scenery: Bay views, woodlands, marshlands

Exposure: About one-third open (along beaches); mostly shady elsewhere, but less so in winter

Traffic: Usually light; moderate in picnic area on warm-weather weekends, holidays

Trail surface: Mostly sand, boardwalk along beaches; dirt on bluffs, in woods, with some rooty stretches

Hiking time: 2.5–3.5 hours (including beach pauses)

Access: Open daily, 8 a.m.–dusk; entrance fee

Maps: USGS Fort Belvoir, Indian Head

Facilities: Toilets, water, at picnic area (near visitor center); water, phone at visitor center

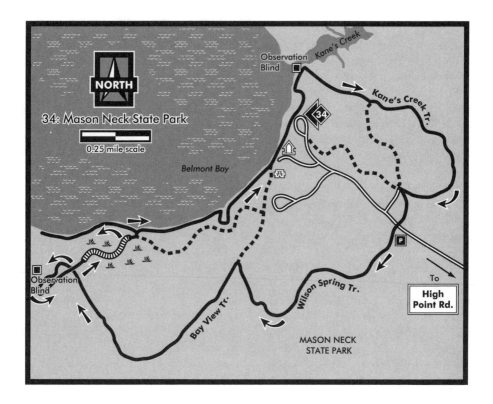

much of the Mason Neck peninsula green, as well as helping restore the area's bald-eagle population. The park and the adjoining Mason Neck National Wildlife Refuge, together with other public lands, now cover most of the peninsula. They are managed cooperatively as a vast nature preserve, providing various recreation opportunities.

Lying some 25 miles south of Washington, the 1,813-acre park is largely an area of rolling woodlands. Although much of it remains closed to the public, several short but lightly used trails pass through attractive scenery. This 3.6-mile hike makes the most of them. So take along binoculars and a reference book, and remember that winter is eagle-spotting time.

The trails are named and nominally color coded, even though you'll see only a few blazes. But they're also signposted and well maintained, so you're not likely to get lost.

To get started from the parking lot, pick up the paved bluff-top trail next to the trailer-style office some 50 yards downhill from the visitor center. On passing a replica of a bald eagle's nest, read the sign and contemplate why some eagles decorate their nests with a single green sprig. Continue past a campfire program area, staying to the right. Then, descend some broad steps, and turn left onto a dirt trail leading to a sandy beach on Belmont Bay, a Potomac River inlet.

Turn right and walk roughly north along the beach for almost half a mile. It's usually passable, even at high tide. Along the way, observe the low, wooded bluffs to your right. Note the exposed tree roots, as well as the trees that have already bitten the sand. The park loses one to two feet of shoreline each year to erosion. Water pollution has killed the aquatic plants that would otherwise reduce the erosive action of waves. Also note the signs warning that the water is unsafe for swimming.

When you see an observation blind on the bluffs, continue past it, and then take the easy path up. Step inside. Scan the skies and also marsh-rimmed Kane's Creek to your right—and possibly spot bald eagles or ospreys. If it's summer, look for an impressive display of American lotus.

Leaving the blind, head inland on a dirt trail that eases uphill and then undulates through oak/hickory/beech woods. After a third of a mile, turn left at a sign marking Kane's Creek Trail (nominally blue blazed). Continue for another third of a mile, then turn left onto the Wilson Spring Trail (nominally green blazed). You'll soon cross the entrance road (note the parking lot) into a hillier and more open area. At a T-junction, turn left onto the Bay View Trail (nominally red blazed) just past the hike's halfway point. Proceeding, pass several information boards that explain the local ecosystem.

On reaching a four-way intersection. Cross it and head for a nearby overlook and then an observation blind, both of which provide good views across a marshy inlet. Follow the trail as it curves left and cuts back across the four-way intersection. It then drops downhill in a short flight of steps to reach the hike's first section of boardwalk. This is a woodsy marsh area where beavers have left their marks.

At the end of the boardwalk, leave the trail and walk a few yards to the beach. Turn left and head down the beach for about a third of a mile on an out-and-back detour. Take in views across the bay to your right, and into the wooded marsh on your left. Watch for birds—and other wildlife. Once, on that beach, I felt my neck hairs tingle; spinning around, I found I was being tracked by a red fox. It quickly skulked into the marsh, leaving me to wonder if it was hungry or just curious. Turn back where the marsh gives way to bluffs.

Continue northward along the low wooded bluffs. The trail includes boardwalk sections, plus inviting overlooks. At the edge of the picnic area, follow the fence line and stay to the left on the grass. Just past bluebird birdbox no. 1, turn left onto a narrow downhill trail, with steps. At the bottom, turn sharply left to follow the trail clockwise around a tidal pond. Reach and cross a waterside parking area. Then ascend some shallow steps to reach the bluff top near the visitor center and the trailhead. Contact the park for more information, (703) 550-0362, (703) 550-0960, or www.dcr. state.va.us/parks/masonnec.htm.

NEARBY/RELATED ACTIVITIES

The visitor center has informative exhibits and staffers. Ask about programs such as the guided canoe trips both by day and moonlight. (The center is open all week in the warm-weather months; otherwise, only on weekends.) Combine this hike with a visit to the national wildlife refuge next door (see hike no. 33, p. 119).

#35
Massanutten Mountain and Shenandoah River

IN BRIEF

Well west of Washington lie scenic Massanutten Mountain and the Shenandoah River's lovely South Fork. They're so well arranged that a hike on one can be paired with a canoe trip on the other.

DIRECTIONS

From Capital Beltway (Interstate 495) in Merrifield, Virginia, take Exit 49 onto I-66 heading west. Proceed for about 56 miles and take Exit 13, at Linden, onto VA 55 heading west. Proceed for 5.3 miles to Front Royal. There, turn left and south onto US 340 and drive 9.3 miles to Bentonville. There, just past a post office (on left), turn right onto VA 613 (Indian Hollow Road) and drive 0.8 miles to either of two outfitters at Bentonville Landing (see text).

DESCRIPTION

This out-and-back outing is grandly distinct from all of this book's other hiking excursions, and not just because it dents the book's titular perimeter. As created by Springfield Cliff, it consists of a 12-mile trek along a rocky mountain ridge, followed by a 12-mile canoe ride on a beautiful, rapids-dotted river.

The ridge is a lofty one atop Massanutten Mountain, a massive, free-standing range in the Shenandoah Valley some 65 crow-miles west of Washington. The river is the Shenandoah River's unspoiled South Fork, meandering

KEY AT-A-GLANCE INFORMATION

Length: About 12 miles each on trail, river

Configuration: Out by trail and back by river

Difficulty: Difficult to extremely difficult

Scenery: Upland woods, Shenandoah Valley vistas and peeks, river views

Exposure: Mostly shady on trail, less so when trees shed; shadeless on river

Traffic: Usually very light on trail, river

Trail surface: Mostly dirt, with long rocky stretches plus unpaved road; moving water, with rapids, rocks

Hiking time: 4.5–5 hours at above-average pace; plus 3–5 hours on river (see text)

Access: No restrictions on trail; outfitter's rules on river

Maps: USGS Bentonville, Rileyville; PATC Map G

Facilities: Toilets, water, phone, camp store at trailhead (outfitters, when open); toilet at Seek Ford Landing

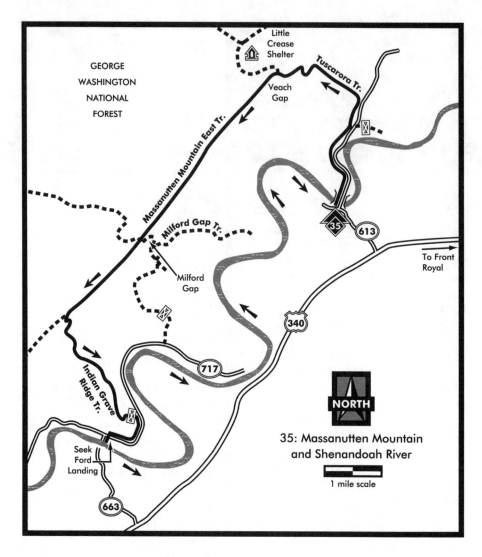

GEORGE
WASHINGTON
NATIONAL
FOREST

Little
Crease
Shelter

Tuscarora Tr.

Veach
Gap

Massanutten Mountain East Tr.

Milford Gap Tr.

Milford
Gap

35

613

To Front
Royal

340

717

Indian Grave
Ridge Tr.

Seek
Ford
Landing

663

NORTH

**35: Massanutten Mountain
and Shenandoah River**

1 mile scale

northward along the eastern foot of the range. The transfer point is Seek Ford Landing, where, by arrangement, the trekkers ford the river to switch to canoes (or kayaks) delivered by a trailhead outfitter.

The hike-and-paddle combo is a long day's journey into delight, especially when organized as a group activity. It provides a strenuous and satisfying workout for both the upper and lower body, as well as for the senses. And it's best suited for people who can hike fairly fast

for close to 5 hours while enduring about 4,100 feet of elevation change—and then paddle for 3 to 5 hours.

Plan on doing the outing when the weather is warm, the river level is right, the outfitters are open, hunters are absent (the Massanutten is part of George Washington National Forest), and you are well prepared.

The best weather is usually from June through September, although the two outfitters at the trailhead operate from April through October. They are

Shenandoah River Trips, (800) 727-4371 or www.shenandoah.cc, and the Downriver Canoe Company, (800) 338-1963 or www.downriver.com. Contact them to discuss your plans and options, and to make reservations. Also check with the Lee District on the hunting situation.

Check with the outfitter on river conditions and schedules. Very low water isn't good because the river is naturally shallow, and very high water is dangerous. But as Cliff says, "Ninety percent of the time, the water level's just fine." That's why you're likely to have an exhilarating and current-aided ride downstream, over rapids that even novices can negotiate safely. One possible scenario is to get there around 7:30 a.m. to sign in, get fitted with a paddle and lifejacket, obtain a river map, and learn the river's secrets; to be on the trail by 8. a.m.; to be on the water by 1 p.m.; and to finish by 6 p.m. You may want to spend the previous night in nearby Front Royal or Luray.

Prepare for the outing's posthike phase: Take along wading footgear (or plan to canoe in wet boots), plus sunblock or protective clothing; put valuables in waterproof bags; and remember to tie down everything when you're in the boat.

To get started, leave the outfitter's and head for the blue-blazed Tuscarora Trail (formerly the Big Blue Trail), which happens to pass right by as VA 613 (Indian Hollow Road). Cross the low causeway spanning the South Fork. Keep going, and bear left at a fork about 50 yards down the road. Walk a third of a mile and then bear right at a fork onto Panhandle Road (which takes over as VA 613). Go straight through the junction after that.

Passing through an area of fields, as the road curves away from the river, you'll begin to ascend and be hemmed in by scrubby woods. At a clearing, turn left—or roughly west—to stay on the blue-blazed Tuscarora Trail. Coming up next will be a second clearing, a "Road Closed" sign, and a gate across the trail (roughly 1.75 miles into the hike). Walk past the gate and head up a dirt trail amid oaks, maples, and mountain laurels. You will still be on the Tuscarora Trail, but the path gets steeper, the pines more prevalent, and the sky more visible.

Continue on a long, straight, steep, rocky, open trail. Savor the panoramic views to the south and east, and look for the curlicue South Fork 1,000 feet below and Shenandoah National Park spread across the horizon. Look more closely and try to discern your trailhead, some 2 crow-miles away. And search the sky for hawks, turkey vultures, ravens, and crows.

Trekking upward, you'll finally slide into a shady area and a trail junction. There, say goodbye to the Tuscarora Trail and turn left onto the orange-blazed Massanutten Mountain East Trail. At that point, you'll be done with the hike's most arduous uphill, over half of its elevation gain, and almost a third of the way to the river.

Staying on or close to the crest of a long ridge, the trail extends south for almost 5 miles as one of the finest and wildest stretches of mountain trail in this book, if not the metro area. It has beguiling scenery that's more rockscape than landscape as well as some distracting vistas. The trail bumps up and down quite a bit and the surface ranges from rocky to very rocky, but you won't face any stiff climbs.

Be especially attentive at four places along the ridge trail. First, at a trail fork about 2 miles down the trail, swing left, as the blazes do. This rocky, below-the-crest trail has gorgeous views to the left. After that, emerge onto the crest and look through the trees for your first views of the Massanutten's western ridges.

Second, thread your way carefully through the intersection at Milford Gap, the hike's 7-mile mark. There, the ridge trail crosses an old road that was once part of a stagecoach route across the Massanutten. That road—now the Milford Gap Trail—slides downhill at the intersection. But you should follow the orange blazes uphill and south.

Third, heading downhill out in the open, stop at a huge rock and take in what I think is one of the ridge trail's best vistas.

Finally, after negotiating the hike's rockiest stretch, watch for a small oak coated with lichen and daubed with orange and purple blazes. There, turn left onto the purple-blazed Indian Grave Ridge Trail to follow the hike's last segment.

The 2.5-mile Indian Grave Ridge Trail follows a wooded side ridge that pushes east between two loops of the river (as is visible on a map, but not on the trail). The reputed burial mound is said to be somewhere in the woods and well plundered.

Initially, the trail is steep and rocky. But the pitch slackens as the trail traverses a wet, muddy, and ferny area near the head of a small stream. It then veers to the right, away from the stream, and proceeds along a rocky hillside, where it's reassuring to see purple blazes again.

After going steeply downhill again, the trail becomes flatter, wider, and less rocky. It then passes through an unattractive, dishevelled area and reaches a gate and "Road Closed" sign. Walk around the gate and across a clearing. Proceed for about 40 yards on an old unpaved road, and then turn right onto a newer, gravel road. That's tree-lined VA 717, which leads slightly downhill and around several curves for just over a mile.

As the road curves south and west, the high ridge bearing the ridge trail south of the colorful oak will loom directly ahead. At the end of an open field, and after passing a couple of telephone poles, turn left onto an unpaved side road—the first you'll encounter on VA 717. Walk a few hundred yards on the level and shady road. Where it curves to the left, watch for a dirt trail going right for about 15 yards to Seek Ford Landing.

Next, ford the rocky-bottomed, 200-yard-wide river. Aim for a small sandbar slightly upstream on the far side, which is where canoes are typically left. Wear appropriate footgear and with empty pants pockets, cross the river as a group (if you have one). Once across, get going on your 12-mile cruise to the trailhead.

If you'd prefer a less-rigorous outing, start with an out-and-back hike on the Tuscarora Trail between the trailhead and the trail's junction with the ridge-top trail. That'll give you an aerobic outing of 7.4 miles, about 2,600 feet in elevation change, and lovely views of the South Fork and beyond. Then have the outfitter launch you 3 miles or 7.5 miles upriver so that you can also spend time on the water.

For more information on Massanutten Mountain, contact the the US Forest Service's Lee District headquarters in Edinburg, (540) 984-4101; for more information on the trails, contact the Potomac Appalachian Trail Club, (703) 242-0693 or www.patc.net.

NEARBY/RELATED ACTIVITIES
Make the most of canoeing down a gorgeous river. For instance, tie up en route to have a picnic and a swim.

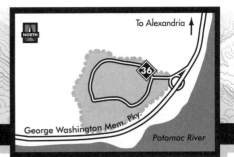

#36
Mount Vernon Trail and Fort Hunt Park

IN BRIEF

Augmented by a turn through Fort Hunt Park, the Mount Vernon Trail south of Alexandria provides hikers with a lovely parkland outing along the Potomac River.

DIRECTIONS

From Capital Beltway (Interstate 495 and I-95) in Alexandria, take Exit 177B to get on northbound US 1. At first traffic light, turn right onto Franklin Street, drive three blocks, and turn right onto South Washington Street, which becomes George Washington Memorial Parkway. At city's southern end, proceed on parkway for 5.6 miles, and take exit ramp to Fort Hunt Park. Enter park, turn right onto loop road at T-junction, and then take first left, into parking lot (about 7 miles from beltway Exit 177B).

DESCRIPTION

First, in the nineteenth century, George Washington's former Mount Vernon estate became a de facto national shrine. Then, in the 1930s, the federal government created the scenic George Washington Memorial Parkway to carry motor vehicles down to Mount Vernon. Then, in 1973, it added the Mount Vernon Trail, a paved strip of right-of-way for people who like to locomote by muscle power.

Today, the trail attracts bikers, hikers, and other muscle-power users and serves

KEY AT-A-GLANCE INFORMATION

Length: 8.4 miles

Configuration: Modified out-and-back

Difficulty: Easy/moderate

Scenery: Parklands, woodlands, river views

Exposure: Mostly open

Traffic: Light; heavier on warm-weather evenings, weekends, holidays

Trail surface: Nearly all pavement; some dirt

Hiking time: 3.5–4.5 hours

Access: Trail closes at dark; park open daily, 7 a.m.–sunset

Maps: USGS Mt. Vernon; ADC Northern Virginia; sketch map in free trail brochure

Facilities: Toilets, phones near trailhead, elsewhere in park, at Mount Vernon (cafeteria too); toilets, water, phones along trail

Special comments: Park's gates close at sunset

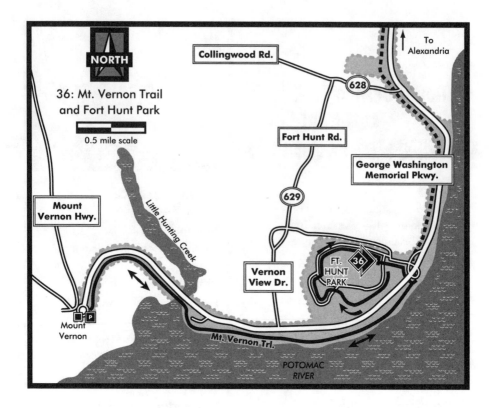

NORTH

36: Mt. Vernon Trail
and Fort Hunt Park

0.5 mile scale

Collingwood Rd.

To
Alexandria

628

Fort Hunt Rd.

George Washington
Memorial Pkwy.

Mount
Vernon Hwy.

Little Hunting Creek

629

Vernon
View Dr.

FT.
HUNT
PARK

36

Mount
Vernon

Mt. Vernon Trl.

POTOMAC
RIVER

as a major element in the metro area's growing trail network. It's also a route segment for most of this hike and for parts of three others (hikes no. 18, 40, and 48).

This 8.4-mile, mostly out-and-back and level hike uses the trail's lowermost portion. That's where the southbound Potomac River turns west and the Virginia riverbank becomes a picturesque corridor of open parklands, woods, and across-the-water views. The hike also includes part of Fort Hunt Park. Located on former Washington-owned land, the fort existed from the 1890s to about 1920 to guard the river approach to the capital. It was converted into a park in the 1930s. Like the trail, it's managed by the National Park Service (NPS) as part of the parkway.

To get started from the trailhead parking lot, head back toward the park entrance. But at the T-junction, walk straight on the loop road, keeping to the right in the reserved-for-foot-traffic lane. Where the road curves right, swing left onto a dirt trail heading into the woods.

Ignoring a side trail on the left, follow the main trail as it swings right and gently uphill. Where it levels off and becomes rather faint, keep bearing left along the edge of the woods until you're heading downhill on a well-defined trail. Continue, across a small bridge. At the next junction, turn right onto an unpaved path that ascends gently to an abandoned paved road. Turn left and follow it to the end. There, turn left to walk clockwise around the mostly open loop road, again staying to the right.

After passing the trailhead, turn left at the T-junction and head for the park entrance. On the way, take an optional

Winter hikers have the lower Mt. Vernon Trail to themselves.

detour to look more closely at an 1890s gun emplacement, on the right. Or visit another one, down a short trail just outside the entrance. In both cases, there's no river view but much poison ivy.

Outside the park, carefully head downhill and cross a traffic intersection to reach the Mount Vernon Trail at an information board. Turn right and follow the trail. Stay to the left where it joins a roadway to curve through an underpass (that's the parkway above). Then turn left to rejoin the trail at the hike's 2-mile mark. Just over half a mile later, pass milepost 2, one of the trailside markers that count down to Mount Vernon. Remember to keep to the right and out of the way of other trail users.

Proceed on the undulating, open riverbank trail and savor the river views. Watch for geese and ducks on the water, ospreys on the hunt, and bald eagles on the wing. Pause at Riverside Park to look for the resident eagles nicknamed George and Martha.

After Riverside, the trail leaves the shore, acquires a tree canopy, and uses a long uphill slope to reach milepost 0 and the Mount Vernon parking lot. Traverse the lot, bear right, and pass the estate gates to get to the newly expanded visitor center, oddly labeled "Shops." It's one-third of a mile beyond milepost 0. Then, make the 3.4-mile return journey to the trailhead. For more information on both the trail and park, contact the George Washington Memorial Parkway office, (703) 289-2500 or www.nps.gov/gwmp.

NEARBY/RELATED ACTIVITIES

En route, take an extended break at Mount Vernon by paying to tour the mansion and grounds, or take a round-trip, summer-weekend ferry ride to Piscataway Park (see hike no. 39, p. 140). In summer, attend a posthike Sunday evening concert at Fort Hunt. Finish hiking by 7 p.m., relax on the grass, and let the sounds of music creep in your ears.

#37
Northwest Branch
Parklands

IN BRIEF

The Northwest Branch valley in suburban Maryland just north of Washington has some rough, little-used trails on which hikers can get a physically and navigationally challenging outing.

DIRECTIONS

From Capital Beltway (Interstate 495), take Exit 31A and head north on Georgia Avenue (MD 97) for about 3 miles. Turn right onto Randolph Road, proceed for 0.3 miles, and then turn right onto Glenallan Avenue. Drive past Brookside Gardens parking lot, and then turn right into Brookside Nature Center parking lot (at 1400 Glenallan Avenue, about 0.6 miles from Randolph).

Or use Metro to do hike. Take Red Line train to Glenmont station. From corner of Glenallan and Layhill Road, walk southeast on Glenallan sidewalk for 1 mile, crossing Randolph, to nature center parking lot (no sidewalk for last 0.2 miles, so walk on left side of road). Contact Metro, (202) 637-7000 or www.wmata.com.

DESCRIPTION

Rising in a rural part of eastern Montgomery County, Northwest Branch flows southward through an increasingly urbanized area. Remarkably, most of it is enveloped by parkland that provides a wonderful, wilderness-tinged venue for hikers.

KEY AT-A-GLANCE INFORMATION

Length: 7.4 miles

Configuration: Elongated loop

Difficulty: Moderate

Scenery: Parklands, water views, signs of suburbia

Exposure: Mostly shady; less so in winter

Traffic: Very light to light; heavier on warm-weather weekends, holidays; heaviest in, near park

Trail surface: Mostly dirt or sand; gravelly, paved, or rocky in places

Hiking time: 3.5–4.5 hours (including route finding time)

Access: Open daily during daylight hours

Maps: USGS Kensington; ADC Montgomery County

Facilities: Toilets, water, phone near trailhead (nature center)

Special comments: Best in dry weather (see text)

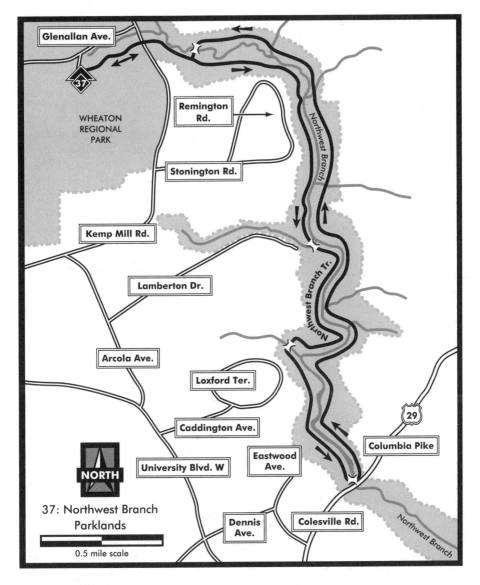

Glenallan Ave.

37

WHEATON
REGIONAL
PARK

Remington
Rd.

Stonington Rd.

Kemp Mill Rd.

Lamberton Dr.

Arcola Ave.

Loxford Ter.

Caddington Ave.

University Blvd. W

Eastwood
Ave.

Columbia Pike

29

NORTH

37: Northwest Branch
Parklands

0.5 mile scale

Dennis
Ave.

Colesville Rd.

Northwest Branch

Northwest Branch Tr.

Northwest Branch

    Northwest Branch is one of two
headwaters of the Anacostia River,
which flows into the Potomac River. It
converges with the Northeast Branch at
Bladensburg. So do the trails that parallel
their lower courses as part of an ambitious plan to develop the Anacostia
watershed's recreational potential and
clean up its polluted waters. One of
those trails, the Northwest Branch Trail,
ends at Wheaton Regional Park.

    This hike is a 7.4-mile elongated loop
that starts at the park and involves taking
the Northwest Branch Trail downstream
on the west bank as far as US 29. It then
turns upstream on an unnamed east-
bank trail. The west-bank trail is
unpaved, adequately marked, and a bit
rough in places. The east-bank route also
is unpaved, but unmarked and rougher.

    If the east-bank route sounds unap-
pealing, do an out-and-back hike on the

west-bank trail instead. Either way, take basic precautions: Check beforehand on trail and weather conditions, guard seasonally against ticks and other bugs, and avoid the poison ivy.

To get started at the Wheaton park, look for a paved trail just behind the information sign at the east end of the parking lot. Head east on the trail and enter the woods. After crossing a service road, look for a trail junction and conspicuous trail marker (a sign mounted on a big wooden post, like others in the park). There, head left to proceed along the Oxbow Trail.

The trail winds and undulates through a fern-dotted area and then straightens out at a junction. There, swing right, proceed to a second signposted junction, and turn left onto a horse trail that follows a creek. After passing a spur trail to the horse stables on the left, reach another signposted junction. There, turn left and head for Kemp Mill Road (the park's eastern boundary).

Cross the road carefully onto a trail that leads into Northwest Branch Park. As the path curves gently right, you will see Northwest Branch to your left. Just beyond the first visible houses on the right, a trail leads left and to a bridge across the stream; this is the direction you will come on the return portion of the loop.

Continue straight ahead (southbound) on the mostly flat and tree-shaded west-bank trail for 3.4 miles. En route, watch for sewer lines, common in most of the metro area's close-in stream valleys. Usually, you'll be alerted by visual cues, such as manholes; in some, though, the cues will be olfactory.

Also watch and listen for wildlife. Birmingham Bud encountered "turtles, chipmunks, squirrels, as well as many birds (heard more often than seen),

including owls, great blue herons, and kingfishers. Once I was surprised by—and surprised—a deer. And several times I caught a sharp whiff of skunk that made me forget the manholes."

About a mile along the trail, notice a yellow poplar (tulip tree) that, says Bud, "is astoundingly large and with a trunk that would take three people to encircle." You'll then pass a ridge and the first of several mica-flecked rock outcroppings. At a muddy stretch where the main trail appears to split, walk either way, but left is usually best. It leads to slightly higher ground and better views. Shortly thereafter, watch for signs of trail maintenance—a series of berms set between pieces of wood to provide dry footing.

As you proceed, more ridges will appear, at first to your left and then to your right, although you're not likely to feel pinned in. An occasional rock outcropping on the far bank is clearly visible. After you pass some plastic cylinders that serve as deer-proof tubes for growing tree seedlings, another rock outcropping will appear on your right. The trail, too, gets rockier. The trail then curves to the right and crosses a bridge over an intermittent tributary. The bridge is almost 2 miles into the hike and about halfway down its west-bank portion. Next you'll pass two side trails, plus a trail sign indicating that Lamberton Drive is off to the right. That's where a hidden spur of parkland juts deep into a residential area.

Continuing downstream, you may find blowdowns on the trail. Either clamber over them or detour around them. The trail then narrows as the landscape becomes more valley-like and more intimate. Subsequently, temporarily part company with Northwest Branch but remain on the trail as it takes a sharp turn to the right and follows a rivulet up a small valley. As the trail widens, watch for a wider spur trail on the left. Use it for a quick detour to get a pleasing view of the stream. Then return to the main trail, turn left, and continue downstream.

Approach a directional sign and turn left. Dip down into a very muddy spot, cross a bridge, and arrive at a junction and trail sign. Loxford Terrace is off to the right, and you'll have done almost 3 miles. Continue left.

The trail's next half-mile crosses three tributary creeks, each spanned by a sewer line and companion footbridge. For part of the way, you'll be on a bluff, maintaining your elevation as Northwest Branch drops away. At one point, rounding a curve, watch for a nice view of the no-longer narrow stream, backed up almost half a mile behind a downstream dam.

Soon after crossing the third tributary creek, you'll reach a signposted intersection offering a side trail to Lockridge Drive off to the right. Instead, turn left, and follow the main stream toward the sound of traffic. After passing the old dam, stay on the trail as it crosses a gully to reach US 29 (which is Columbia Pike to the east and Colesville Road to the west). Turn left along the roadside and then cross Northwest Branch on the road bridge, which is the hike's 3.7-mile and halfway point. Then turn left into a parking lot behind a brick building.

Then get ready to face the challenge of staying on course on the east bank, with its unmarked intersecting trails and dead-ends. The first half-mile is the trickiest stretch. Bud, who went astray the first time, offers this advice: "It really isn't that hard. Be patient, keep the water on your left and the ridges on your right, stay to the left at most trail forks, jump across or detour around tributary creeks, and use a bit of trial and error."

Start by heading toward a small stand of pines beside the dam. Look around for an obvious path, get on it, and then take some steps down to the riverbank. Proceed upstream through a moist and grassy area. At a tributary creek, jump across, pass to the right of a large fallen tree, and follow the trail uphill. Proceed about a hundred yards and turn left at a junction. Watch for a rock outcropping that looks like a perfect place to jump into the stream. But don't; the water quality is dubious. Then, where the trail splits, take either fork; they soon reunite. Later, it's mostly a level and sandy waterside path winding northward through mature hardwoods.

When you're close to the water in summer, try sniffing for fish. As Bud says: "If you have a keen nose, you may be able to smell the shallow-water nests set up by local populations of bluegill."

After the trail swings sharply right and passes a huge blue manhole cover, you'll notice a very rocky stretch of trail peeling off to the right and uphill. But don't walk that way. Instead, find and take a trail going left. At a tributary creek, take a short detour upstream to cross and return to the main trail, where three small manholes on the left will confirm you're on course.

As the stream and trail swing to the left and westward, the two separate. The trail leaves the woods to cross a wide field. When you again have trees overhead, you'll also have the stream nearby. At a trail junction, turn left to cross the bridge, turn right onto the Northwest Branch Trail and return to the trailhead.

For more information on the trail and park, contact the Montgomery County Department of Parks and Recreation, (301) 699-2407.

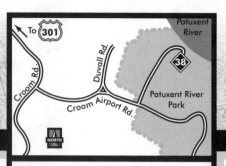

#38
Patuxent River Park

IN BRIEF

Plants and wildlife thrive in the scenic Jug Bay section of Patuxent River Park, in Prince George's County, Maryland. Another life-form that does well in that setting is the visiting hiker.

DIRECTIONS

From Capital Beltway (Interstate 495 and I-95), take Exit 11 and head roughly southeast on MD 4 (Pennsylvania Avenue) for about 7.5 miles to Upper Marlboro. There, turn right onto US 301 and head roughly south for 3.5 miles to junction marked by traffic light. There, turn left onto Croom Road and proceed for almost 3 miles, going east and then south. At a Patuxent State Park sign, turn left onto Croom Airport Road. Drive east for about 3 miles, passing Duvall Road. On reaching another park sign, turn left onto park entrance road. Drive 1.6 miles to parking lot near visitor center and park office.

DESCRIPTION

The Patuxent River, Maryland's longest in-state waterway, wriggles south for over 100 miles through woodlands, wetlands, and farmlands—and urbanized areas—to reach Chesapeake Bay. Like the rest of the bay's watershed, it suffers from poor water quality and other environmental ills. Even so, under a program launched in the early 1960s, much of its river valley is protected

KEY AT-A-GLANCE INFORMATION

Length: 7.3 miles

Configuration: Modified loop

Difficulty: Easy/moderate

Scenery: Wooded hills, meadows, tidal marshes, river views

Exposure: Mostly shady; less so in winter

Traffic: Usually very light to light; heavier on warm-weather weekends, holidays near visitor center, in nature study area

Trail surface: Mostly hard-packed sand; some pavement; short stretches of boardwalk, wood chips, mud

Hiking time: 3–4 hours (including viewing time)

Access: Open daily, 8 a.m.–posted closing time; day-use fee

Maps: USGS Bristol, Lower Marlboro

Facilities: Water, toilets, phone at visitor center

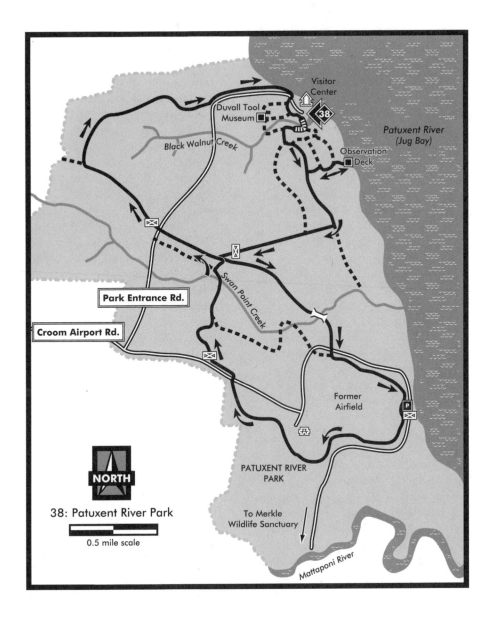

Visitor
Center

Duvall Tool
Museum

38

Patuxent River
(Jug Bay)

Black Walnut Creek

Observation
Deck

Swan Point Creek

Park Entrance Rd.

Croom Airport Rd.

Former
Airfield

P

NORTH

38: Patuxent River Park

PATUXENT RIVER
PARK

0.5 mile scale

To Merkle
Wildlife Sanctuary

Mattaponi River

as publicly owned and limited-use open space.

The program has also resulted in some fine hiking venues, such as Patuxent River Park. The park consists of several areas of great natural beauty dotted along the lower Patuxent. Of those, my choice is the delightful 2,000-acre Jug Bay section, some 20 miles southeast of Washington.

Named for a lake-like stretch of the river, the Jug Bay Natural Area is well equipped with both scenery and trails. Except for birders, though, most visitors focus on other attractions. Those close to the trailhead—and also worth a hiker's time—include a visitor center, nature study area, antique-tool museum, and reconstructed colonial-era village.

Adjoining the Jug Bay section is the Merkle Wildlife Sanctuary, a large, state-owned preserve renowned for its bird life. Together, the two areas form one of the finest mid-Atlantic birding spots, so don't forget your binoculars. The two areas are also linked by the worth-taking Chesapeake Bay Critical Area Driving Tour.

This 7.3-mile hike consists of a modified loop, or pair of stacked loops. The mostly woodland trails wind through rolling hills and wetland marshes, and past the site of a historic airfield. Mud, bugs, and poison ivy are common, but steep hills are not.

To get started from the trailhead parking lot, head down a gravel path in the direction of the W. H. Duvall Tool Museum. After passing an old Chesapeake log boat on the right, turn left onto a narrow woodland path surfaced with wood chips. Follow it through a vine-covered arch and into the Black Walnut Creek Study Area, a lush area of ferns, vines, and dense undergrowth.

Then drop down into a little valley onto a sandy path. At a trail junction, turn left and head east, toward the bay. Go past a wooden door (another entryway into the study area) and turn right, reaching a boardwalk shortly thereafter. The boardwalk crosses Black Walnut Creek and curves back westward. It winds along the foot of a steep hill, on the left. Watch and listen for a pond on the right. It's filled with cattails and other aquatic plants, as well as noisy amphibians.

At a set of steps on the left, climb them, pausing at an observation platform. Then continue to the top of the rise on a rather rooty path that soon gives way to a wide trail of hard-packed sand with large trees overhead. At a junction, note the first of numerous

directional signs you'll see on the hike. Also, turn left and head roughly south, passing through another junction.

At the junction after that, turn left off the main trail to take a detour of about 200 yards round-trip. Walk about 10 yards along the side trail, follow a path to the left and downward (using several short boardwalks), and turn right at the next junction. Then follow a boardwalk that'll take you to an observation deck overlooking Jug Bay's freshwater tidal marshes. See if you agree with Birmingham Bud that, were it not for a distant farmhouse and occasional passing boat, one would feel transported to a bygone wilderness.

Return to the main trail, turn left, and continue south through the woods on a low ridge. In the fall, as the leaves start to tumble, look for views of the bay off to the left. At the next junction, turn right and head west on a trail that ranges from level to undulating. Arriving at yet another junction, go straight and be prepared for mud if there's been rain recently. About 35 yards after a gate, find the intersection that serves as the hike's central node—and to which you'll be returning.

Turn left there and go straight at a junction about 35 yards down the trail. About a quarter-mile along, there's an often wet and muddy stretch of trail. Approaching Swan Point Creek, you'll go downhill. Don't take the apparent path to your right, but step carefully along the wider, rooty section on the left. Cross the bridge spanning the creek, keep going, and then ascend the creek bank to level ground.

After passing through an open area, reach Croom Airport Road (part of the driving tour route). Cross the road, duck into the trees on the other side, and turn left at a directional sign onto a wide, grassy path. Then you'll be out in the open. Note the distant barn to your right, a landmark during the hike's next portion, which traces three sides of what was the country's first black-owned and operated airfield. Opened as Riverside Field in 1941 by John W. Greene Jr., it was used for wartime flight training until 1944. Later reopened by Greene as the Columbia Air Center, the facility was permanently closed in 1958.

Along the second and third sides of the airfield, the trail and paved road keep close company but leave a ribbon of grass for your feet. Pass Shelbys Landing and a dirt trail, then stay on the grassy swath as it curves to the right, leaving the road behind. Continue along the grassy path, which dips under some tree cover and then opens up to offer views of the barn ahead.

At a picnic area, pass to the left and then slide back under the trees. Next, follow a muddy stretch of trail that crosses a grassy road, passes a stand of pines on the right and then two ravines on the left, and crosses another grassy road. At a junction and directional sign, turn right and north. You'll soon reach Croom Airport Road again and, roughly, the hike's halfway point.

There, turn left and walk along the road. Watch for a gate on the right, opposite a trail. Turn off past the gate onto yet another muddy stretch of trail. It swings left and then sharply right to reach a junction. There, ignore the gate on the right, and stay to the left. Proceeding, cross entrenched Swan Point Creek again; approach on a steep length of trail surfaced with very light colored pebbles, and leave on a very rocky and rutted portion. Turn right at the next junction, walk about 70 yards to another

one, and turn left there. Proceed along that trail for about 70 yards to get to the junction that's the hike's central node. Go straight through to reach the park entrance road.

Cross the road, walk through a gate, ignore a trail that takes off immediately to your right, and head toward the northwest. Initially, you'll be on an old roadway, set between steep banks. But then the trail rises and levels off. At the next junction, turn right. The trail leads to a field and a grassy path. There, turn right and continue across the partly open field, and then scoot back under the trees.

As the path curves east, go past several side trails on the left and then get a final go at a very muddy stretch of trail. At the park entrance road, swing left and follow it for about a third of a mile to the trailhead.

For more information on the Jug Bay section, contact the park, (301) 627-6074.

NEARBY/RELATED ACTIVITIES

Within the Jug Bay section, roam the rest of the study area, and visit the tool museum, Patuxent Village, and visitor center. In warm-weather months, sign up for a guided birding trip or nature hike, or (best of all) a scheduled sunset boat tour. Or take a rental canoe or kayak out on the bay. Call the park for details.

Explore Merkle Wildlife Sanctuary (entrance fee). For information and directions, call the sanctuary, (301) 888-1410. Take the 4-mile Chesapeake Bay Critical Area Driving Tour between Jug Bay and Merkle. Call the park or sanctuary for details.

#39
Piscataway Park

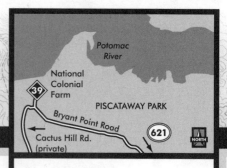

IN BRIEF

Piscataway Park, in Prince George's County, Maryland, preserves the view across the Potomac River from Mount Vernon. But hikers can also use it to trek through both the past and present.

DIRECTIONS

From Capital Beltway (Interstate 495 and I-95) in Oxon Hill, take Exit 3 onto southbound MD 210 (Indian Head Highway). Proceed for about 9.5 miles, and then turn right onto exit ramp leading to Bryan Point Road. Follow service road, and turn right onto Bryan Point Road. If you miss exit ramp, turn right at next traffic light onto Livingston Road; then turn right onto Biddle Road and left onto Bryan Point Road. Proceed for 3.5 miles. After passing Cactus Hill Road on left, continue for about 200 yards. At "All Visitors" sign, turn right onto gravel road and proceed 100 yards to parking lot near visitor center (pay entrance fee there). On leaving park, use Biddle and Livingston to get back onto MD 210.

DESCRIPTION

In the late eighteenth century, the view across the Potomac River from George Washington's Mount Vernon estate was one of woods and cultivated fields. More than two centuries later, it still is.

A mix of private and public actions saved the shoreline only 14 miles south

KEY AT-A-GLANCE INFORMATION

Length: 8.5 miles

Configuration: Modified out-and-back

Difficulty: Easy/moderate

Scenery: River vistas, woodlands, fields, wetlands

Exposure: Mostly open; more so in winter

Traffic: Very light to light; heavier on warm-weather weekends, holidays at colonial farm

Trail surface: Chiefly dirt or grass (muddy in places when wet); marsh boardwalk, short stretches of gravel, pavement

Hiking time: 4–5 hours

Access: Open daily, dawn to dusk; entrance fee

Maps: USGS Mount Vernon

Facilities: Toilets, water at visitor center (near trailhead); toilets along Piscataway Creek trail

Special comments: Stay on trails. Although park is under National Park Service, much of it is privately owned property on which scenic easements control land use. To learn more, contact Accokeek Foundation at Piscataway, (301) 283-2113 or visit www.accokeek.org.

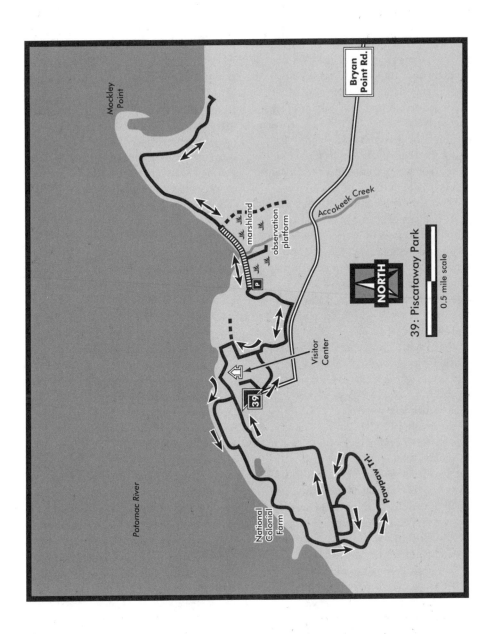

NORTH

0.5 mile scale

Bryan Point Rd.

Accokeek Creek

Mockley Point

marshland

observation platform

P

Visitor Center

39

Pawpaw Trl.

Potomac River

National Colonial Farm

of the White House. In the early 1950s, local groups and citizens launched an effort to protect it. Then, in 1961, Congress authorized Piscataway Park to preserve "the historic and scenic values ... of lands which provide the principal overview." The present-day park extends along the riverbank for 7 miles and covers about 5,000 acres.

This hike is a country ramble in an area where past and present mingle. It includes a reconstructed colonial-era farm featuring rare crops and livestock breeds, as well as a modern organic farm. Among its other attractions are views of Mount Vernon, a Native American ceremonial site, an arboretum, and a marsh. The mostly level, 8.5-mile hike is only

141

partially blazed and signposted, so follow my directions closely, especially on the segment after the colonial farm. Also, expect little shade and a bit of mud.

To get started from the trailhead parking lot, walk back to the paved road. Turn left onto the grassy shoulder and walk along the edge of the woods for about 50 yards. Turn left onto the Blackberry Trail at a half-hidden trail sign. Follow the purple blazes through the woods.

At the far side, you'll reach the fenced-in Robert Ware Straus Ecosystem Farm. It develops improved methods of intensive and sustainable organic farming. Like the colonial farm, it's run by the Accokeek Foundation at Piscataway Park, which also manages the park's trails and visitor center.

Touch not the electrified anti-deer fence. Turn right to walk along it. At the end, turn right onto an open gravel road. At a paved road (Bryan Point Road), turn left, and follow it for 200 yards, staying left. Then, at the "Tayac" sign, turn left onto a dirt road guarded by orange gates. Follow that road through fields going wild. Cross a parking lot onto a woodland path, then settle in for a scenic hike of just over a mile along the river. It begins with a large freshwater tidal marsh fed by Accokeek Creek, spanned by a boardwalk.

In the warm-weather months, the marsh is a green carpet dotted with color, mostly the red, pink, or white blooms of flowering plants and the wing patches of red-winged blackbirds. Water birds ply the shore. Insects create a sonic background for the boom of a bullfrog or the whistle of an osprey. In winter, you'll mostly experience browns, grays, and silence. The browns may well include bald eagles.

After the marsh, pass through a small wooded swamp and then step off the planks and onto a paved woodland path. About 20 yards later, step into the open at a junction with an unpaved farm road. Turn left and follow the road along the riverbank to the site of a large, precolonial Piscataway village. The area remains sacred to the villagers' descendants, who gather there each spring for a ceremony. Pause to view the ceremonial wigwam, other artifacts, and the plaque honoring Chief Turkey Tayac (1895–1978).

Continuing, stay near the river, which is shielded by thickets. The passing fields are part of a special farm where schoolchildren learn about farming and ecology. Eventually, enter some woods and leave the river as the road swings right. When you next reach the water, it'll be at Piscataway Creek's estuary—also the turnaround spot, 2.25 miles into the hike.

Look around. In the warm-weather months, deep in the sunny thickets, dragonflies seemingly hang like blue threads in the still air. On the estuary's far side, see Fort Washington, built in 1824 to guard the river approach to the capital.

Then begin your return to the ecosystem farm. En route, take a detour just after the end of the boardwalk, on the left. It's a quarter-mile round-trip into the marsh on a trail bordering Accokeek Creek. Watch on the left for an observation platform. Observe and walk back.

At the ecosystem farm, again, change course. First, you'll proceed along the fence all the way to the end. Then turn right along a second fence line. Turn left at the second side trail, near bluebird box no. 42; and walk to the riverbank. There, at the farm's solar power generator, eyeball Mount Vernon, turn left, and follow the grassy riverbank path.

At a trail junction (that's the Blackberry Trail again, on the left), proceed on the signposted Pumpkin Ash Trail. A half-mile long and named for an uncommon tree, the yellow-blazed woodland trail leads to the visitor center. From the center, head west on a dirt path. Just before getting to an avenue of cedars, turn right onto the signposted Riverview Trail. It's an open, blue-blazed, and mowed-in-season grassy trail, but shielded from the river by thickets.

On approaching a fenced enclosure, leave the trail to turn right and then right again to take a stairway to the boat dock. The dock provides a view of Mount Vernon year-round, and ferry service there on summer weekends (tickets are sold at the visitor center).

Back on the main trail, detour to the enclosure. The farm's "Museum Garden," it features displays of plants used by the colonists. Leaving the garden, turn left, walk to the end of the fence, and turn right onto a gravel road. After passing a woodshed and driveway on the right, leave the road and swing right onto a grassy, blue-blazed trail. Follow it past a pond on the left. Then swing sharp right and head into the woods on a dirt trail.

After crossing a stream, you'll be in the open again at a three-way junction. Turn right onto a broad grassy trail, and follow the blue blazes past overgrown fields. Turn right at the next, albeit blaze-less, junction. At the third junction, turn left, then pass a reassuring blaze, and continue through open woodlands. At the fourth junction, out in the open, turn right onto a broad grassy trail—and again pass a blue blaze. At the fifth junction, ignore the trail sign pointing straight ahead to the Bluebird Trail. Instead, turn right and walk about 50 yards uphill—to a sixth junction.

There, turn right and then left onto the signposted and white-blazed Paw-paw Trail. It's a narrow dirt trail that arcs for half a mile through a hilly and heavily wooded area. Watch for labeled trees, mature trees, baby trees (especially pawpaws), wildflowers, and poison ivy.

The Pawpaw Trail ends at the upper edge of a mowed area dotted with labeled young trees and shrubs representing over 125 species that grew in southern Maryland in the colonial era. They make up the park's Native Tree Arboretum, started in the 1980s.

Then, walking on the grass, follow the edge of the woods westward (away from the Pawpaw Trail). Reach a gravel road, which is part of the Bluebird Trail. You'll turn left onto the road, walk 10 yards, and turn left again onto a grassy path. The path follows the edge of the woods in a semicircle around what park literature says is a chestnut grove.

Continuing, you'll see a familiar place: the junction of the Pawpaw Trail and the short trail up from the Bluebird Trail. This time, turn right onto the short trail and then right again onto the blue-blazed Bluebird Trail and out into the open. Follow the road east, between a pasture on the left and the lower part of the arboretum on the right. At the end of the pasture, turn sharp left to stay on the gravel road and Bluebird Trail.

Heading north, follow the road as it swings right past some stables and reaches a junction. There, turn sharp left and continue, following the blue blazes past the farm's livestock area. Then pass the driveway again—and realize that both the Riverview Trail and Bluebird Trail are blazed blue. Continue, keeping the Museum Garden on your left, and head down the cedar avenue that leads to the start of the Riverview Trail. At the end of the avenue, detour through a gate on the right to circle by the old farmhouse, out-kitchen, smokehouse, "necessary" (outhouse), and kitchen garden. Then return to the trailhead.

Potomac Heritage Trail and C&O Canal Towpath

G. Washington Memorial Pkwy.

40

Theodore Roosevelt Island

Potomac River

Theodore Roosevelt Memorial Br.

63

NORTH

IN BRIEF

This book's only key-chain hike combines two very different riverside trails, one in Virginia's Arlington County and the other in Northwest Washington.

DIRECTIONS

From Washington's Mall area, access Constitution Avenue heading west. Proceed across Theodore Roosevelt Memorial Bridge, staying to right. Then take first exit to right followed immediately by another right onto westbound George Washington Memorial Parkway. Take first exit (within 400 yards) into Theodore Roosevelt Island parking lot on right. To get there from parkway's eastbound lanes, cross into Washington, turn around, and follow directions given above. *Note:* To return to Washington or eastbound lanes after hike, drive west (upriver) on parkway for 0.7 miles and take first exit, on left, onto Spout Run Parkway; then take first exit, on left, and access eastbound parkway.

Or use Metrorail and your feet to get to trailhead. Take Orange or Blue Line train to Rosslyn Metro station and then walk 0.7 miles to trailhead: From main entrance, turn left and walk downhill on North Moore Street, cross North 19th Street, turn right alongside Lee Highway, cross North Lynn Street, turn left onto North Lynn, and cross Lee Highway; at far corner, turn right onto Mount Vernon Trail and follow it downriver to

KEY AT-A-GLANCE INFORMATION

Length: 9.3 miles

Configuration: Loop

Difficulty: Easy/moderate

Scenery: River/canal views, woodlands

Exposure: Mostly open; more so in winter

Traffic: Extremely light on PHT; mostly light to moderate on towpath, but heavier on warm-weather evenings, weekends, holidays

Trail surface: Mostly dirt and rocks, with rooty, grassy patches, on PHT; packed dirt on towpath; paved bridges

Hiking time: 4–5 hours

Access: Open daily, dawn to dusk

Map: USGS Washington West

Facilities: Toilets near trailhead; toilets, water, phone, warm-weather snack bar at Fletcher's; phone at Chain Bridge; emergency phones on towpath downriver from Fletcher's

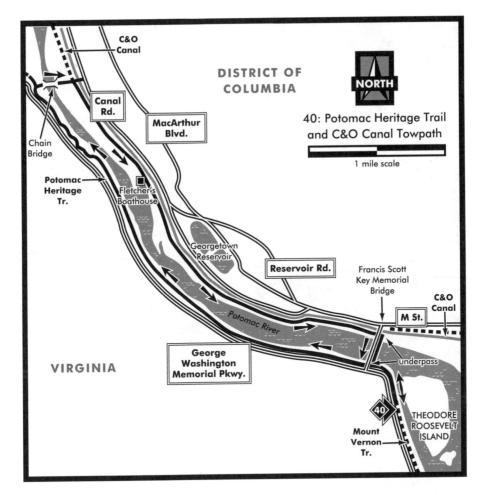

DISTRICT OF
COLUMBIA

NORTH

40: Potomac Heritage Trail
and C&O Canal Towpath

1 mile scale

C&O
Canal

Canal
Rd.

MacArthur
Blvd.

Chain
Bridge

Potomac
Heritage
Tr.

Fletcher's
Boathouse

Georgetown
Reservoir

Reservoir Rd.

Francis Scott
Key Memorial
Bridge

C&O
Canal

M St.

Potomac River

VIRGINIA

George
Washington
Memorial Pkwy.

underpass

40

THEODORE
ROOSEVELT
ISLAND

Mount
Vernon
Tr.

trailhead. Contact Metro, (202) 637-7000 or www.wmata.com.

Alternatively, start hiking at Fletcher's Boathouse, which is accessible by road and Metro.

DESCRIPTION

Each side of the Potomac River between Francis Scott Key Memorial Bridge and Chain Bridge has an unpaved trail that's set within federal parkland and linked to the other trail by both bridges. Knowing hikers use the trails and bridges to enjoy a close-in, 9.3-mile circuit—veterans call it the "Key-Chain Hike"—that ranges in ambiance from almost wild to urban.

The trail on the Virginia side is part of the Potomac Heritage Trail (PHT). It mostly follows the base of the wooded bluffs that carry the George Washington Memorial Parkway through Arlington County. Invisible from the parkway, the PHT seems much like a riverbank path in a wilderness or rural woodland.

Although reliably blue blazed, the trail itself is narrow, twisty, rocky, root strewn, nettled, rich in poison ivy, somewhat overgrown, and faint in places. Predictably, it's slow going. It's also little used. Over a decade, the only other people I've seen have been my companions—plus a few Potomac Appalachian

Milepost 4 is made of stone and wood.

Mountain Club volunteers clearing the trail. PATC maintains the trail, which it built for the National Park Service (NPS) in the mid-1980s.

Bad weather can make the PHT hazardous, flooding the trail, making streams impassable, and glazing rocks with ice. So, be prudent and prepared to turn back.

The trail on the Washington riverbank is also NPS property, being part of the C&O Canal National Historical Park. However, it's a broad, smooth, level, and elevated path flanked by the restored canal and mostly screened from the river by thickets. And like the adjoining Capital Crescent Trail, it's very popular with a variety of trail users.

To get started on the hike, head upriver from the Roosevelt Island parking lot, pass beneath the cross-parkway footbridge, cross the grass, and head into the

woods on the blue-blazed PHT. Within half a mile, you'll pass beneath Key Bridge and then travel upriver for 4-plus more miles.

In warm-weather months, the narrow floodplain is a colorful tangle of trees, bushes, blooms, and darting birds. In spring, pause at the shore to watch for the silvery glint of migrating shad. On winter afternoons, see if a certain slant of light presses you to wait, as though the land around you is listening.

Heading upriver, you'll have the Potomac swirling by on your right. The view to the left is mostly trees and cliffs broken by stream valleys. The streams can range from paltry trickles to powerful flows roaring down gullies or cascading over cliffs as mist-shrouded waterfalls. The largest ones, all signposted, are Windy Run, Donaldson Run, and Gulf Branch.

Just after Gulf Branch, watch for some stone steps on the left. Ascend them and keep going up what becomes a steep-in-places dirt trail. At a fork, go either way; both paths lead to an overlook. At the top of the hill, some 200 feet above the river, the trail flattens out and proceeds upriver for about half a mile, close to the noisy parkway.

The trail then slides under the parkway and descends to a road (Glebe Road). Cross very carefully, and turn right onto a protected walkway (saying goodbye to the PHT, which continues upriver). Cross VA 123 at the traffic light and head across Chain Bridge. Built in the mid-1930s, it's the flood-susceptible site's sixth bridge in 140 years. An earlier one had a roadway suspended from huge chains slung from stone abutments— hence the enduring name.

On the bridge, pause to look upriver, noting the riffles that are part of Little Falls. About two-thirds the way across, turn left onto a ramp that leads down to the towpath. Turn right, adjust to watching for other trail users but not your feet, and proceed downcanal on the towpath for over 3 miles. You'll soon see milepost 4—twice. Next to the standard wooden marker is the now-battered stone one that, until the C&O Canal was closed in 1924, told travelers it was "4 MILES TO W. C." (Washington City). Only a few other stone towpath markers remain.

About three-quarters of a mile farther down the towpath, watch for a footbridge across the waterway and a large stone house painted white. They mark Fletcher's Boathouse, the towpath's most popular gathering place inside the beltway. The white-sided Abner Cloud House, built in 1801 and the towpath's oldest existing building, is run by the Colonial Dames of America as a by-appointment-only museum.

It's worth lingering a while or longer at Fletcher's. It's the first spot on the towpath south of Chain Bridge where one can see the river and walk down to the water. A spacious riverside picnic area beckons in warm weather, when the snack bar is open and rental boats are available.

The next stretch of the towpath is closely paralleled by part of the paved Capital Crescent Trail (CCT), which agreeably tends to draw bikers and

in-line skaters away from the towpath. After the CCT veers away and just before the towpath reaches Key Bridge, watch on the right for the remaining piers of the Alexandria Aqueduct, built in the 1840s to link the C&O Canal with a canal extending to Alexandria. Over several decades, the aqueduct was rebuilt to serve variously as a roadway, dual canal/roadway, and railroad bridge. It was replaced by Key Bridge in 1924, but remained standing until the 1930s.

After passing under Key Bridge and by milepost 1, turn left onto a cross-canal footbridge. Ascend some steps, and cut left through a small park—also named for Francis Scott Key—to reach the bridge. Cross it, taking in the sweeping views. Then turn left onto the sign-posted Mount Vernon Trail to do the half-mile back to the trailhead.

For more information on the PHT, contact NPS's George Washington Memorial Parkway, (703) 289-2500 or www.nps.gov/gwmp, and PATC, (703) 242-0693 or www.patc.net. For more information on the towpath, see hike no. 10 (p. 33).

NEARBY/RELATED ACTIVITIES

En route, pause at Fletcher's to picnic or paddle. Later, at Francis Scott Key Park, make a gastronomic detour down Georgetown's M Street to Dean & Deluca, near 33rd Street.

NORTH

Constitution Ave.

Madison Dr.

14th St.

7th St.

NATIONAL MALL

41

Jefferson Dr.

Indepedence Ave.

12th St.

IN BRIEF

Extending south from the Mall, Washington's Potomac Park is just the place for a hike featuring paved paths, waterfront views, the Tidal Basin, cherry trees, memorials, and much open space.

DIRECTIONS

Head for Mall area. Park near trailhead-Smithsonian Metro station entrance within Mall (near Independence Avenue and 12th Street SW). Arrive early on crowded warm-weather weekends and holidays, beware local parking regulations (read signs carefully). Or use Metro: Smithsonian station is on Orange, Blue Lines; Metrobuses operate on nearby streets. Contact Metro, (202) 637-7000 or www.wmata.com.

DESCRIPTION

Potomac Park is world-famous for its Tidal Basin rimmed with Japanese cherry trees and memorials. In springtime the basin is filled with blossoms and upturned faces. Year-round, visitors stream through the memorials dedicated to presidents Thomas Jefferson (opened in 1943) and Franklin Delano Roosevelt (opened in 1997). In a few years, there will be a third one, honoring civil rights leader Martin Luther King Jr.

However, the park also includes a larger and little-visited area to the south. Originally a huge mound of dredging spoils, it's now a landscaped peninsula

KEY AT-A-GLANCE INFORMATION

Length: 8.2 miles

Configuration: Figure eight

Difficulty: Easy/moderate

Scenery: Parklands, waterfront views, street scenes

Exposure: Mostly open

Traffic: In Tidal Basin area, moderate to heavy in cherry-blossom season especially on weekends, holidays, and lighter at other times; elsewhere, light year-round

Trail surface: Pavement

Hiking time: 4–5 hours

Access: No restrictions

Maps: USGS Washington West; ADC Metro Washington

Facilities: None at trailhead; toilets, water, phones at Tidal Basin memorials, elsewhere in park, in Mall museums

Special comments: Finish hike by dusk

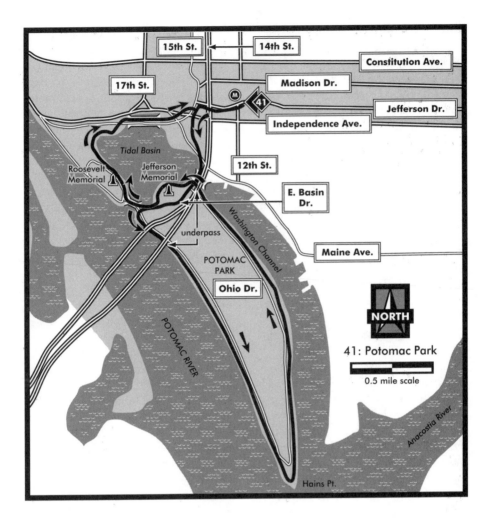

Labels on map: 15th St. · 14th St. · Constitution Ave. · 17th St. · Madison Dr. · 41 · Jefferson Dr. · Independence Ave. · Tidal Basin · Roosevelt Memorial · Jefferson Memorial · 12th St. · E. Basin Dr. · underpass · Washington Channel · Maine Ave. · POTOMAC PARK · Ohio Dr. · POTOMAC RIVER · NORTH · 41: Potomac Park · 0.5 mile scale · Anacostia River · Hains Pt.

dotted with playing fields, grassy areas, and a paved perimeter path.

This 8.2-mile, hill-free hike first loops around the peninsula and then circles the Tidal Basin. So you'll be able to get a good workout on a scarcely used waterside path, followed by an inevitably slower cherries-and-memorials tour. Each season has its pleasures, so don't limit yourself to when the cherry trees are in bloom or when the tourists are gone. By way of a hint, the peninsula has cherry trees that bloom later.

To get started from the Smithsonian Metro station on the Mall, head south (toward Independence Avenue) for about 20 yards. Turn right onto the paved path alongside Jefferson Drive. Follow it across 14th and 15th Streets NW, then turn left and follow 15th Street to Independence. Cross to continue on Raoul Wallenberg Place (in back of the US Holocaust Memorial Museum). Then cross Maine Avenue, walk a few yards, and swing left onto the paved path alongside the Tidal Basin. Stay on the path as it becomes a sidewalk that, flanked by a green handrail, bumps over the basin's hidden outlet and continues along East Basin Drive.

After passing the Jefferson Memorial, off to the right, reach the drive's junction with Ohio Drive, near the basin's inlet. There, turn left and cross East Basin Drive to visit a bronze George Mason sitting casually on a stone bench in a flower garden. Also tour the garden, which is ablaze with color in the spring. Then cross Ohio Drive, cut across the grass toward the Potomac, and turn left onto the paved path at the river's edge. Keep going until you pass under the bridge spans known collectively as the 14th Street Bridge, or George Mason Bridge.

Then settle in for a 2.3-mile excursion to the peninsula's southern tip, Hains Point. There, pause to watch the gulls, ducks, and other water birds. You may even spot a bald eagle or osprey. Continuing on the riverside path, celebrate the hike's halfway point by drawing abreast of "The Awakening." Created by J. Seward Johnson Jr., it's an aluminum statue of an enormous and mostly buried man lying on his back, with only his head and limbs visible, thrusting skyward.

Back on the path, continue walking along the Washington Channel. Across the channel is Fort McNair's manicured grounds, where the National Defense University looms. Just north of the fort is the Washington Marina and a popular fish market. Stay on the path as it cuts left to become a sidewalk that passes under the 14th Street Bridge spans. Just after the last span, leave the side-walk and cross East Basin Drive to complete the first loop of the figure-eight hike.

Walk across the grass to the Tidal Basin, and turn left to follow the cherry trees and path to the Jefferson Memorial. John Russell Pope's classic memorial will provide you with fine views inside and out. While there, contemplate a little puzzle: Why does the first panel of Jefferson's quotations slightly mangle the Declaration of Independence?

Leaving the memorial, continue clockwise around the Tidal Basin. After crossing the bridge over the basin's inlet, reach the Roosevelt Memorial. Either take a quick tour of the memorial or plan to go through it more thoroughly while doing hike no. 48 (p. 173). Continuing, either stop to read the plaque marking the site of the Martin Luther King Jr. memorial or detour around the construction site.

Then, after passing a Japanese stone lantern on your left, reach Kutz Bridge, which carries Independence Avenue over the northern tip of the Tidal Basin. Turn right to walk across the bridge and then keeping going along the avenue. If it's spring or summer, though, detour through the flower garden just beyond the bridge. Then follow the avenue to 15th Street and, from there, head for the trailhead or your car. For more information on Potomac Park, contact National Capital Parks—Central, (202) 619-7222 or www.nps.gov/nacc.

NEARBY/RELATED ACTIVITIES
Take a rental paddleboat out on the Tidal Basin. Detour to the lively Maine Avenue Fish Market, near the Tidal Basin's outlet; it has ready-to-eat food, too. Visit one of the nearby museums.

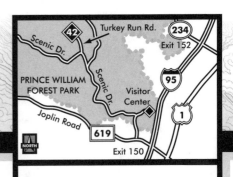

#42
Prince William
Forest Park

IN BRIEF

Prince William Forest Park, in Prince
William County, Virginia, is a huge nature
preserve that provides a wonderful habitat
for plants, wildlife, and visiting hikers.

DIRECTIONS

From Capital Beltway (Interstate 495 and
I-95), take Exit 57A onto I-95 heading
southwest, toward Richmond. If you start
from Washington, head southwest on
Shirley Memorial Highway (I-395) to
automatically be on I-95 when you cross
beltway. From beltway, go almost 20 miles
on I-95, watch for road sign announcing
park, and take Exit 150B to VA 619. Head
west on VA 619 (Joplin Road) for 0.4
miles. Then turn right onto park entrance
road. Stop at fee-collection kiosk. Continue for 0.5 mile, and then left onto
Scenic Drive. Proceed for 2 miles, and
turn left, at sign for Turkey Run campground, onto loop part of Scenic Drive.
Go 0.3 miles and turn right onto Turkey
Run Road. Continue for 0.3 miles, past
campground, to parking lot at Turkey
Run Educational Center.

DESCRIPTION

Located about 20 miles southwest of the
Capital Beltway, Prince William Forest
Park ranks as the metro area's largest
park. Covering 18,571 acres, it's also the
largest woodland expanse within 50
miles of Washington. And I claim that

KEY AT-A-GLANCE
INFORMATION

Length: 12.3 miles

Configuration: Loop

Difficulty: Quite difficult

Scenery: Rolling woodlands,
stream valleys

Exposure: Over half open; more so
in winter

Traffic: Usually light or very light;
heavier in warm-weather season,
especially on weekends, holidays

Trail surface: Mostly dirt, with
some rocky, rooty stretches; one
dirt/gravel road

Hiking time: 4.5–6 hours

Access: Open daily, dawn to dusk;
entrance fee

Maps: USGS Joplin, Quantico;
sketch map in free park brochure

Facilities: Toilets, water, phone at
trailhead; toilets, water at Oak
Ridge

Special comments: Use bug
repellent; check for ticks after hike

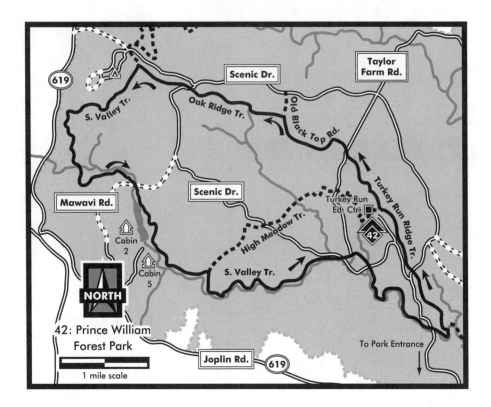

it's the only one worthy of being called a forest, even if it is a young one.

The area was well forested in pre-colonial times, but over two centuries of farming left the land badly eroded. In 1933 the federal government made it one of the country's 50 or so demonstration projects for restoring the environment and developing inexpensive recreation facilities. The Civilian Conservation Corps (CCC) seeded slopes, created trails, and built facilities.

Eventually, in 1948, the area became a national park. Decades of recovery have transformed the depleted farmland. Trees, bushes, wildflowers, and ferns flourish, making springtime treks along the stream valleys a particular delight. Deer, beavers, squirrels, and other wildlife are plentiful. Their habitat extends into the adjoining Quantico Marine Corps

Base, much of which is managed as a natural preserve.

This hike is a 12.3-mile counterclockwise loop with about 1,800 feet of elevation change, but only one steep hill. The trails are blazed and signposted (and do stay on them to avoid the poison ivy). You'll get scenic views rather than vistas; there are open areas but no high overlooks. Trail traffic is usually light; most visitors seem to be there to camp, picnic, fish, or take short strolls.

The hike works best in the spring and fall. Summer can be muggy and buggy. Winter, though, can be wonderful. My best time there was a cold but sunny day with snow on the ground, deer on the move, and the pileated woodpecker's "great god-call" (to use nature writers Bill and Phyllis Thomas's lovely phrase) echoing through the forest.

To get started from the trailhead, step onto the undulating, dirt-and-gravel-surfaced Old Black Top Road (opposite the parking lot's entrance). Head northwest for 1.8 miles in open country. After crossing Taylor Farm Road and a small stream, watch on the left for the hike's first concrete signpost. There, turn left onto the yellow-blazed Oak Ridge Trail. Follow it for 1.6 miles through the open forest (take care when crossing Scenic Drive).

At a junction, turn left onto the white-blazed South Valley Trail, which will be your path for the next 7.5 miles. First, head roughly south through a fairly open area for almost 2 miles until you reach the South Fork of Quantico Creek. From there, follow the trail as it wiggles southeast close to the tree-lined stream. Cross Mawavi Road (a fire road near the hike's halfway point) and watch for a large beaver lodge in a broad, swampy area. Then, pass two man-made lakes used for canoeing and fishing by summertime campers staying in the nearby CCC-built cabins. Below the second lake, the stream valley is postcard pretty and one of the park's most attractive trail segments.

Continuing, cross Scenic Drive for the second and third times, hike up and over the hike's only significant hill, and pass side trails leading off to parking lots C, B, and A. Then, cross Scenic Drive again and take the first left onto the 1.4-mile Turkey Run Ridge Trail. Follow the dark-blue-blazed trail uphill, heading northwest. Cross Scenic Drive one last time. Then traverse a hilly and forested area to reach the trailhead. Contact the park for more information, (703) 221-7181 or www.nps.gov/prwi.

This beaver lodge lies near Mawavi Road.

RELATED/NEARBY ACTIVITIES

Visit the park's visitor center, off the entrance road. It has nature exhibits, maps, books, and friendly rangers. After the hike, explore historic Dumfries, at the head of Quantico Creek's estuary. To get there, stay on VA 619, cross I-95, and turn north onto US 1 at Triangle. In Dumfries, visit the Weems-Botts Museum (703) 221-3346. In winter, drive along the estuary on Possum Point Road to see migratory tundra swans. They leave on about March 19 (oddly, that's when the swallows return to San Capistrano). If you're hungry, try Tim's Rivershore Restaurant & Crabhouse (703) 441-1375, on Cherry Hill Road.

#43
Red Rock Wilderness Overlook Regional Park

IN BRIEF

In this secluded vest-pocket park on the Potomac River in Loudoun County, Virginia, you'll find small-scale pleasures that are riverine, hilly, colorful, arboreal, aloft, afoot, and seasonal.

DIRECTIONS

From Capital Beltway (Interstate 495) in McLean, Virginia, take Exit 45A and access Dulles Toll Road heading northwest. That feeds into Dulles Greenway (another toll road). At greenway Exit 4 (roughly 22 miles from beltway), turn right onto Belmont Ridge Road (VA 659). Proceed for about 3.8 miles and turn left onto VA 7 (Harry Byrd Highway). For toll-free route that's shorter but slower, start at beltway Exit 47A and access VA 7 (there called Leesburg Pike). Either way, from VA 7's intersection with Belmont Ridge Road, drive about 1.2 miles toward Leesburg. Then turn right onto River Creek Parkway, which runs into Edwards Ferry Road. Turn sharp left where the four-lane divided road becomes a two-lane road. Two miles from VA 7, turn right into inconspicuous park entrance flanked by stone pillars. Drive to parking lot.

DESCRIPTION

Loudoun County's once-rural Leesburg area continues to be built up and over, but a few close-in green spaces remain. One of them is Red Rock Wilderness

KEY AT-A-GLANCE INFORMATION

Length: 2 miles

Configuration: Modified loop

Difficulty: Very easy

Scenery: Hilly woodlands, river vistas

Exposure: Mostly shady; less so in winter

Traffic: Usually very light to light; light to moderate on warm-weather weekend, holiday afternoons

Trail surface: Mostly hard-packed dirt; can be wet, muddy on floodplain

Hiking time: 1.5–2.5 hours (including dawdle time by river)

Access: Open daily during daylight hours

Maps: USGS Leesburg; so-so sketch map in free park brochure

Facilities: None

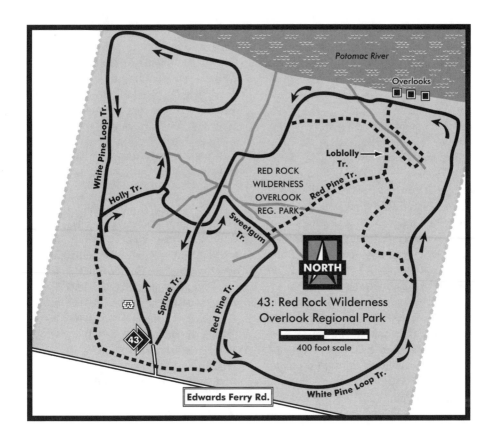

43: Red Rock Wilderness Overlook Regional Park

Overlook Regional Park, opened in 1977. It lies on the Potomac River just east of Leesburg and about 25 miles northwest of Washington.

The park's name seems extravagant. There's hardly any red rock or wilderness, and "regional" doesn't fit a 67-acre area. But "overlook" is apt since there are river vistas. And visitors with scaled-down expectations can expect to see beauty in small proportions (just as life can be perfect in short measures).

The park consists of a tract of hilly, mostly deciduous woodlands crisscrossed by short, well-maintained trails. The six main trails are color blazed and named. Oddly, though, the names appear only on maps and paper, not on trailside sign-posts. I've incorporated five of the main

trails into a 2-mile loop that accumulates about 700 feet of elevation change.

To get started from the parking-lot trailhead, head for the white-blazed White Pine Loop Trail, near a picnic table. Walk gently downhill through the trees, which include gorgeous-in-spring dogwoods and pines. At the first trail junction, turn right onto the blue-blazed Holly Trail and continue downhill. At the next junction, turn left onto a curving and undulating section of the white-blazed trail. Close to the river, you'll reach a junction where the white-blazed trail goes uphill and an unblazed side trail drops to the river. McLean Claire recommends detouring to the floodplain for fine views from beneath the leafy leaning trees.

Back on the white-blazed trail, head uphill. When you reach the blue-blazed trail, turn left to repeat its 100 yards. But then turn right onto another section of the white-blazed trail. Undulate past the green-blazed Spruce Trail, on the right, to reach a small bridge. There, turn right onto the orange-blazed Sweetgum Trail and ascend a lovely stream valley.

At the next junction, cross a small bridge and turn right and uphill onto the red-blazed Red Pine Trail. Keep going, and reach the hike's halfway point—a junction where you'll turn left onto yet another section of the white-blazed trail. Mostly level and flanked by pines, this half-mile-long and pine-needle-covered section passes the yellow-blazed Loblolly Trail and then leads to the first of three fenced cliff-top overlooks. There, enjoy a panoramic view of the Potomac swirling eastward through rolling fields and woodlands.

The trail then picks its way upriver and downhill, taking you to the other two overlooks, each offering a slightly different but fence-filtered perspective on the riverscape. McLean Claire likes to walk to the far end of the fence at the second overlook. There, she sits on a log and enjoys a lovely fence-free view.

After the third overlook, the trail pitches steeply downhill to the floodplain. On the way down (carefully), eyeball the cliff wall, where red sandstone makes a tiny contribution to the park's name. And in the warm months, watch for cliff-side wildflowers engaged in the art of vertical living. At the bottom, proceed along the floodplain for roughly 75 yards. Then, swing left to take an unblazed trail that climbs a short but very steep slope. At the top, on reaching yet another section of the white-blazed trail, follow it uphill and away from the river.

After a second stream crossing (ignore the Sweetgum Trail on your left), you'll be on a short stretch of the white-blazed trail that you did earlier in the opposite direction. But this time turn left onto the short and green-blazed Spruce Trail, which will deliver you to the trailhead.

For further information on the park, contact the offsite office, (703) 737-7800, the Northern Virginia Regional Park Authority, (703) 352-5900, or visit www.nvrpa.org/redrock.html.

NEARBY/RELATED ACTIVITIES

At the parking lot, explore the nearby buildings, including an icehouse and carriage house. They're remnants of a nineteenth-century estate. Between late August and the end of October, wander through the amazing 5-acre cornfield maze at Temple Hall Farm Regional Park, about 5 miles north of Leesburg. Call for details, directions, and cost, (703) 779-9372.

#44 Riverbend Park and Great Falls Park

IN BRIEF

Riverbend Park and Great Falls Park in Fairfax County, Virginia, offer hikers Great Falls, great vistas, and a great time in a magnificent Potomac River setting.

DIRECTIONS

From Capital Beltway (Interstate 495) in McLean, Virginia, take Exit 44 onto Georgetown Pike (VA 193) heading roughly west. Stay on pike for 4.7 miles. Then turn right onto River Bend Road (VA 603). Drive 2.2 miles and turn right onto Jeffrey Road (VA 1268). Proceed for 1.3 miles, past Riverbend Park's main entrance, to parking lot at end of gated road, next to park's former nature center. *Note:* Nearing gated road's end, note posted closing time—to avoid staying overnight in park.

DESCRIPTION

Only about 15 miles from downtown Washington, the Great Falls area is probably the metro area's finest close-in natural attraction. There, the broad and smooth Potomac River suddenly tumbles almost 80 feet in a series of rapids, and then squeezes through a narrow, mile-long, and sheer-walled gorge. National Park Service (NPS) lands protect both banks and provide riveting views of nature at work.

On the Virginia side, Great Falls Park stretches the length of the gorge and beyond, and inland too. It covers 800

KEY AT-A-GLANCE INFORMATION

Length: 9.5 miles

Configuration: Modified loop

Difficulty: Moderate/difficult

Scenery: Wooded uplands, river vistas, waterfalls, historic remains

Exposure: Mostly shady; less so in winter

Traffic: Usually light, but heavy to crowded in falls area on warm-weather weekends, holidays

Trail surface: Mostly dirt; some pavement, gravel; very rocky in places

Hiking time: 5–6 hours (including overlook time)

Access: Riverbend open daily, 7 to 5–8:30 p.m. (closing time varies); Great Falls open daily, sunrise to sunset (closed December 25)

Maps: USGS Rockville, Seneca, Vienna, Falls Church; PATC Map D; ADC Northern Virginia; so-so sketch maps in free park brochures

Facilities: Toilets, water, phones at visitor centers; snack bar at G.F. center; toilets, water at Matildaville

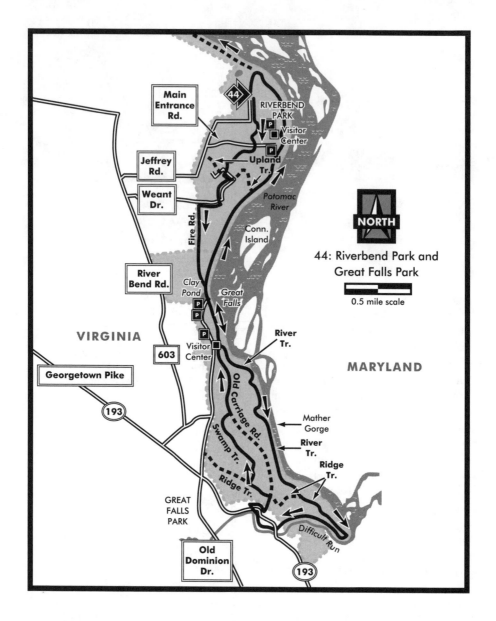

Main
Entrance
Rd.

44

RIVERBEND
PARK

Visitor
Center

Jeffrey
Rd.

Upland
Tr.

Weant
Dr.

Potomac
River

Conn.
Island

NORTH

44: Riverbend Park and
Great Falls Park

0.5 mile scale

Fire Rd.

River
Bend Rd.

Clay
Pond

Great
Falls

River
Tr.

VIRGINIA

603

Visitor
Center

Georgetown Pike

MARYLAND

Old Carriage Rd.

193

Mather
Gorge

Swamp Tr.

River
Tr.

Ridge
Tr.

Ridge Tr.

GREAT
FALLS
PARK

Difficult Run

Old
Dominion
Dr.

193

acres of rocky shoreline and wooded
uplands. It also has hiking trails, but
nearly all of the park's 500,000 annual
visitors concentrate on the falls-and-
gorge area, especially on warm-weather
weekends and holidays.

Adjoining the NPS park to the north
lies 409-acre Riverbend Park. It's a Fairfax County park that has wooded

uplands, hiking trails, and a pretty floodplain shoreline. It too is popular in warm
weather, when picnickers cluster near its
riverbank visitor center.

This hike is a two-park, 9.5-mile loop
leading through the uplands, to the falls,
along the gorge, and onto the floodplain.
You'll experience assorted scenery, impressive vistas, and about 2,200 feet of

elevation change. The route has limited blazes and signposts, so follow directions closely—and stay out of the poison ivy.

To get started from the trailhead, hike back along the entrance road to a bulletin board. There, turn left and head downhill on a dirt trail. Then turn right onto the red-blazed Upland Trail. This undulating trail will take you through scenery common to much of both parks: rolling hills and stream valleys clothed in good-sized oaks, hickories, and beeches, with an understory of mountain laurels, dogwoods, and assorted wildflowers.

On the Upland Trail, you'll cross the park's entrance road and then encounter a series of signposted trail junctions. Stay on the Upland Trail until you reach a junction where there's a post promising that it's 3.4 miles back to the visitor center (Riverbend's) and 0.2 miles to the river. There, turn right to leave the Upland Trail and head uphill.

Avoiding several side trails, follow the unmarked trail as it levels off and goes mostly and gently downhill. It emerges from the woods at the intersection of two gravel roads, one L-shaped, the other gated. Turn right onto the L-shaped road and head uphill to where it becomes a paved road (Weant Drive) and forms a junction with a two-sign gravel road ("Fire Road" and "Private Drive"). There, turn left onto the signed road.

Follow it mostly downhill to reach the Great Falls visitor center's vast parking area and Clay Pond (read the explanatory label). Cross the lot to take a short path leading toward the river. At the end of the path, turn right onto a broad and gravelly path that parallels the ruined Potowmack Canal.

The canal was one of five built by the Potowmack Company, starting in 1785, to make the Potomac navigable and open up waterborne trade with the interior. The company's first president was an ardent advocate named George Washington. After four years, though, he left to become the first president of a larger entity.

The Great Falls canal was opened in 1802. For two decades, it had enough boat traffic to support the adjoining town of Matildaville, started by Henry "Light-Horse Harry" Lee (Matilda was his first wife; Robert E. was his son). But the town, canal, and company foundered.

You'll soon reach the park's big visitor center. Do what you must, and then continue on the gravelly path. Turn left to cross a footbridge spanning the old canal bed, and proceed on a dirt-and-gravel path through an open cliff-top area of parkland. Short trails lead left to two overlooks, built almost a century ago as part of a private amusement park.

Visit both overlooks to see the river, falls, gorge, and possibly people at the Olmstead Island overlook on the far side. Overlook no. 2 is the best. Then visit the cliff-top post on which record flood levels are marked. Imagine being there and able to breathe only by standing up straight (as in 1972) or by wearing scuba gear (as in 1985 and 1996).

Continue downriver, but not on the main path. Instead, get on a twisty cliff-top trail. It runs into the blue-blazed River Trail, which you'll be on for 3 miles. En route, detour left on short side trails to peer down into Mather Gorge. The 200-foot-wide gorge is a two-million-year work in progress, being created by the erosive river cutting down through bedrock.

At a signless and blaze-less intersection, go straight and cross a stream valley on wooden stairs. A little farther on, the trail swings abruptly right and away from the cliff. Cross the old canal bed to reach a trail that parallels the canal. There, turn left and proceed, passing a deep man-made rock cleft where Locks 3, 4, and 5 once stepped the canal down to the river.

Continuing along the gorge, you'll notice the scenery gets wilder, the trail rockier, and the going slower. But the views of the gorge are superb. From the semi-overgrown Cow Hoof Rock over-look, near the end of the gorge, the trail angles inland and climbs uphill steeply, as you should. Then turn left onto the Ridge Trail. At a junction, turn left and walk down a very steep hill. At the bottom, turn left and proceed to a lovely off-the-beaten trail place—Difficult Run's mouth on the Potomac. Then follow the streambank inland. Don't hike back up the very steep trail, but stay left and take the less-steep gravelly fire road alongside the picturesque stream.

Where the road levels off, bear left at a trail sign onto a muddy-when-wet dirt trail that follows the stream under trestled Georgetown Pike (VA 193). At a roadside parking lot, you'll be just past the hike's halfway point. There, cross the pike very carefully (blind curves hide the speeding cars). Turn right and walk about 200 yards along the edge of the road even more carefully. Then turn left, bypass a gate, and head into the woods on a gently ascending fire road.

At the first intersection, turn left onto and up the Ridge Trail. At the top, turn right and walk through a gate onto an unnamed trail. It undulates through deep woods and then levels out near a sign-posted junction. There, turn left onto the summer-scenic Swamp Trail. At the next junction, turn left onto the mostly level Old Carriage Road near what's left of Matildaville. Continuing, pass the visitor

center again. Then swing right to the trail along the canal, and head upriver. Beyond the canal, jog left onto a gravel path, and proceed to leave one park and reenter the other.

Negotiate a short stretch of very rocky and tree-rooty trail, then walk along 2 miles of some of the best riverside hiking I know. You'll be on the floodplain where the Potomac makes the big bend for which the park is named. The mostly smooth but sometimes muddy trail is flanked by mature sycamores, cotton-woods, and maples, as well as pawpaws, bushes, and wildflowers. And watch for springtime songbirds, summertime but-terflies, wintertime water birds, and any-time bald eagles (they reside on Conn Island).

After passing the Riverbend visitor center, walking softly on flood-deposited silt, and crossing a footbridge, watch for a trail fork. There, take the left-hand tine to start the hike's final half-mile. Walk uphill and past a pond, staying to the left. At a signpost banning horses and bicycles, turn left onto a narrow trail leading to the trailhead.

In the fall and winter, try reversing the hike route so you're doing the riverside trail in the morning sunshine.

For more information, contact River-bend Park, (703) 759-9018 or www.co.fairfax.va.us/parks and Great Falls Park, (703) 285-2966 or www. nps.gov/gwmp/greatfal.

RELATED/NEARBY ACTIVITIES
Explore other trails, such as Riverbend's Meadow Trail and Great Falls' Matil-daville Trail. Stop by at both visitor centers to see the nature exhibits and confer with eager-to-help staffers. Try some of the many year-round program offerings.

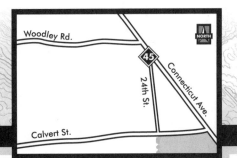

#45
Rock Creek Park: Arboreal Southern Section

IN BRIEF

Rock Creek Park's tree-rich southern section and western outliers enable hikers to loop through Northwest Washington on mostly shady trails.

DIRECTIONS

Head for Northwest Washington. Park near trailhead—Woodley Park-Zoo/Adams Morgan Metro station entrance on Connecticut Avenue (just north of Connecticut and Calvert Street NW). Heed posted street parking regulations. Arrive early on warm-weather weekends and holidays. On weekdays, consider starting hike at no-time-limit parking lots at Pierce Mill or zoo.

Or use Metro to do hike: Woodley Park-Zoo/Adams Morgan Metro station is on Red Line (as are close-to-hike-route Cleveland Park and Tenleytown-AU stations); Metrobuses operate on nearby streets. Contact Metro, (202) 637-7000 or www.wmata.com.

DESCRIPTION

Washington, DC, has long been called the City of Trees. Despite a net tree-cover loss of roughly 60 percent since 1980, the name still applies. The parks remain mostly wooded. Residential streets, yards, and gardens sport canopies of leaves. Vacant lots, rights-of-way, and nooks quickly follow suit if left alone.

This hike celebrates the District's arboreal heritage. It winds through the

KEY AT-A-GLANCE INFORMATION

Length: 8.9 miles

Configuration: Loop

Difficulty: Moderate

Scenery: Mostly wooded parklands, with intervening street scenes

Exposure: Mostly shady; less so in winter

Traffic: Light to moderate on Rock Creek Trail, but heavier on warm-weather evenings, weekends; light elsewhere

Trail surface: Roughly half pavement; rest mostly dirt; rooty, muddy in places

Hiking time: 3.5–4.5 hours

Access: Parks open daily, dawn to dusk; zoo grounds' hours are similar

Maps: USGS Washington West; PATC Map N; ADC Metro Washington; sketch map in free Rock Creek Park brochure

Facilities: Toilets, water, phones near Pierce Mill, at eateries on major streets

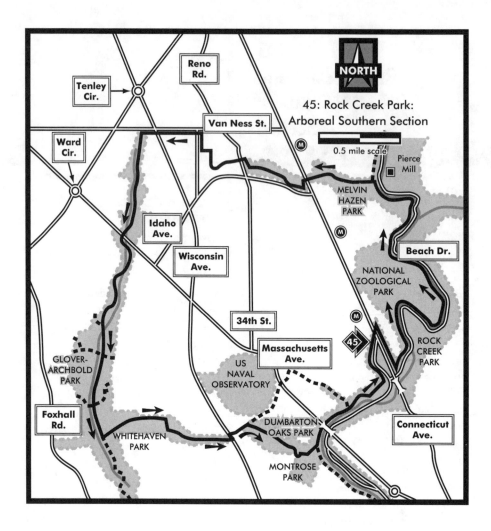

well-wooded parklands and residential areas of Northwest Washington. Administratively, the parklands are all part of the National Park Service's Rock Creek Park. However, like the hike, they also include four separate units—Melvin Hazen, Glover-Archbold, Whitehaven, and Dumbarton Oaks Parks.

Most of the trees along the hike route are deciduous, such as oaks, hickories, maples, dogwoods, and sycamores. Hikers will also find more exotic varieties along the way, with wildflowers and birds adding further color and interest to the trailside parklands.

The 9.2-mile counterclockwise loop is only partially signposted and blazed, so pay attention to the description. Most of the route is fairly level or undulates gently, but it does have a few steep but short uphill stretches—and about 1,600 feet of elevation change. When you're on the busy Rock Creek Trail, stay to the right. On city streets, use the sidewalks and be careful when you cross.

To get started from the Woodley Park-Zoo/Adams Morgan Metro station, walk over to 24th Street as it angles downhill from Connecticut to Calvert Street. Cross Calvert and head down into Rock

162

Creek Park, staying to the left of the roadway. After crossing a twin-laned side road, turn left onto the paved Rock Creek Trail. Head generally north, alongside Rock Creek Parkway and southward-bound Rock Creek. Just before you reach a road tunnel, turn left and follow the trail for half a mile through the gated outer grounds of the zoo—formally, the National Zoological Park.

Emerging from the zoo, swing left onto the trail and proceed. At a trail fork, stay to the right and follow the trail downhill and under a low green bridge. At a signposted junction, take the Valley Trail, which crosses Rock Creek on a bridge and continues upstream next to the parkway. After a third of a mile, another bridge will take you back over the creek and into an open field.

Off to the left is the signposted Melvin Hazen Trail. Before taking it, detour to the other end of the field to see the restored Pierce Mill, dating from 1820 and the only surviving gristmill along Rock Creek. Housed in another old building nearby is the Rock Creek Gallery, long known as the Art Barn.

On the Melvin Hazen Trail, in the narrow wooded park of the same name, follow a rocky stream valley uphill and generally westward for half a mile. Starting there, watch your step on the hike's dirt trails, which can be get muddy or icy. At Connecticut Avenue, turn right to cross it at Sedgewick Street. On the far side, turn left and proceed back down the avenue. At a "Dead End Street" sign, turn right into an alley. At the end of the alley, descend some steps to rejoin the Melvin Hazen Trail. At a junction, turn right onto a yellow-blazed trail. Then, at a fork, follow a streamside trail to Tilden Road just before its junction with Reno Road.

Cross Reno and walk up Springland Lane. At the end of the lane, head up the nearby steps. Then turn right onto a broad unpaved path that leads to a signless street (it's Idaho). Proceed along the street and turn left at the next intersection onto Tilden Street (again, no sign visible). At the intersection after that, turn right onto 37th Street (no sign) and proceed for two blocks. Then turn left onto Van Ness Street.

Next, head for Wisconsin Avenue, a major thoroughfare with bathroom-equipped eateries. Cross the avenue, continue along Van Ness for about 100 yards, and then walk left onto a short paved road. At a stop sign, swing right onto a grassy area and cross to the northern end of both Glover-Archbold Park and the Glover-Archbold Trail, the hike's halfway mark.

Head south on the blue-blazed woodland trail for 1.5 miles, crossing Massachusetts, Cathedral, and New Mexico Avenues along the way and avoiding the side trails. Then, at a signpost pointing to the Whitehaven Trail, leave the G-A Trail and turn left and east into wooded Whitehaven Park. Follow the buff-blazed trail uphill and then along the edge of an athletic field, staying close to the boundary fence. At the end of fence, turn right and then bear left. Then descend with the trail and cross an open picnic area to reach 37th Street.

Cross the street carefully. On the far corner, go left and then right onto a steep but short flight of steps. At the top, stay to the right and continue along the Whitehaven Trail. It will deliver you to the corner of 35th Street and Whitehaven Parkway. Follow the parkway to nearby Wisconsin Avenue (for bathroom-equipped eateries, head left, up the avenue).

Cross the avenue, turn left, and then turn right onto Whitehaven Street. At the end of the street, access the signposted Dumbarton Oaks Trail, in the park of the same name (not be confused with the adjoining estate called Dumbarton Oaks—well worth a visit at another time). This trail winds through a lovely stretch of parkland that has more of a wilderness flavor than any other segment of the hike.

Stay on the main trail. Where that gets somewhat faint, in an open area, stay to the right, jump over a small stream, and continue along the trail on the far side.

Leaving the park, walk past a stone gatepost and start the final mile of the hike by reaching a trail junction. There, take the buff-blazed trail (marked with a no-bikes sign) that heads downhill toward Rock Creek Park proper. Stay on the trail as it turns to the left and goes upstream alongside Rock Creek. Cross a small bridge and stay to right. Then turn left onto the Rock Creek Trail. Just past some exercise stations, swing left and uphill to reach and cross Calvert Street.

Then walk up 24th Street to the trail-head or go find your car. As this hike is a loop, you may prefer to select your own trailhead (see under Directions).

For more information on parks along hiking route, contact Rock Creek Park, (202) 282-1063 or www.nps.gov/rocr.

NEARBY/RELATED ACTIVITIES

During or after the hike, visit Pierce Mill, (202) 426-6908, and the Rock Creek Gallery, (202) 244-2482, if they're open. During the hike, on leaving the Whitehaven Trail, refuel at one of the nearby Wisconsin Avenue eateries; try Faccia Luna, (202) 337-3132. After the hike, decompress at one of the Connecticut Avenue restaurants near the trailhead; try Tono Sushi, (202) 332-7300. Or walk one Metro stop north to the avenue's Cleveland Park eateries; try pan-Asian Ivy's Place, (202) 363-7802.

#46
Rock Creek Park:
Rocky Central Section

IN BRIEF

As this easy hike in Northwest Washington reveals, the chief natural attraction of Rock Creek Park's central section is a rocky stream valley set amid hilly woodlands.

DIRECTIONS

Head for Northwest Washington. From intersection of Connecticut and Nebraska Avenues, head northeast on Nebraska for 0.4 miles. Turn easy (not sharp) right onto Military Road and drive east for 0.7 miles. Then turn right and south onto Glover Road to enter Rock Creek Park. Proceed for 0.4 miles, swinging left at fork and then taking first left to get to parking lot for Rock Creek Nature Center and Planetarium.

Or use Metro and your feet: From either Friendship Heights Metro station (Red Line) or Fort Totten Metro station (Red, Green Lines), take Metrobus E2 or E3 along Military Road. Get off at Oregon Avenue (opposite Glover Road). From southeast corner of intersection, walk uphill on paved path for 400 yards to reach trailhead. Contact Metro, (202) 637-7000 or www.wmata.com.

DESCRIPTION

Rock Creek Park forms a big wedge that follows its namesake creek from Washington's northern apex down to the creek's mouth on the Potomac River. The park's central section features

KEY AT-A-GLANCE INFORMATION

Length: 4.5 miles

Configuration: Loop

Difficulty: Easy

Scenery: Gently rolling woodlands, rocky creek

Exposure: Mostly shady; less so in winter

Traffic: Usually light; heavier on warm-weather evenings, weekends, holidays

Trail surface: Mostly dirt or stony dirt; some pavement, grass; rocky, rooty in places

Hiking time: 2.5–3 hours

Access: Open daily, dawn to dusk

Map: USGS Washington West; PATC Map N; ADC Metro Washington; sketch map in free NPS Rock Creek Park brochure

Facilities: Toilets, water, phone at nature center (limited hours)

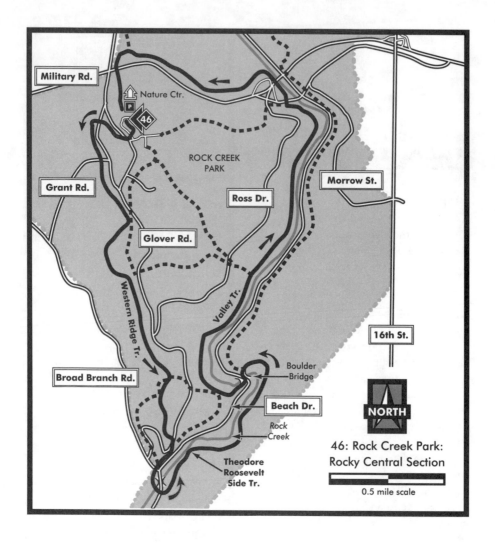

Map labels:
- Military Rd.
- Nature Ctr.
- 46
- ROCK CREEK PARK
- Grant Rd.
- Ross Dr.
- Morrow St.
- Glover Rd.
- Western Ridge Tr.
- Valley Tr.
- 16th St.
- Broad Branch Rd.
- Boulder Bridge
- Beach Dr.
- NORTH
- Rock Creek
- Theodore Roosevelt Side Tr.
- 46: Rock Creek Park: Rocky Central Section
- 0.5 mile scale

a rocky and superbly scenic creek valley. This easy woodland loop provides hikers with 4.5 miles of horizontal tromping and about 1,000 feet of elevation change. This hike will give hikers a restorative dose of outdoor activity, plus a sampling of the park's natural charms.

Follow the directions closely; some trails are unmarked, unblazed, and unnamed. Wet weather leads to puddling and muddiness, especially on trails used by horses. Throughout the hike, stay on the trail and out of the poison ivy.

To get started on the counterclockwise loop, leave the nature center's parking lot by the exit road (at the south end). Turn right onto the short side road connecting it to a nearby spur of Glover Road. Walk about 10 yards and then cross the spur road carefully. Turn right on the grass and follow the edge of the woods away from the road and downhill past a picnic area. At an information board close to a road (Glover Road proper), look for greenish blazes on a tree and stumpy post. Turn left to carefully cross the road. Then swing half-left across the grass and toward the woods. There's no signpost, so look for a double greenish blaze on a beech about 40 yards from the road and access the adjacent dirt trail.

The green-blazed Western Ridge Trail takes you south and mostly downhill to Rock Creek, along the flanks of a well-wooded ridge. Watch for mature oaks, yellow poplars (tulip trees), and hickories. And don't be surprised to see deer. Soon, reach and cross—prudently—a paved road (Grant Road) to a trail junction. There, swing right onto a broad, stony trail on which horses are allowed. Then, at a "No Horses" sign, swing right onto another narrow dirt trail.

Nearing a road (Glover, again), the trail broadens into a stony path flanked by picnic areas and then recombines with a horses-allowed trail segment. Emerging from the woods, it passes the Equitation Field, a large fenced area containing corrals and a horse-jumping ring. Follow the edge of the woods to the end of the fence, and then turn right, at a maple, and reenter the woods.

The trail goes stonily downhill. Stay left at a fork. Then, at a parking lot, turn left and head for the nearby road (Glover, again). Cross it with care, turn right, and proceed along the edge for less than 50 yards to get to a steep, unmarked trail on the left. Follow it downhill.

The trail bottoms out near where Broad Branch Road runs into Beach Drive. Head to the left and cross Beach Drive onto a bridge spanning Rock Creek. On the far side, turn left onto the signposted Theodore Roosevelt Side Trail (TR liked to take friends on fast jaunts in the park), a charming and hilly woodland trail with good views of the creek. Watch your step; the trail is also

Rock Creek's trees and trails lure hikers.

narrow, rocky, rooty, and sometimes slippery. At Pulpit Rock, detour a few yards to the left to visit a cliff-top cluster of rock spires.

Continue northward on the blue-blazed Valley Trail. The trail gets very close to the creek, which itself is quite rocky, with both boulders and underwater ledges causing audible riffles that blend well in summer with the cicada serenade. It's like being in a remote mountain valley, even if the water is polluted.

Follow the trail when it turns away from creek and then forks. Turn left there to leave the Valley Trail and reach a nearby road (Beach Drive). Turn left to take the road—carefully—across Boulder Bridge. On the far side, walk about 40 yards and turn right onto an inconspicuous dirt trail heading uphill into the woods. It'll level off atop a ridge, show you the creek, and then reach a broad, stony path—the hike's halfway point. There, turn right onto a creekside trail. At the next junction, turn right again. At the one after that, go straight through to stay close to Rock Creek at its rockiest.

Continuing northward, you'll eventually swing left alongside a paved road that's part of the ramp system linking Military Road to Beach Drive. Watch for three short white posts along the ramp road. There, turn right and carefully cross the road. On the similarly decorated far side, proceed on the dirt trail ahead of you to start the hike's final mile.

After walking under Military Road, turn left at the next intersection. Then head west and uphill across the park on a paved woodland trail that parallels Military Road and terminates at the Western Ridge Trail. There, turn left, walk downhill to Military. Cross safely and proceed uphill to the trailhead.

For more information, contact Rock Creek Park, (202) 282-1063 or www.nps.gov/rocr.

Nearby/Related Activities

Visit the vast and intriguing stone pile I call the Lost City. It consists of most of the Capitol's 1828 east portico, which was replaced in 1958 (to see more of it, head for the US National Arboretum—hike no.56). Drive or walk to the park's maintenance yard—off the spur road just south of the nature center—and ask to see the site; the yard closes at 3 p.m. Roam the eerie assemblage and speculate about what future archeologists may make of it. After the hike, stop at Politics and Prose, a well-stocked and cafe-equipped bookstore, and also at Marvelous Market, which makes unusually good bread in town. Both are on the Connecticut Avenue just south of Nebraska Avenue.

#47
Rock Creek Park: Wild Northern Section

IN BRIEF

The hilly and little-used woodlands of Rock Creek Park's northern section rank as one of Washington's best venues for off-street hiking in a wilderness-tinged setting.

DIRECTIONS

Head for Northwest Washington. From intersection of Connecticut and Nebraska Avenues, head northeast on Nebraska for 0.4 miles. Turn easy (not sharp) right onto Military Road and drive east for 0.7 miles. Then turn right and south onto Glover Road to enter Rock Creek Park. Proceed for 0.4 miles, swinging left at fork and then taking first left to get to parking lot for Rock Creek Nature Center and Planetarium.

Or use Metro and your feet: From either Friendship Heights Metro station (Red Line) or Fort Totten Metro station (Red, Green Lines), take Metrobus E2 or E3 along Military Road. Get off at Oregon Avenue (opposite Glover Road). From southeast corner of intersection, walk uphill on paved path for 400 yards to reach trailhead. Contact Metro, (202) 637-7000 or www.wmata.com.

DESCRIPTION

The same year that Congress accorded national park status to the three big chunks of California known as Yosemite, Sequoia, and Kings Canyon, it also preserved a piece of its own backyard. It

KEY AT-A-GLANCE INFORMATION

Length: 9.2 miles

Configuration: Modified loop

Difficulty: Moderate

Scenery: Gently rolling woodlands, stream valleys

Exposure: Mostly shady; less so in winter

Traffic: Usually very light to light; heavier on warm-weather evenings, weekends, holidays

Trail surface: Mostly dirt or stony dirt; some pavement; rocky, rooty in places

Hiking time: 4.5–5.5 hours

Access: Open daily, dawn to dusk

Maps: USGS Washington West; PATC Map N; ADC Metro Washington; sketch map in free NPS Rock Creek Park brochure

Facilities: Toilets, water, phone at nature center (limited hours); toilets near Riley Spring Bridge

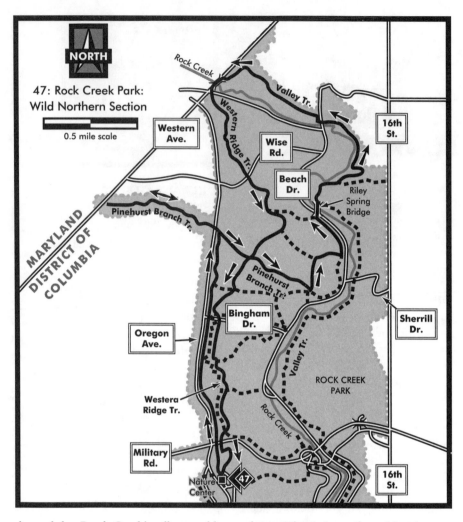

**47: Rock Creek Park:
Wild Northern Section**

0.5 mile scale

NORTH

Rock Creek

Valley Tr.

16th St.

Western Ave.

Western Ridge Tr.

Wise Rd.

Beach Dr.

Riley Spring Bridge

Pinehurst Branch Tr.

MARYLAND

DISTRICT OF COLUMBIA

Pinehurst Branch Tr.

Bingham Dr.

Oregon Ave.

Sherrill Dr.

Valley Tr.

ROCK CREEK PARK

Western Ridge Tr.

Rock Creek

Military Rd.

Nature Center

47

16th St.

---

decreed that Rock Creek's valley would become "a pleasuring ground for the benefit and enjoyment of the people of the United States." That was in 1890.

Today, covering about 2,100 acres, the park consists largely of woodlands and stream valleys that protect the environment and provide habitat for assorted flora and fauna. Most visitors head for various recreation facilities. But informed hikers head for the hills and trails.

The 9.2-mile hike consists of a modified loop that undulates enough to accumulate about 1,600 feet of elevation change. The major trails are blazed, named, and signposted. Rain makes the unpaved ones muddy; horses make them even muddier. Flooding can also be an occasional problem. And do stay out of the poison ivy.

To get started from the nature center's parking lot, pick up the nature trail at the north end (near the center), at an "Edge of the Woods" sign. Bear right onto a paved path next to a labeled chestnut oak. Proceed until you get to a small blue sign opposite a labeled spicebush. There, turn left onto a dirt path that takes the nature trail through the woods.

170

North of Wise Road, Rock Creek winds across a scenic floodplain.

At a paved woodland path (the same one used by Metro riders to get to the trailhead), turn right and head downhill. At Military Road, carefully cross and stay on the path as it goes uphill and back into the woods. For about 2 miles, follow the well-wooded western edge of the park northward. Watch for bikers; the path is one of the park's few off-road trails open to them in the park. The path gently curves, dips, and climbs as it passes through regal stands of mature yellow poplars (tulip trees).

After passing a fenced community garden on the right, you'll reach and cross a paved access road. Jog to the left to pick up the path again and ignore whatever unpaved trails tempt you. Go through the same moves again when crossing a busier road (Bingham Drive). But after that, watch for a trail junction marked by a small yellow post. There, leave the paved path and turn left onto the dirt-surfaced Pinehurst Branch Trail.

The trail follows Pinehurst Branch upstream for about 0.75 miles in a lovely woodland corridor. Within 20 yards, cross Oregon Avenue, carefully. On the far side, look for the trail a few yards up on the right side of a driveway. Follow the yellow blazes as the trail winds through thickets and crisscrosses the stream. When the blazes end, emerge into a residential area along Western Avenue, on the District/Maryland line. Look around, and then walk back along the Pinehurst Branch Trail.

At the paved path, cross and keep going on the Pinehurst Trail for about 0.75 miles. Go straight through where the trail intersects the Western Ridge Trail. Then twice cross the stream—Pinehurst Branch—to a point where several trails merge just upstream from the stream's mouth on Rock Creek. That's roughly the hike's halfway point.

Cross the stream and turn left and then left again onto a narrow and unblazed dirt trail that goes uphill. At the top, turn right and descend on another unblazed trail, staying to the right at two successive forks. Stepping over a rotting log will mean you're on course. At an intersection just before a paved road (it's Beach Drive), turn left onto an unblazed trail heading north. To the right, just across the drive, you'll see and maybe hear the park's northernmost picnic area. The trail stays in the woods and close to the drive. At a junction (past the toilets), turn right, carefully cross the road, and take Riley Spring Bridge across Rock Creek.

At a trail junction about 50 yards on, turn left onto the blue-blazed Valley Trail, the major north-south trail along the eastern side of the park. This northernmost segment is mostly a broad woodland path that curves westward across the park for almost 1.5 miles. In places, the nearby creek gives the impression of being a wilderness stream. Heading uphill, watch for an intersection overlooking a bend in the creek. Detour to the left (but not sharp left) and walk down about 40 yards to a rocky, off-the-beaten-trail spot where the slope is steep and the view is splendid. Then return to the main trail and continue, past what seems to be an official overlook duly hemmed in by a rail fence.

The trail flattens out as it leaves the bluffs and eases across the creek's wooded floodplain. After crossing a wooden bridge over a tributary (Fenwick Branch), either turn left to take the trail along the creek bank and under a road (West Beach Drive), or go straight and cross the road with due care (and dry feet, if the underpass is flooded). Then continue on the reunited trail, staying with the blue blazes but off the side trails.

If it's spring, bear in mind that the stretch of trail leading to the Boundary Bridge passes through one of the District's richest displays of wildflowers. So either soak up the color as you hike by, or slow down to savor whatever takes your fancy. At the bridge, pause to take in the view, and then move on. A short paved path will take you to a small parking lot adjoining Beach Drive. Carefully cross the drive and, having just spent a few minutes in Maryland, head uphill on a narrow dirt trail marked with greenish blazes. It's the Western Ridge Trail, the major north-south trail along the western side of the park and your route back to the trailhead.

On the 2.5-mile southbound journey, you'll pass through mature woodlands. Along the way, watch on the left for a remarkable yellow poplar with five full-sized trunks. At Wise Road, cross wisely. Then press on, past a couple of cross-park trails, the first of which leads to Riley Spring Bridge. After that, reach Pinehurst Branch and its trail—again. This time, cross both.

Walk through another intersection to reach Bingham Drive—again. Then, you'll take the paved path route back to the access road near the community garden. But this time, on emerging from the trees, turn left to walk along the blazed road. Just before reaching a "Do Not Enter" sign, turn right and follow a dirt trail alongside a fenced paddock. When you reach the far corner, turn left onto the reassuringly signposted Western Ridge Trail.

Proceed into the woods and mostly downhill. Turn right at a junction (to the left is another cross-park trail) and continue, mostly upward. At the next junction, turn right (again, to the left is a cross-park trail), and then right again onto a paved trail leading a short distance to the paved trail on which you started out. Turn left and head for the trailhead. For more information, contact Rock Creek Park, (202) 282-1063 or www.nps.gov/rocr.

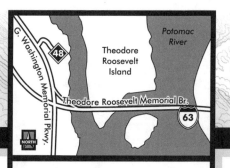

#48
Roosevelt to Roosevelt

IN BRIEF

The close-in Potomac River parklands include two Roosevelt memorials and a nature preserve. Two memorial bridges enable hikers to make some stimulating connections.

DIRECTIONS

From Washington's Mall area, access Constitution Avenue heading west. Proceed across Theodore Roosevelt Memorial Bridge, staying to right. Then take first exit to right followed immediately by another right onto northbound George Washington Memorial Parkway. Take first exit (within 400 yards) into Theodore Roosevelt Island parking lot on right. To get there from parkway's southbound lanes, cross into Washington, turn around, and follow directions given above. *Note:* To return to Washington or southbound lanes after hike, drive north on parkway for 0.7 miles and take first exit to left onto Spout Run Parkway; then either take first exit on left onto southbound parkway, or continue to Lee Highway, which connects to local roads and Interstate 66.

Or use Metro and feet to get to trailhead. Take Orange or Blue Line train to Rosslyn Metro station and then walk 0.8 miles to trailhead: From main entrance, turn left and walk north (downhill) on North Moore Street, cross North 19th Street, turn right alongside Lee Highway, cross North Lynn Street, turn left

KEY AT-A-GLANCE INFORMATION

Length: 9.3 miles

Configuration: Modified loop

Difficulty: Easy/moderate

Scenery: River/canal views, urban views, parklands, swampy woodlands

Exposure: Mostly open; more so in winter

Traffic: Usually light; moderate to heavy on warm-weather evenings, weekends, holidays—more so at FDR memorial

Trail surface: Mostly pavement; rest mostly dirt; some boardwalk, brick

Hiking time: 5–6 hours (including memorial time)

Access: Island open daily, 8 a.m.–dark; MV trail, towpath open until dark

Map: USGS Washington West

Facilities: Toilets, water on island; toilets, water, phones at boat center (warm season), FDR memorial, near towpath; toilet, water at volleyball courts; water along Ohio Drive

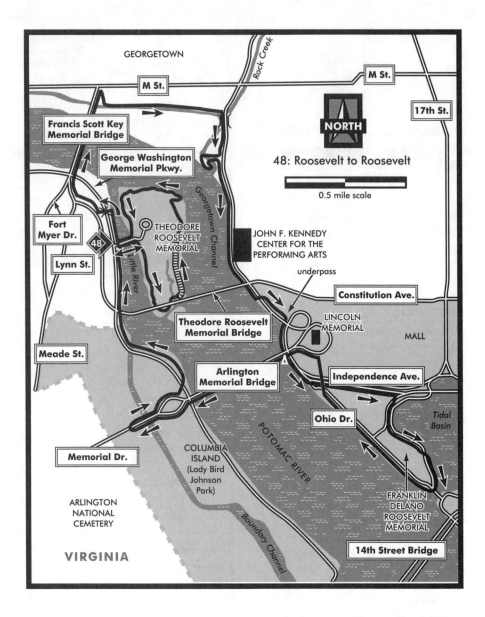

48: Roosevelt to Roosevelt

0.5 mile scale

and walk north on North Lynn, and cross Lee Highway; at far corner, turn right onto signposted Mount Vernon Trail and follow it to trailhead. Contact Metro, (202) 637-7000 or www. wmata.com.

DESCRIPTION

Metro-area hikers owe Theodore Roosevelt and his distant relative Franklin Delano Roosevelt at least a grateful nod. During TR's 1901–09 presidency, the country got a forest service and wildlife refuge system, and the metro area had a hiker in the White House. During FDR's 1933–45 presidency, the country got many new and improved national parks, including the metro area's parklands along both banks of the Potomac River.

This 9.3-mile and hill-less hike loops through these scenic parklands. Managed by the National Park Service (NPS), they include the Franklin Delano Roosevelt Memorial at the Tidal Basin and the Theodore Roosevelt Memorial and nature preserve on Theodore Roosevelt Island. The hike route's trail signs are few, so follow the directions closely. Also be very careful around vehicular traffic.

The hike begins with a mini-loop around TR Island. Long known as Analostan Island, it was a plantation until the Civil War. Thereafter, it was briefly a recreation area. Neglected for decades, it was bought by the Theodore Roosevelt Memorial Association in 1931 and given to NPS. Taken on as a Civilian Conservation Corps project, the island was renamed, stripped of everything man-made, planted with 30,000 trees, and allowed to evolve as a nature preserve. The TR memorial was added in 1967.

To get started, take the footbridge to the heavily wooded island. At a bulletin board, turn right and head south on a broad dirt path for 50 yards. At a fork, turn right onto a narrow dirt trail. Then continue, staying to the right at the next junction. After passing under the Theodore Roosevelt Memorial Bridge (an early 1960s addition), turn right again at the next fork. The trail then swings back under the bridge to reach a junction. There, turn right and head for the nearby boardwalk, which protects both the wetlands and human feet along the island's swampy eastern border. Where the boardwalk ends, proceed on a trail to a junction, turn right and walk to the riverbank.

From the riverbank, scan the Georgetown waterfront. Compare what you see with the grimy 1863 view reproduced on a nearby plaque. Also check the far shore to see the writing on the wall—on

bulkheads near a row of high-school and college boathouses. The painters identify their teams and express their opinions. One repeatable message I remember was "TOLERANCE."

Heading back, take the first side trail on the right, along the island's northern shore. At a junction, go straight onto a trail heading south. Pass the footbridge and follow the curving main path to the TR memorial. That's a large open plaza dominated by a 17-foot-high statue of TR and flanked by large stone tablets inscribed with TR quotations. See if you find it odd to encounter such an edifice in a nature preserve.

From the plaza, return to the trailhead, having hiked almost 2.5 miles. Then set out again, heading upriver on the Mount Vernon Trail and out in the open. After crossing the George Washington Memorial Parkway on a footbridge, you'll reach a sidewalk. Turn right and cross the Francis Scott Key Memorial Bridge. In Georgetown, turn sharp right and walk through Francis Scott Key Park, with its overgrown trellis, colorful plantings, and Key placards. Key once lived nearby. His bridge was opened in 1924. A poem of his became the official national anthem in 1931. His house was dismantled in 1949.

From the park, walk down to the nearby restored C&O Canal, using some steps and a ramp. Head east on the dirt—later, brick—towpath, keeping the canal on your right. After passing several locks and basins and an NPS visitor center, stop at the paved Rock Creek Trail, next to busy Rock Creek Parkway. There, turn right and head south.

At the Thompson Boat Center, detour by turning right into the parking lot and crossing Rock Creek by bridge. At the river, turn left to walk past the center. Then take a footbridge to an off-the-beaten-trail spot that has a concrete post inscribed with "Mile 0" (a C&O Canal towpath marker)—and great views.

Return to the Rock Creek Trail. Turn right and head south along the waterfront. Pass the infamous Watergate complex, developed in the 1960s on the site of a former gas works. Then pass the famous John F. Kennedy Center for the Performing Arts, developed in the same decade on the site of a former brewery.

Going under Roosevelt Bridge will take you past the hike's halfway point and into an area that, until the 1920s, was swampland. That's why most of the hike, including TR Island, is officially in the District.

Near a large flowerbed, turn left and cross the parkway onto a paved path alongside some volleyball courts. Follow it to the riverbank and under Arlington Memorial Bridge. Where the parkway merges into Independence Avenue at Ohio Drive, head east on the paved path alongside the avenue. At a side road (West Basin Drive), cross it, turn right onto a walkway, and proceed across a spur road to the Tidal Basin. Note the plaque about the pending memorial to Martin Luther King Jr. (or detour if work has begun). Swing right onto the basin-side path and proceed amid the cherry trees. Then turn right to enter the FDR memorial.

Completed in 1997, the 7.5-acre memorial is laid out as four walled outdoor enclosures, called "rooms," each devoted to one of FDR's terms of office. Stonework, waterfalls, pools, landscaping, sculpture, and FDR quotations illustrate the years covered, literally and symbolically. Controversy about FDR's concealment of his polio-induced paralysis led to the addition in 2001 of a bronze FDR sitting jauntily in his wheelchair—but minus his customary cigarette holder.

Head for the Tidal Basin, turn right onto the perimeter path, and follow it to Ohio Drive. Cross the drive, turn right, and walk north on the paved and scenic riverbank path for 0.75 miles. At Independence Avenue, recross Ohio Drive, cross Independence, and head up the sidewalk. Ignore the Lincoln Memorial just ahead (that's another outing—hike no. 31, p. 109). Instead, turn left, recross Ohio, cross a busy traffic ramp, and then walk across Arlington Memorial Bridge. Stay on the post-bridge sidewalk, and then turn right to use the crosswalk to cross a busy road. Proceed on the paved path that curves by a traffic circle and becomes a sidewalk.

Soon, reach a statue labeled "The Hiker" and "Spanish American Veterans 1898-1902—Cuba—Porto-Rico—Philippines." Your next stop will be the Seabees memorial, just across the avenue (use the crosswalk). Erected in the 1970s to honor the US Navy's construction battalions, it's one of those rare metro area memorials that explain their subject. From there, take the eastbound path past the traffic circle. Next, very carefully cross a busy road and two very busy parkway roads, and walk down to the riverbank. Turn left onto the Mount Vernon Trail, and head north for about a mile, half of it on boardwalk, to reach the trailhead.

For more information, contact NPS's George Washington Memorial Parkway, (703) 289-2500 or www.nps.gov/gwmp) regarding TR island and the Mount Vernon Trail; the NPS visitor center in Georgetown, (202) 653-5190, regarding the canal and towpath; and NPS's National Capital Parks-Central, (202) 619-7222 or www.nps.gov/nacc, regarding the FDR memorial.

#49
Scotts Run
Nature Preserve

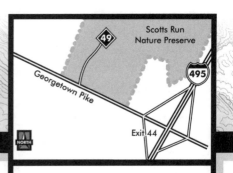

IN BRIEF

Virginia's out-of-sight Scotts Run Nature Preserve, on the Potomac River near the beltway, is well supplied with flora, fauna, river views, and little-used hiking trails.

DIRECTIONS

From Capital Beltway (Interstate 495) in McLean, Virginia, take Exit 44 and access Georgetown Pike (VA 193) heading roughly west. Proceed for 1 mile, passing a small parking lot on right en route, and then turn right into preserve's main parking lot. Turnoff is hidden from view, but is just after Swinks Mill Road sign on left, and just before large sign on right for Betty Cooke Bridge. If lot is full, use small parking lot, and start hike there.

DESCRIPTION

Hidden away amid upscale subdivisions, Scotts Run Nature Preserve consists of a hilly, wildflower-riddled tract of riverside woodlands scarcely 4 crow-miles northwest of Washington. For songbirds and other wildlife, it's a sanctuary. For local people, it's a community park. And for hikers, it's one of the metro area's loveliest close-in venues.

For many years, owner Edward Burling used the area as a weekend getaway, but also allowed hikers to roam his almost 400 acres. After he died, the tract was sold to a developer. But in 1970, local residents and officials finally managed to fold

KEY AT-A-GLANCE INFORMATION

Length: 4 miles

Configuration: Modified loop

Difficulty: Easy

Scenery: Rolling woodlands, river views

Exposure: Mostly shady; less so in winter

Traffic: Light to moderate on main path to river, especially on warm-weather evenings, weekends, holidays; elsewhere, usually light

Trail surface: Mostly dirt or gravel; rocky, rooty near river

Hiking time: 2.5–3.5 hours (including dawdle-at-river time)

Access: Open daily, sunrise to sunset

Maps: USGS Falls Church; trailside maps (see text)

Facilities: None

Special comments: Scotts Run is polluted, so don't touch the water

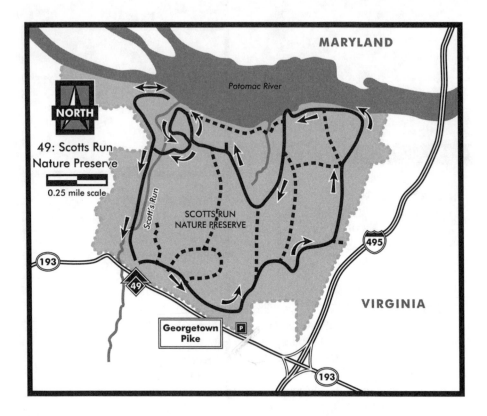

49: Scotts Run Nature Preserve

0.25 mile scale

Scott's Run

SCOTTS RUN
NATURE PRESERVE

MARYLAND

Potomac River

495

193

Georgetown
Pike

VIRGINIA

193

it into Fairfax County's park system as Dranesville District Park. It was later renamed.

This easy, 4-mile hike loops through thickly wooded uplands and reaches the Potomac River in three places. It's hilly enough to provide about 1,900 feet of elevation change. Although there are no trail signs, you'll see a few "You Are Here" trailside maps. They're marginally helpful, so follow this guide carefully. And keep in mind that in wet or icy conditions, the riverside trails can be tricky or even hazardous. Also, do stay out of both the poison ivy and the polluted stream.

To get started from the parking lot, head up a flight of wooden steps and into the woods. Proceed along a winding and undulating dirt trail that roughly parallels Georgetown Pike. Pass two side trails on

the left, bear right at a fork, and cross an eroded gully. Then, at the next fork, turn left and uphill (near the small parking lot, off to the right). At a broad unpaved road, turn left and continue gently uphill. When you reach an intersection marked by a "You Are Here" map, turn right onto a narrow curving trail.

After crossing a bridge spanning a little gully, continue gently uphill. At a T-junction and trailside map near the preserve's eastern boundary, turn left and keep going. At the next intersection, turn right and head downhill to the river. There, beneath a great arc of open sky, you'll find a stretch of unspoiled Potomac shoreline. Over on the Maryland shore, in the Carderock area, lurks part of the Billy Goat Trail. In the river are the shoals known as Stubblefield

Falls. In the moist ground at your feet, hunt for the tracks of deer and other creatures.

Admire but don't touch the biggest nearby tree, a huge, poison ivy-entwined maple. Then head upriver on a narrow trail that's somewhat overgrown. The trail soon becomes a rocky and rooty path that angles uphill, crosses a rock-slab streambed, and then skirts the base of a huge rock. About 60 yards beyond the rock, stop at the first of several spots that offer gorgeous views. It's a one-person, fern-fringed overlook just a few steps off the trail. Note the old and mysterious stone walls in the water below.

Another rewarding overlook occurs just after the main trail is crossed by another trail that sweeps straight downhill. To get there, turn right at the next intersection onto a rocky ledge. Be doubly careful in that the rock can be slippery and is rimmed by poison ivy.

Retrace your steps from the ledge, cross the main trail, and continue uphill. The trail is steep at first and then flattens out and curves through the woods. At an intersection near a concrete-embedded pipe called the Flag Pole, go straight through on a broad trail. At the next intersection and trailside map, take the right-hand trail. At the fork after that, the hike's halfway point, detour to the right to see what's left of Burling's fire-destroyed cabin.

Return to the main trail and follow it downhill to some wooden stairs. Step down and turn right to take a broad gravel path down to the Potomac. There, enjoy more fine river views and reach a lovely, waterfall-fed, and rock-enclosed pool at the mouth of Scott's Run. But resist the temptation to swim or wade.

Start to retrace your route uphill on the gravel path. Then, either keep going, past the wooden stairs, until you reach

McLean Claire shows the way to Scott's Run.

Scott's Run, or do the following instead. When you reach a trash barrel, turn right and head up a very steep dirt trail (you may need to use your hands). Stay on the trail as it levels out. At a junction, turn left and continue along a ridge until you reach the gravel path near the wooden stairs. Turn right and continue to Scott's Run.

Then cross the stream on the concrete stepping posts. Turn right onto a fairly flat trail. Continue, staying to the right wherever the trail forks. At a steep slope, ascend it to reach the top of a ridge. Pause to view the river, then follow the trail down to the mouth of Scott's Run. Be careful because the trail is steep, rocky, and rooty—and hemmed in by poison ivy. Enjoy the pool and waterfall and then head back.

At the stream in the stepping-posts area, don't step across. Rather, turn right onto the broad gravel trail that goes gently uphill for half a mile to the trail-head. That's when you may encounter other people, mostly local strollers, dog walkers, and riverbound teenagers. For more information on the preserve, contact nearby Riverbend Park, (703) 759-9018.

NEARBY/RELATED ACTIVITIES

Explore nearby Great Falls Park and Riverbend Park. To get there, continue west on Georgetown Pike and watch for the park signs.

SENECA CREEK STATE PARK

270

50

Exit 11

Clopper Rd.

Quince Orchard Rd.

Exit 10

Clopper Lake

NORTH

IN BRIEF

Seneca Creek State Park, in west-central Montgomery County, Maryland, has one of the Metro area's most attractive around-the-lake trails.

DIRECTIONS

From Capital Beltway (Interstate 495), take I-270 northwestward (toward Frederick, Maryland) for 12 miles. Get off at Exit 10 in Gaithersburg and head west on Diamond Avenue West, which becomes Clopper Road, for 2 miles. Turn left into park. Take first right and drive 0.2 miles to visitor center's parking lot. If lot is full, look for space at another lot and start hike from there. *Note:* Visitor center's parking lot is free year-round, but admission fee is charged on weekends and holidays for using other lots.

Or use Metro and your feet to get to trailhead: Take Red Line train to Shady Grove station, Montgomery County Ride-On bus 61 along Clopper Road, and then walk 400 yards to trailhead. Contact Metro, (202) 637-7000 or www.wmata.com.

DESCRIPTION

In the early 1950s, this area some 20 miles northwest of Washington consisted of farmlands and small communities such as 1,800-person Gaithersburg and even smaller Germantown. Five decades later, the farms are mostly gone and the

KEY AT-A-GLANCE INFORMATION

Length: 6.1 miles

Configuration: Modified loop

Difficulty: Easy

Scenery: Woodlands, stream valley, lake views

Exposure: Mostly shady; less so in winter

Traffic: Usually very light to light; light to moderate on warm-weather weekends, holidays; heaviest near boat center

Trail surface: Mostly hard-packed dirt; very rooty all around lake

Hiking time: 2.5–3 hours

Access: Open daily, 8 a.m.–sunset (but closed on Thanksgiving Day, December 25)

Maps: USGS Germantown, Gaithersburg, Seneca; sketch map in free park pamphlet

Facilities: Toilets at visitor center (check hours), off-trail at picnic areas

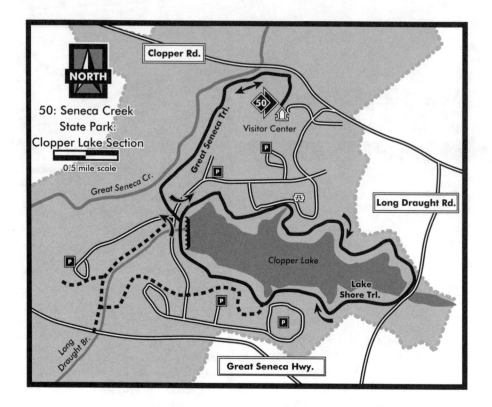

Clopper Rd.

NORTH

50: Seneca Creek State Park: Clopper Lake Section

0.5 mile scale

Great Seneca Trl.

50

Visitor Center

P

P

Great Seneca Cr.

Long Draught Rd.

Clopper Lake

Lake Shore Trl.

P

P

P

Long Draught Br.

Great Seneca Hwy.

two communities, each with around 50,000 residents, are among Maryland's largest (after Baltimore).

What now keeps Gaithersburg and Germantown apart is the northern portion of Seneca Creek State Park. Starting in the 1950s, the state government slowly acquired 6,609 acres of old fields and woodlands along Seneca Creek. Opened in 1980, the ribbony, creek-valley park winds across the county for roughly 16 miles from north of Gaithersburg to the Potomac River at Seneca. Only the park's northern section has been developed. Its centerpiece is woodland-enveloped, 90-acre Clopper Lake. During the warm-weather months, the lake area attracts boaters, anglers, picnickers, and strollers. Most of them head for the picnic areas and nearby boat center.

This hike is a 6.1-mile, modestly hilly water-side excursion with about 550

feet of elevation change. It passes through oak and hickory woods that also harbor dogwoods, redbuds, pines, and mountain laurels. It offers lake and creek views, plus a multi-hued array of wildflowers and birds. The trails are named, color-coded, signposted, and blazed. The blazes are a bit sparse in places, so follow these directions closely.

To get started from the parking-lot trailhead, head away from the visitor center and walk north toward Clopper Road. Access the signposted Great Seneca Trail, marked by orange or reddish-orange blazes. For a way, it's coextensive with the park's longest trail, the end-to-end, bluish-green-blazed Greenway Trail.

The dual trail swings left and downhill across a power-line right-of-way and into the woods, eventually reaching Great Seneca Creek, which is Seneca

Creek's chief headwater. There, turn left onto the creek-side trail and proceed on a lovely wooded floodplain set between low bluffs. Follow the trail as it leaves the creek, goes gently uphill to the left, and then crosses a pair of broad, open, and grassy utility-line rights-of-way. At the far side of the second one, head steeply uphill for a hundred yards or so (ignore the Old Pond side trail). Then, proceed along a level path at the edge of the woods. Stay to the right, following the blazes.

Remain on the trail as it turns left into the woods and descends the creek. You'll follow the creek, regain elevation, and eventually reach a paved-road T-junction. There, leave the trail, sidle to your left, and carefully cross the main road. Then walk gently downhill for about 100 yards, toward the dam that retains Clopper Lake.

Just before reaching the dam, turn left to start your clockwise circuit on the blue-blazed Lake Shore Trail. Begin by ascending some wooden steps embedded in a sandy trail, which levels off at about 30 feet above the water. Then skirt the base of Kingfisher Overlook, the most popular lakeside viewing spot (it's easily reached by car). Proceed through the woods to reach a grassy area that slopes down to the water and ends at the boat center. On a warm-weather weekend, you'll have to thread your way through the picnickers. After passing the boat center (roughly the hike's halfway point), look for the blue-blazed trail on the far side, next to several parking spaces.

The woodland trail takes the long way—2.7 miles—around the lake to the dam. It follows the shore closely, but

pulls away in four places to accommodate large inlets and their feeder streams.

This undulating trail segment has more tree roots than any other trail I know in the metro area. Pick up your feet, follow the blue blazes, and whenever you're in directional doubt, turn right, toward the lake. At what appears to be the eastern end of the lake, take a railing-flanked paved path across twin tunnels that carry the lake beneath nearby Long Draught Road. The actual end of the lake lies on far side of the road, hidden from view. From the elevated, paved path, you'll have good views far down the lake.

Swing right onto a dirt trail and head west along the lake's southern shore. At a trail junction where a white-blazed trail (the Mink Hollow Trail) comes in from the left, stay to the right, on the joint blue- and white-blazed trail. Then cross a sloping meadow and head for the dam. Cross the dam to complete the Lake Shore Trail loop. Then return to the trailhead on the Great Seneca Trail.

Contact the park for information, including current trail conditions, (301) 924-2127.

NEARBY/RELATED ACTIVITIES
If you see too few wildflowers, offset your sorrow by visiting the park's wealth of globèd peonies. They dazzle the eye with white, red, pink, and magenta blooms in May and June, and with crimson foliage after Labor Day. Look for them in a display garden just north of the lake's eastern end, and also sprawled across several nearby acres.

Return to the park to attend its annual Shaker Forest Festival in September.

SENECA CREEK STATE PARK

28

Darnestown Rd.

Black Rock Rd.

51

To 270

Berryville Rd.

NORTH

IN BRIEF

The unspoiled and little used Greenway Trail in Maryland's Seneca Creek State Park is one of the metro area's best close-in trails.

DIRECTIONS

From junction of Capital Beltway (I-495) and I-270, proceed northwest for about 6 miles (toward Frederick, Maryland). Get off at Exit 6B and proceed generally west on MD 28 (which becomes Darnestown Road in part). About 6.4 miles along MD 28 and 1 mile past Germantown Road (MD 118), turn right onto Black Rock Road. Proceed on narrow and twisty road for 0.7 miles. Turn left into small parking lot at Black Rock Mill. If lot is full, cross bridge and park on shoulder on right.

DESCRIPTION

Running the length of Seneca Creek State Park in west-central Montgomery County, the 16-mile Greenway Trail is one of the finest close-in hiking trails I know. It accompanies its namesake creek through a mostly pastoral landscape of wildflower-dappled floodplain areas, thickets, and wooded hills flanked by farmlands.

This out-and-back hike uses part of the middle third of the trail, about 20 miles northwest of Washington. The path threads through a serene and picturesque area where deer, smaller

KEY AT-A-GLANCE INFORMATION

Length: 8.8 miles

Configuration: Out-and-back

Difficulty: Easy/moderate

Scenery: Stream valley, woodlands, rural views

Exposure: Half shady; less so in winter

Traffic: Usually very light, even on warm-weather weekends, holidays

Trail surface: Hard-packed dirt; rooty in places

Hiking time: 4–5 hours

Access: Open daily, 8 a.m.–sunset (but closed Thanksgiving Day, December 25)

Maps: USGS Germantown, Gaithersburg, Seneca; sketch map in free park pamphlet

Facilities: None

Special comments: Beware of flooding (see text)

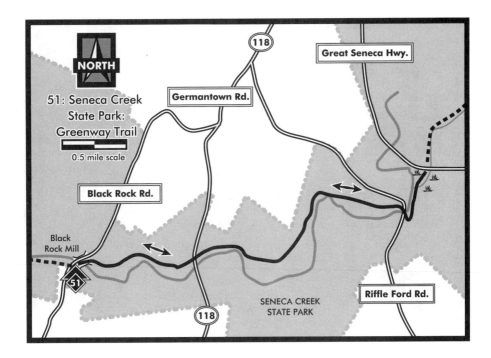

four-footed creatures, birds, and wild-flowers are plentiful. Humans are not, maybe because the trail, finished in 1999, is still little known.

Before hiking, check with the park on trail conditions, because the creek sometimes floods. Also, anticipate encountering long grass, so take anti-tick measures. And remember that, although the trail is quite well blazed and signposted, the posted distances are misstated by 200 to 600 yards (a result of route changes).

Before getting started, take a look at Black Rock Mill, now a roofless shell with thick fieldstone walls and glassless windows. Use the second-story walkway to peer into the interior. Read the chain-suspended display boards outlining the mill's century of operations starting in 1815, as well as the effects of flooding. Note the marked flood levels, some of them above your head.

The hulking mill is a spooky sight at dusk. Rising tall and black against the western sky and topped by gallows-like rafters, it seems dark and diabolical, in contrast with the green and pleasant land around it. Some scenes for *Blair Witch Project* were filmed nearby.

To get started from the mill, cross the creek bridge, bear right, and walk along the road for 50 yards. Pass a "Seneca Creek Greenway Trail" sign, and march between a pair of bluish-green blazes to head upstream and generally eastward on a floodplain where the oak/hickory woods are brightened by dogwood and redbud blossoms—and warblers—in the spring and display darker hues in the fall.

Half a mile into the hike, the trail switchbacks up to the left, leaving the creek behind. It'll be the first of the ups and downs that will enable you to accumulate 800 feet of elevation change on the hike. The trail then stays roughly level for another half-mile and then turns right to descend alongside a stream gully.

Almost two centuries old, Black Rock Mill still looms over Great Seneca lake.

Following the bluish-green blazes, turn left to cross the gully by bridge and then head uphill through some pines. The trail then levels off and eases down hill through a large hemlock grove to the floodplain. Out in the open, you'll cross a thicket that's abuzz with chickadees, flycatchers, songbirds, and insect during the warm-weather months.

Then you'll reach busy Germantown Road, 1.6 miles into the hike. Cross with care and proceed on a broad, flat, and more open floodplain area, heading mostly northeast along the edge of the woods. The trail stays quite close to the creek, except in the few places where it takes a shortcut across or around a low hill or ridge. It's flanked by woods on the right and by fields on the left.

As you hike, listen for chattering kingfishers along the creek and the staccato calls of woodpeckers in the woods, and watch for beaver-felled trees. In muddy places, where deer tracks are common, see if you can tell the difference between males and females (females leave prints that are more pointed).

At Riffle Ford Road, 4 miles into the hike, cross carefully. Then turn right to take the bridge over the creek, and turn left onto a broad and level dirt path. It doubles as a stretch of both the Greenway Trail and Long Draught Trail, so you'll see both yellow and bluish-green blazes.

Follow the path to an open wetland straddling Long Draught Branch. There, climb up the low observation deck to look around and listen. In warm-weather months, watch for eastern bluebirds, which make good use the wetland's insect population and nesting boxes. Then scurry back to the mill before dark. Contact the park for more information, (301) 924-2127.

#52
Sky Meadows State Park

IN BRIEF

Sky Meadows State Park, in Virginia's portion of the Blue Ridge, lives up to its name. Up there, too, hikers can enjoy woodlands, wildlife, exercise, and an Appalachian Trail segment.

DIRECTIONS

From Capital Beltway (Interstate 495) in Merrifield, Virginia, take Exit 49 and access I-66 heading west. Proceed for about 47 miles; take Exit 23 and access US 17 North. Proceed for 7.3 miles, and turn left into park on Edmonds Lane. Drive 0.7 miles to fee-collection kiosk, and then 0.6 miles to parking lot at visitor center.

DESCRIPTION

Sky Meadows State Park, some 60 miles west of Washington, is a wonderfully tilted place. Suspended from the Appalachian Trail, it spreads across the Blue Ridge's eastern flanks down to the Piedmont. It consists of almost nothing but slopes. Some support broad meadows reminiscent of the Alps, with vistas unsurpassed in the metro area. Others carry woodlands harboring a wealth of flora and fauna. Throughout the park are canted trails conducive to the release of endorphins and sweat in hikers.

The park covers 1,842 acres of unspoiled countryside along the border between Fauquier and Loudoun Counties. The landscape is one of woodlands

KEY AT-A-GLANCE INFORMATION

Length: 10.3 miles

Configuration: Modified out-and-back

Difficulty: Quite difficult

Scenery: Vista-rich upland meadows; woodlands

Exposure: Mostly shady; less so in winter

Traffic: Mostly very light to light; heavier on warm-weather weekends, holidays

Trail surface: Mostly dirt; some gravel, grass; rocky, rooty in some places

Hiking time: 6.5–7.5 hours (including overlook looking)

Access: Open daily, 8 a.m.–dusk; entrance fee

Maps: USGS Upperville, Ashby Gap; PATC Map 8; sketch map in free park pamphlet

Facilities: Toilets, water, phone at trailhead; toilet near fee-collection kiosk

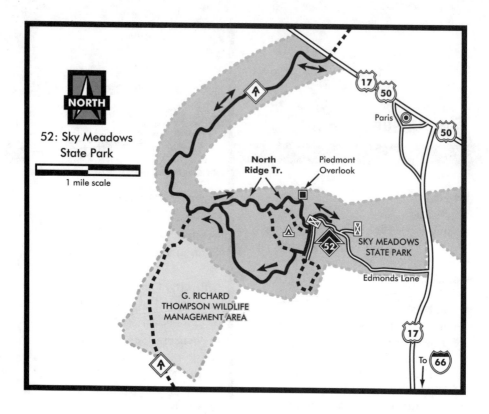

52: Sky Meadows
State Park

1 mile scale

North
Ridge Tr.

Piedmont
Overlook

SKY MEADOWS
STATE PARK

Edmonds Lane

G. RICHARD
THOMPSON WILDLIFE
MANAGEMENT AREA

17
50

Paris

50

52

17

To 66

and fields dotted with an occasional pond or farm building and crossed by a few ribbons of country road. It seems ageless, tranquil, and inviting.

As farmland, the park's core area has a heritage dating back three centuries. A series of families raised crops, livestock, and children there. Their cumulative history is preserved in the restored main building—called Mount Bleak—and other structures near the current parking lot.

Sky Meadows beginnings as a park date back to the mid-1960s, when philanthropist and local resident Paul Mellon (son of Andrew, who gave us the National Gallery of Art and other treasures) saved the area from becoming a subdivision. He donated the property to the state of Virginia in 1975. After the park was opened in 1983, the state added 248 acres to encase a stretch of the Appalachian Trail.

The 10.3-mile hike described here consists of a clockwise meadow loop broken by an out-and-back excursion on the park's AT corridor. It's a rewarding hike, with the seasons providing a continuum of change and an occasional surprise (my best so far: a bluebird in the snow). It's also a challenging hike, with about 3,800 feet of elevation change. Most hikers relish the meadow segment, but a few dislike the AT segment. "It's boring" declared College Park Scott after rechecking the full hike for me.

The park's trails are named, color coded, well marked, and generally well maintained. When in the woods, where poison ivy lurks, stay on the trail. When in the meadows, steer clear of long grass (tick-tick-tick) and cow pies. Although animals are protected in the park, adjoining areas are open to hunters, so wear orange in the fall, especially on the AT.

To get started from the parking-lot trailhead, head for the nearby "Hiking Trails Campground" sign. Follow the dirt path for about 140 yards and then turn left onto a country lane. At a trail junction just past a stream (Gap Run), turn right onto the orange-blazed Gap Run Trail by climbing over a stile, the first of several you'll encounter. Then, walk about 100 yards and turn left onto the yellow-blazed South Ridge Trail. Follow it for 1.5 miles as it gains 600 steep feet in elevation, mostly in the woods. Along the way, pause at gaps in the tree cover to take in the long view.

At a trail junction, turn left onto the blue-blazed North Ridge Trail and continue uphill. At a spot, 2.5 miles into the hike, look for the AT and a bench in a clearing. There, turn right and head generally northeast on the AT to Ashby Gap, almost 3 miles distant. Follow the AT's distinctive white blazes as you traipse through the woods on dirt trails and old roads. Head downhill, gradually at first and then more steeply. A few hundred yards down the AT, watch for the only decent long-distance vista—off to the west.

Approaching Ashby Gap, a major passageway through the Blue Ridge, follow the trail as it clears the woods and slips through a stone wall to reach the highway shoulder. There, you'll be just over halfway through the hike. Rest if you want to, and then start the long climb back.

At the AT bench, turn left onto the North Ridge Trail. At the junction with the South Ridge Trail, stay to the left. Also stay left at the Gap Run Trail, and then turn left onto the red-blazed

Piedmont Overlook Trail, which is somewhat rocky.

Proceed uphill, following a fence line along the upper edge of a huge meadow, until the grassy path levels out and delivers you to a couple of benches and the park's best overlook. Depending on the season and weather, you'll have views across the Piedmont to the east and south. Linger a while at what Scott rightly calls the "very best of the hike's overlooks."

Then head downhill through the meadow for over half a mile, following a line of trail markers and a seasonally mowed path. When cattle are present, the area resembles Europe's alpine pastures in several biological respects, so watch your step if cows are not your passion. But be grateful that their appetites and teeth help keep the meadows from reverting to woodland.

Near the bottom, the trail resumes and swings to the right, past an old shed, to reach the North Ridge Trail. Turn left and head for your last stile. There, turn left onto the old country lane, and return to the trailhead. Contact the park for more information, (540) 592-3556 or www.dcr.state.va.us/parks /skymeado.htm; for more information about the AT in general, contact the Appalachian Trail Conference, (304) 535-6331 or www.appalachiantrail.org.

NEARBY/RELATED ACTIVITIES

During the warm-weather months, tour Mount Bleak and sample the park's events and programs. Among them are the two-day Delaplane Strawberry Festival (late May), full-moon walks on the Piedmont Overlook Trail, and astronomy programs featuring telescopes, experts, and the dark night sky. Contact the park.

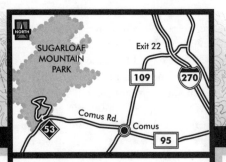

#53
Sugarloaf Mountain

IN BRIEF

Washington's nearest mountain is vista-rich Sugarloaf Mountain located in southern Frederick County, Maryland. One can hike up, around, and down it in half a day.

DIRECTIONS

From Capital Beltway (Interstate 495), take I-270 northwest (toward Frederick, Maryland) for about 23 miles. Exit at Exit 22, turn right onto MD 109, and head west for about 3 miles. At Comus Inn, turn right onto MD 95 (Comus Road) and proceed for about 5 miles to small parking lot at base of mountain, just outside entrance gate. If lot is full, drive to one of upper lots and start hike there (see map). *Note:* Gated entrance road closes one hour before sunset.

DESCRIPTION

Sugarloaf Mountain looms above rolling farmlands about 30 crow-miles northwest of Washington. Privately owned, it's managed as both a nature preserve and public recreation area. Although it attracts many visitors, they're mostly sightseers and picnickers who prefer the roadside overlooks and the summit.

For hikers, the 3,300-acre property offers good trails, a lungs-and-muscles workout, and a beguiling natural setting. At its best, it's wildflower pretty in spring, green-bower scenic in summer, turning-leaf colorful in autumn, and snow-dusted

KEY AT-A-GLANCE INFORMATION

Length: 8.1 miles

Configuration: Loop

Difficulty: Quite difficult

Scenery: Upland woodlands; sweeping vistas

Exposure: Mostly shady; less so in winter

Traffic: Usually light; heavier on warm-weather weekends, holidays, especially on and near summit

Trail surface: Roughly half hard-packed dirt, half rocky and rooty

Hiking time: 3.5–4.5 hours

Access: Open daily, sunrise to sunset; road within park opens 8 a.m., closes 1 hour before sunset

Maps: USGS Urbana, Buckeystown, Poolesville; map on free preserve flyer

Facilities: Water, phone at trailhead; toilets near parking lots; summer snack bar near top lot (weekends, holidays)

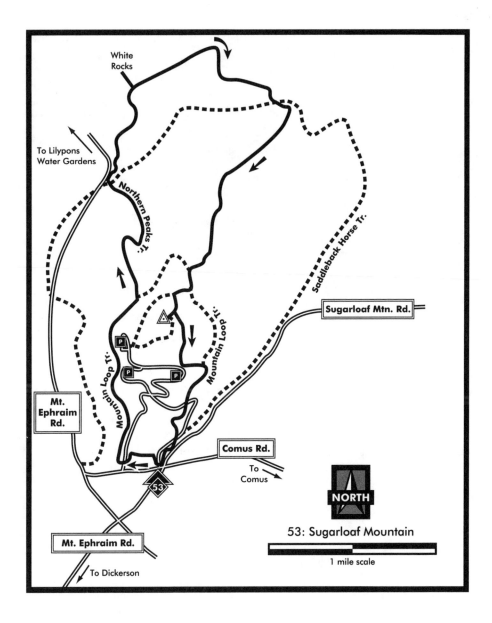

White
Rocks

To Lilypons
Water Gardens

Northern Peaks Tr.

Saddleback Horse Tr.

Sugarloaf Mtn. Rd.

Mountain Loop Tr.

Mountain Loop Tr.

P

P

P

Mt.
Ephraim
Rd.

Comus Rd.

To
Comus

53

Mt. Ephraim Rd.

To Dickerson

NORTH

53: Sugarloaf Mountain

1 mile scale

ethereal in winter. Birds, deer and other four-footed creatures are plentiful, and so are copperheads and rattlers.

The preserve exists because Sugarloaf intrigued vacationing cyclist Gordon Strong when he pedaled by in 1902. He acquired the mountain piecemeal, and turned it into a private preserve, complete with vacation mansion. He opened

the grounds to the walking public on weekends. He retired there in 1936. When he died in 1954, the estate was already in the hands of the present owner and his nonprofit foundation called Stronghold Inc.

The 8.1-mile hike described here is a fairly strenuous clockwise loop featuring impressive overlooks and 4,000 feet of

Hikers atop Sugarloaf learn to be wary of local residents, such as copperhead snakes.

elevation change. The well-maintained trails are named, blazed, color coded, and signposted.

To get started from the parking-lot trailhead, walk up the paved entrance road, pass between two small buildings, and turn left onto a paved path. Proceed past a "Smokey Says" sign, toilet, and maintenance shed. At the next paved road, turn left and follow it downhill for about 50 yards. Then turn right onto the combined white-blazed Mountain Loop Trail and yellow-blazed Saddleback Horse Trail.

The two-in-one trail will take you into the oak-dominated woods typical of the hike route. At the next junction, go straight, staying on the gently climbing white-blazed trail. At the following junction, turn left onto the combined white-blazed trail and blue-blazed Northern Peaks Trail.

At the junction after that, stay to the left, on the blue-blazed trail and follow it through the back country for several

miles. Head downhill initially, and then level off on a short stretch of blue-blazed gravel road. Then turn right onto a dirt trail and follow the blazes steeply uphill. At the next signposted junction, go straight (on what is actually a side trail), and proceed to the White Rocks overlook. Just over 3 miles into the hike, it's a superb place to linger and admire the Frederick Valley.

From there, return to the main, blue-blazed trail. Swing left and follow its undulating course for about 2.5 miles. En route, you'll cross the yellow-blazed horse trail and encounter an assemblage of rocks that gets reworked by passing hikers. Later, after skirting or crossing several rocky outcrops, you'll traverse a dark grove of conifers.

At the next junction, stay left on what is again the combined blue- and white-blazed trail. Then, at the junction after that, turn right and head steeply uphill on the blue-blazed trail. At an intersection, turn right and head for the nearby

Sugarloaf Mountain's distinctive shape makes it a regional landmark.

overlook. Look around, and retrace your steps.

Cross the blue-blazed trail, and head uphill on the red-blazed Monadnock Trail (geologically, Sugarloaf is a monadnock —an outlier of the Blue Ridge). Walk sharply uphill for several hundred yards to the summit, a flat and massive rock slab covering about an acre. Head for the tree- and bush-rimmed edge in search of viewing spots. At 1,282 feet above sea level, you'll be some 800 feet above the surrounding farmlands.

From the summit, head back down the red-blazed trail to the first junction, turn right onto the orange-blazed trail, and then walk down a steep hill. At East View, a popular picnicking area over 400 feet lower than the summit, pause to take in more fine views. Then, turn left (eastward) onto a short connecting trail,

and then turn right onto the white-blazed trail. Follow the white blazes downhill, carefully crossing a paved road twice (that's the road leading to the upper parking lots and areas of the mountain). On the way down, watch on your left for a glimpse of Gordon Strong's mansion, which is off-limits but can be rented for weddings and other events.

For more information on the preserve, contact Stronghold Inc., (301) 869-7846.

NEARBY/RELATED ACTIVITIES
Make a warm-weather, 6-mile detour to visit Lilypons Water Gardens, started by an opera buff and now run by his grandsons. Roam through 300 colorful acres of water-lily and lotus ponds. Call for directions, (800) 999-5459. Then, refuel at Comus Inn, (301) 428-8593.

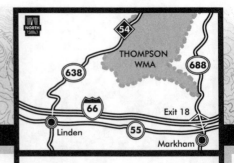

#54
Thompson Wildlife Management Area

IN BRIEF

The Thompson Wildlife Management Area, in Virginia's Fauquier County, is richly supplied with trees, wildflowers, and wildlife, and enough trails to make it a rewarding hiking venue.

DIRECTIONS

From Capital Beltway (Interstate 495) in Merrifield, Virginia, take Exit 49 onto I-66 heading west. Proceed for about 52 miles, and then take Exit 18, at Markham, and access VA 55 heading west. Proceed for 4.3 miles to Linden. There, turn right onto VA 638, drive 4.2 miles, and pull into parking area 4, on right.

DESCRIPTION

The G. Richard Thompson Wildlife Management Area covers almost 4,000 acres on the eastern slopes of the Blue Ridge. Lying about 10 miles east of Front Royal and 60-plus miles west of Washington, the state-owned, well-wooded WMA is managed chiefly to provide habitat for deer, black bears, and other creatures.

For hikers, the habitat is the major draw, especially in spring, when trilliums are in bloom. The WMA is graced with what is probably North America's largest trillium stand (up to 30 million). Other wildflower blooms color the woods from late spring to late fall.

Fall is also the main hunting season, when it's best to hike elsewhere. You

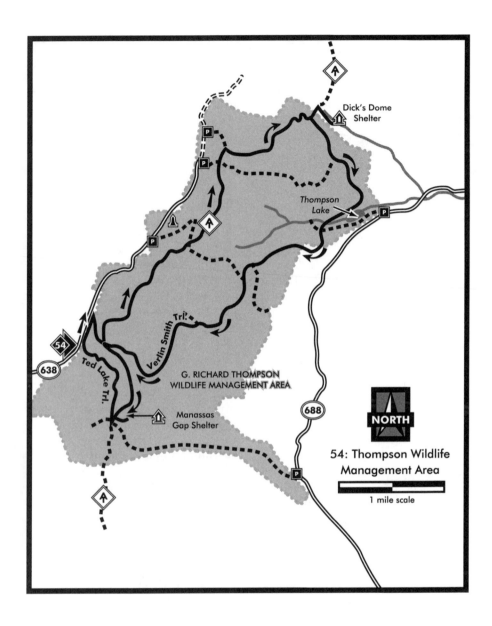

Thompson Lake

Dick's Dome Shelter

Verlin Smith Trl.

Ted Lake Trl.

G. RICHARD THOMPSON
WILDLIFE MANAGEMENT AREA

Manassas
Gap Shelter

54

638

688

NORTH

54: Thompson Wildlife
Management Area

1 mile scale

should check with the state game department or Appalachian Trail Conference on dates. Even so, Sunday is officially a no-hunting day throughout Virginia.

The hike described here consists of a 10.3-mile clockwise loop that includes an Appalachian Trail segment and approximately 3,200 feet of elevation change. As signposts and blazes are not abundant, use these directions well.

To get started from the parking-area trailhead, head northeast along VA 638 for about 300 yards. At a small unmarked parking area on the right, look for an old dirt road signposted as the Verlin Smith Trail. Head south on it for almost half a mile. Then turn left onto the white-blazed AT and follow it for 3.6 miles, traveling generally north with the Blue Ridge crestline on the left. En route, in late April and May, watch for trilliums, with their three broad leaves and three large white or pink petals. Most belong to the species called large-flowered trillium.

In trillium areas, stay on the trail. The plants grow slowly, taking up to eight years to produce their first flowers. They're easily killed by a heavy foot or grasping hand

After passing a large rock on the right and easing downhill for about half a mile, reach a three-way junction. There, turn left to stay on the AT. After a few hundred yards, leave the AT and turn right onto a blue-blazed trail. Follow it and a small stream (Whiskey Hollow Creek) downhill. Reach Dick's Dome Shelter, a stopover for AT thru-hikers. Peruse the logbook (trail register) for information and amusement.

From there, retrace your steps to the AT and then back to the three-way junction. This time, turn left, onto an unblazed trail that wanders generally south and downhill. After almost half a mile, reach another junction—and be about halfway through the hike. There, bear left onto a seasonally overgrown road. After about half a mile, reach Thompson Lake. Follow the trail around the 10-acre lake's western shore and pass some stone ruins. In high summer, watch for butterflies, then, in a muddy area, the lake's feeder stream.

At the next intersection, turn left and hike up a steep hill. At a junction marked by an old red barn, turn right to follow the WMA boundary and enjoy what College Park Scott calls "bucolic views." At the next junction, turn right to begin a long woodland ascent. After a third of a mile, reach a pair of trail junctions. Turn right at the first one, and then left at the second one, marked by a metal shack in ruins.

Continuing uphill, the dirt path is seasonally flanked by overgrown grass. After passing more stone ruins, reach a stream (Wildcat Hollow Creek). For about 50 yards, the stream and trail often vie for the same space, so try to step inventively. After that, you'll be on the lower end of the Verlin Smith Trail. Swing sharply right, stop climbing, and again have trilliums for company. At the next junction, turn left onto the AT to start the hike's last leg by going downhill for almost a mile. Then detour 70 yards to your left on a blue-blazed trail to visit the Manassas Gap Shelter and its logbook.

Continuing on the AT, the trail soon intersects with the Ted Lewis Trail. Turn right onto the Lewis trail, an old dirt road that's nominally blazed blue. Follow it uphill for about three-quarters of a mile to reach the trailhead and your car. For more information about the Thompson WMA, contact the Virginia Department of Game and Inland Fisheries office in Fredericksburg, (540) 899-4169. For AT information, contact the Appalachian Trail Conference, (304) 535-6331 or www.appalachiantrail.org.

NEARBY/RELATED ACTIVITIES
Visit the family-run Apple House, (540) 635-2118, in Linden. It's an eccentric mix of restaurant, gift shop, general store, and apple stand, plus bathrooms. It's also the home of a nonalcoholic fizzy cider called Alpenglow. To get there from VA 638, follow VA 55 west for 1.4 miles. On leaving, access I-66 at nearby Exit 13.

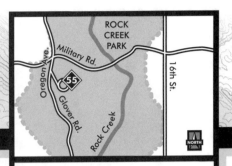

IN BRIEF

March across northern Rock Creek Park and through streets. Check fort attacked in only Confederate raid on Washington. Pay respects at Union cemetery. Retreat through woods. Regroup at civilian cabin. Reconnoiter second fort. Disband.

DIRECTIONS

Head for Northwest Washington. From intersection of Connecticut and Nebraska Avenues, head northeast on Nebraska for 0.4 miles. Turn easy (not sharp) right onto Military Road and drive east for 0.7 miles. Then turn right and south onto Glover Road to enter Rock Creek Park. Proceed for 0.4 miles, swinging left at fork and then taking first left to get to parking lot for Rock Creek Nature Center and Planetarium.

Or use Metro and your feet: From either Friendship Heights Metro station (Red Line) or Fort Totten Metro station (Red, Green Lines), take Metrobus E2 or E3 along Military Road. Get off at Oregon Avenue (opposite Glover Road). From southeast corner of intersection, walk uphill on paved path for 400 yards to reach trailhead. Contact Metro, (202) 637-7000 or www.wmata.com.

DESCRIPTION

Hiking not only meshes well with other interests, but also can lead to new discoveries. That's how I came across Fort

KEY AT-A-GLANCE INFORMATION

Length: 7.3 miles

Configuration: Loop

Difficulty: Easy/moderate

Scenery: Rolling woodlands, creek valley, city streets, historic sites

Exposure: Over half shady; less so in winter

Traffic: Generally very light to light

Trail surface: About half dirt, half pavement; stony, rocky, rooty in places

Hiking time: 3.5–4.5 hours (including historic-site time)

Access: Rock Creek Park, Fort Stevens, cemetery open daily, dawn to dusk

Maps: USGS Washington West (USGS); PATC Map N; sketch map in free NPS Rock Creek Park brochure

Facilities: Toilets, water, phone at nature center (limited hours); toilets, water near Miller Cabin

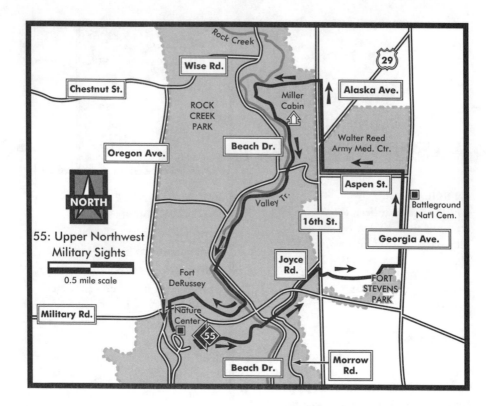

Stevens and Fort DeRussey in upper Northwest Washington and learned about the only Civil War attack on the city. Later, after finding other historic sites, I devised this hike.

The 7.3-mile hike is a counterclockwise loop with about 1,100 feet of elevation change. It starts and ends in the rolling woodlands of northern Rock Creek Park. In between, it winds through city streets, with stops at Fort Stevens, a Union cemetery, and Walter Reed Medical Center. Back in the park, it reaches Fort DeRussey.

While in the park, don't go astray. The hike route mostly uses horse trails. Oddly, they're not signposted or blazed, but may be marked with no-bike symbols. Also, they're muddy when wet, so choose wisely if faced with on-trail mud versus off-trail poison ivy. And do be careful when crossing streets.

To get started from the nature center's parking lot, walk south to the lot's entrance. There, turn left onto the road leading to the park's horse center. Then turn left again to traverse a parking lot and reach a short paved road leading to a fenced riding ring. At the fence, turn left and head for an open, unpaved path that enters the woods. Follow it downhill for half a mile. If you encounter equestrians, step aside and let them pass.

After carefully crossing Ross Drive, follow the trail that swings right alongside an unnamed ramp road. Then leave the trail to take the road over Rock Creek. After crossing Beach Drive, head uphill on tree-shrouded Joyce Road. Stay on Joyce as it swings left at a fork, glides under Military Road, and ascends to reach a T-junction. There, turn right, keep walking, and leave the park at 16th Street and Rittenhouse Street.

The Miller Cabin has been linked to poets and poetry since the 1880s.

Turn right and walk south for one block to Fort Stevens Drive. Turn left and east onto the drive and follow it gently uphill for three blocks to Piney Branch Road. There, cross over and climb the grassy rampart to enter Fort Stevens Park. Managed by the National Park Service as part of Rock Creek Park, the fort site is now a grassy open area partially rimmed by a reconstructed and cannon-dotted parapet. A scale model depicts the original fort, and a streetside display board provides related information.

The fort was one of the Civil War hilltop defenses built around Washington. In July 1864, it was attacked by a small force under Jubal Early, sent north to draw off the Union troops around the Confederate capital, Richmond. After two days of fighting, Early's troops were driven off, and Washington was saved. But the episode may have prolonged the war by six months or more.

On the parapet, locate a plaque commemorating Abraham Lincoln's visit to the besieged fort. It shows Captain (later Justice) Oliver Wendell Holmes grabbing Lincoln's arm. Holmes is supposed to have yelled, "Get down, you damned fool!" But a more reliable story has the fort commander telling the President to keep down.

Return to Piney Branch Road, turn right, walk north to the next corner, and turn right (east) onto Rittenhouse Street. At the end of the block, turn left onto Georgia Avenue and head north. After crossing Van Buren Street, watch for and turn right to enter Battleground National Cemetery. A one-acre burial ground for Union soldiers who fought at Fort Stevens, it was dedicated by Lincoln on the conflict's second day. While walking around, try reading the much-weathered headstones.

Continue north on Georgia Avenue until you reach Aspen Street and Walter Reed Army Medical Center. The 110-acre campus is worth visiting. Named for a medical hero, it's a military facility dedicated to saving lives, with attractive gardens, a remarkable medical museum, and a Fort Stevens connection.

On weekdays, enter at the Aspen security gate (carry a photo ID). A hundred yards in, pause at a "Lincoln under Fire" plaque on the right. It marks the site of the Sharpshooter's Tree (later toppled by a storm) from which snipers shot at Fort Stevens. Then head west across the campus to the 16th Street gate. On weekends or holidays, when the only gate open is four blocks north, skip the grounds and take Aspen across to 16th Street.

There, turn right and head north, with Rock Creek Park on your left. At Holly Street, you'll be halfway through the hike. Nearby, just south of the intersection, find a trail sign and a dirt trail. Follow them downhill into the woods.

At a trail junction, walk straight ahead on the Pine Trail. At the next one, turn left onto the Valley Trail. Stay on it for 1.5 miles as it follows Rock Creek downstream. Although not always close to the water, it's the hike's loveliest segment. After passing Rolling Meadow Bridge, the trail may be churned-up muddy, thanks to horse traffic. At the next fork, where a trail sign points left and warns, "Foot Travel No Horses," turn right and leave the Valley Trail. At the next fork, turn left and then cross a paved road (Beach Drive).

Then swing left onto a paved and parallel path. Walk about 200 yards and turn right to circle a dark and sinister looking log cabin with a pitched roof, as I did one gray winter afternoon with District Brigitte. There's no explanatory sign, but she explained: "It's the witch's house!" (as in Hansel and Gretel).

Later, I learned that it's the Miller Cabin. Now almost forgotten, poet Joaquin Miller was very popular in the post-Civil War era. But when he lived in the cabin in the 1880s, it was located on 16th Street. Decades later, the cabin was moved to the park as a gift to the nation.

From there, walk back upstream on the paved trail and cross the bridge spanning the creek. Then, turn left to ease down an embankment. Turn left again onto an old road running into the creek at Millhouse Ford. But stay dry by turning right beforehand onto a horse trail heading downstream. At a junction, turn right onto another horse trail. After trekking uphill and roughly west through the woods, reach a side trail with a "No Horses Permitted" sign. Turn right and walk just a few yards to visit the ruins of Fort DeRussey.

As a trailside plaque says, the fort "commanded the deep valley of Rock Creek." Perched about 350 feet above sea level, on what is now the park's highest point, it did just that. During the Confederate attack, its guns were fired almost 200 times. Walk just beyond the plaque and turn right onto an elevated perimeter path atop the now-overgrown earthen ramparts. Make a bumpy circuit on the path.

Return to the main trail and turn right to continue. At a signposted junction, go straight, on the Western Ridge Trail. Ignore a paved path coming in from the left. Turn left at the next junction, next to a display board about Fort DeRussey. Then head downhill, cross Military Road, and proceed uphill to the trailhead. For more information on both parks and the cemetery, contact Rock Creek Park, (202) 282-1063 or www.nps.gov/rocr.

NEARBY/RELATED ACTIVITIES
Attend Rock Creek Park's Civil War-related and other ranger-led programs. Call the nature center, (202) 426-6829. Or attend Miller cabin poetry readings. For details visit www.wordworksdc.com.

#56
US national Arboretum

IN BRIEF

The US National Arboretum, hidden away in Washington's eastern section, is an exotic locale where hiking can be an unusual and moving experience.

DIRECTIONS

From downtown Washington, access New York Avenue NE (US 50) heading out of town. Turn right onto Bladens-burg Road. Drive about 0.4 miles and turn left onto R Street, which ends in 0.3 miles at arboretum's main entrance. Drive through gates to parking lot. Or, while on New York Avenue, cross Bladensburg Road to swing right onto service road leading to other gated entrance; once inside, bear right and follow Hickey Lane to R Street parking lot. *Note:* To access westbound New York Avenue after hike, get back on R Street, turn right onto Bladensburg Road, and then take first left, onto Montana Avenue, which runs into New York Avenue.

Or travel by Metro. Take Orange or Blue Line train to Stadium Armory Metro station, transfer to Metrobus B2, leave bus at Bladensburg Road and R Street, and walk 0.3 miles along R Street. On weekends and holidays, Metrobus X6 runs from Union Station (on Red Line) to arboretum's R Street parking lot. Contact Metro, (202) 637-7000 or www.wmata.com.

KEY AT-A-GLANCE INFORMATION

Length: 7.5 miles

Configuration: Modified loop

Difficulty: Moderate

Scenery: Woodlands, open spaces, river views, exotic plantings

Exposure: Mostly open

Traffic: Generally very light to light; much heavier on spring week-ends along Azalea Road

Trail surface: Mostly paved road-way; some dirt, gravel, mulch, grass

Hiking time: 4–6 hours (allowing for lingering caused by flora, vistas, labels)

Access: Open daily, 8 a.m.–5 p.m. (closed on December 25)

Maps: USGS Washington East; map in free arboretum brochure

Facilities: Toilets, water at admin. center, near gift shop, and (warm-weather months only) along hike route

Special comments: Remember that museum closes at 3:30 p.m.and arboretum gates clang shut at 5 p.m.

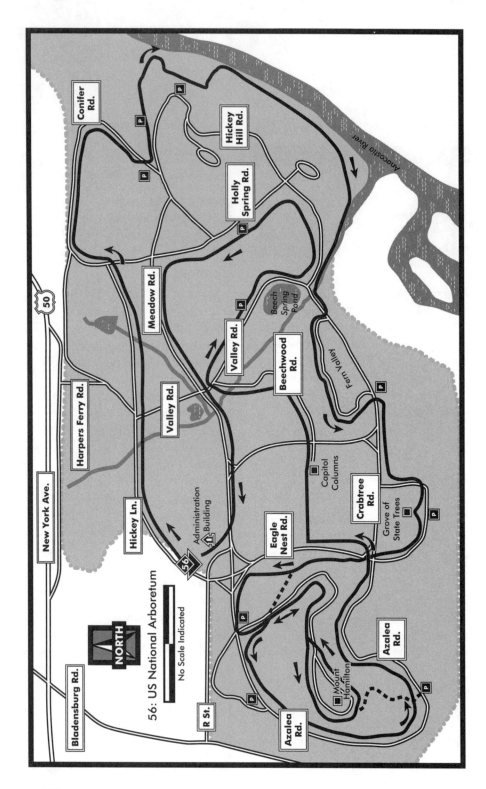

56: US National Arboretum

No Scale Indicated

NORTH

Anacostia River

Conifer Rd.

Hickey Hill Rd.

Holly Spring Rd.

Meadow Rd.

Beech Spring Pond

Valley Rd.

Beechwood Rd.

Fern Valley

Harpers Ferry Rd.

Valley Rd.

Capitol Columns

Administration Building

Eagle Nest Rd.

Crabtree Rd.

Grove of State Trees

New York Ave.

Hickey Ln.

Mount Hamilton

Azalea Rd.

Bladensburg Rd.

R St.

Azalea Rd.

50

56

Once part of the Capitol, these columns now support the sky over the arboretum.

DESCRIPTION

The US National Arboretum is one of the city's finest outdoor treasures—and a wonderful hiking venue, too.

This hike is a 7.5-mile convoluted loop with 2,200 feet of elevation change. It's mostly on paved roads that are well signposted and usually used only by a few strollers, joggers, bikers, and car-enclosed sightseers, as well as arboretum security patrols. Preface your hike by visiting the administration building to get the "Hort Hot Spots" brochure.

Take Hickey Lane heading away from the R Street entrance. Follow it across Valley Road and swing left at the next junction. Continuing, turn right onto Conifer Road—and into the remarkable Gotelli Collection, a Lilliputian forest of dwarf conifers. They're naturally occurring small and slow growing forms of their full-sized ancestors. Detour on the grassy side paths, and let the weeping blue Atlas cedar amaze you.

At the next road junction, stop at a grove of dawn redwoods. As a plaque

explains, when the species was discovered in fossil form in China in the 1930s, it was classified as extinct. A few years later, though, living specimens were found. The arboretum acquired some in 1948, the year before it opened.

Then turn left onto Hickey Hill Road and walk gently uphill. Veer left through a small parking lot, and take a paved path to a three-bench circle. Then head downhill on the grass, staying to the right, to reach an Anacostia River overlook. Look over, and then head back uphill for about 30 yards onto a mulch-surfaced trail going to the left and uphill.

Where the trail branches, next to two yellow poplars (tulip trees), stay to the left and proceed gently downhill and deep into the impressive Asian Collection. Just past a bench, swing right onto the lower of two trails and proceed. If it's fall, you'll see a large and late blooming snow camellia, and an unlabeled Chinese quince that bears fragrant yellow fruit. As the trail angles uphill, turn left at the buttercup winterhazel, pass a lovely

Japanese maple, turn left again, and cross a paved circle. Where the trail forks, turn left, head down some steps, and pass a deodar cedar and alongside a scenic ravine guarded by dawn redwoods to reach a small red pagoda.

From the pagoda, take a stepping-stone path downhill and turn left to continue on a curving, plant-lined concrete path. At the bottom, near the river, turn right onto on a broad gravelly path. Leave the path at Hickey Hill Road. Walk to and turn left onto Crabtree Road, and head for the first dirt trail on you right. Take it to enter Fern valley, a wooded stream valley filled with labeled native American plants. Cross the stream, turn left and follow the dirt trail uphill. After recrossing the stream, turn right at a small shed to return to Crabtree Road. Turn right and continue. Then swing left to visit and study the State Grove of Trees.

Head for the intersection of Crabtree, Azalea, and Eagle Nest Roads. There, turn left onto Azalea Road, turn right to ascend some brick steps, and pause at a rare lace-bark pine from China. Walk up more brick steps to the B.Y. Morrison Garden with its rich azalea collection shaded by dawn redwoods. Staying to the right, take a woodland path to the azalea-filled F. P. Lee Garden. Then swing right and descend to where Eagle Nest Road meets Azalea Road again.

After walking about 200 yards along Azalea Road, turn left onto a paved woodland path. It'll take you to the tree-shrouded top of Mount Hamilton, 240 feet above sea level and the city's third highest point of land. There, look for the distant Capitol through the trees, and visit a nearby clearing to see two broken and former Capitol columns.

Return to, and turn left onto, Azalea Road. Follow it for about a mile as it loops leftward around Mount Hamilton.

If it's spring, you'll see in bloom some of the 15,000 azaleas planted by Morrison, the arboretum's first director. And if it's summer or even fall, you'll see late-blooming azalea varieties.

At the end of Azalea Road, turn left onto Eagle Nest Road and proceed alongside a large meadow to an ex-Capitol capital and plinth, and explanatory plaque. Then, head across the meadow to an astonishing site: 22 capital-topped sandstone columns arranged in austere, Acropolis-like splendor on a low knoll. The columns were installed there in 1990, 32 years after completing their first assignment—supporting the Capitol's east portico for 130 years.

Linger, especially if you have a camera. Then head down to Ellipse Road, cross it, and follow Beechwood Road to Valley Road. Turn right and proceed, but look to the left for some unlabeled trees with red-stemmed, heart-shaped leaves and big clusters of drooping orange-red berries (Idesia polycarpa). Continuing, pass Beech Pond, turn left onto Hickey Hill Road, left onto Holly Spring Road, and then left onto Meadow Road. Watch for unlabeled Japanese apricot trees that flower in winter. Near Valley Road, detour to the left to a towering willow oak; over 200 years old, it's probably the facility's oldest tree.

Returning to the road, follow it to the exquisite Bonsai and Penjing Museum (penjing is a Chinese precursor of bonsai). There, savor what's very small, very old, and very lovely. (As the museum closes at 3:30 p.m. consider starting your hike there).

Then, roam the National Herb Garden. Finally, return to the trailhead before the arboretum gates shut at 5 p.m. For more information, contact the arboretum, (202) 245-2726 or www.usna.usda.gov.

#57
Virginia State Arboretum

IN BRIEF

The Virginia State Arboretum lies amid the farmlands of northwestern Virginia. As a year-round hiking venue, it is novel, uncrowded, and picturesque.

DIRECTIONS

From Capital Beltway (Interstate 495) in Merrifield, Virginia, take Exit 49 and get on I-66 heading west. Proceed for about 47 miles, and take Exit 23 onto US 17 north. Go 8.9 miles, and turn left onto US 50 west (also US 17 north). Continue for 7.9 miles to brown "Arboretum" sign on right. Get in left lane immediately and 0.2 miles later, turn left into arboretum on Blandy Farm Road. Drive 0.5 miles to main parking lot.

DESCRIPTION

The Virginia State Arboretum covers 172 acres of gently rolling Clarke County countryside just west of the Shenandoah River and roughly 60 crow-miles west of Washington. Officially, it's the Orland E. White Arboretum and part of a 700-acre agricultural research station operated by the University of Virginia.

Although hiking here is physically unchallenging, it offers superlative aesthetic pleasures. The core setting consists of open woods and broad meadows. The woods range from dense research plots to spacious groupings of native trees, shrubs, and associated nonnative species. The meadows furnish serene vistas all

KEY AT-A-GLANCE INFORMATION

Length: 5.3 miles

Configuration: Modified loop

Difficulty: Easy

Scenery: Gentle hills, meadows, open woods, farmlands, ephemeral ponds

Exposure: Mostly open

Traffic: Very light; heavier on warm-weather weekends, holidays near trailhead

Trail surface: Mostly grass; some dirt, gravel, pavement

Hiking time: 3–4 hours (scenery gazing and label reading included)

Access: Open daily, dawn to dusk

Maps: USGS Boyce; sketch maps in free facility pamphlets (accuracy iffy)

Facilities: All near trailhead: toilets, water, emergency pay phone at Quarters; water at picnic area

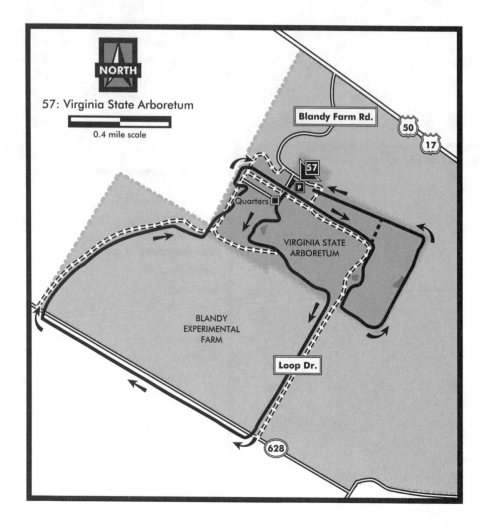

57: Virginia State Arboretum

0.4 mile scale

NORTH

Blandy Farm Rd.

50

17

57

P

Quarters

VIRGINIA STATE
ARBORETUM

BLANDY
EXPERIMENTAL
FARM

Loop Dr.

628

year and erupt in vivid wildflower color in warm-weather months.

This core area is surrounded by the research station's other lands, which in turn are encircled by commercial farms. Consequently, an arboretum hike is a journey through a countryside stretching to the horizon.

It also can be wonderful beyond the colorful attractions of spring and fall. In summer, one can freely roam the colorful meadows on broad mowed pathways. In winter, crossing the withered grasslands under a slate sky can evoke starkly beautiful images of Western plains or

Brontean moors. In good weather at any season, try ending your outing by walking across the meadows and into the sunset when the evening seems spread out against the sky.

Yet another year-round pleasure is that the arboretum offers solitude and tranquillity. Visitors are mostly researchers, gardening enthusiasts, and a few tourists, none of whom seem to go very far. As yet, the only hikers I've met have been my companions.

This easy, 5.3-mile hike covers most of the arboretum and a bit of the research station. In using the following description, keep in mind that distances are short, many trees are labeled, and the bluebird nesting boxes are numerous—as are the birds, so take along binoculars.

You'll also see gnarled trees, stone walls, old roads, and other signs that the area is rich with history. In the 1830s, Joseph Tuly had a large mansion built on his plantation here and named it Tuleyries (possibly a playful variant on the name of the famous French palace). Eventually, a stockbroker named Graham Blandy acquired the property. When he died in 1926, he left most of his 900 acres to the University of Virginia. The mansion and remaining acreage remain in private hands.

The following year, Orland E. White joined the university faculty as a professor of agricultural biology and director of the new Blandy Experimental Farm. Gradually, he transformed the property into a renowned research institution. After he retired in the mid-1950s, the arboretum was named in his honor. It was also designated Virginia's state · arboretum in 1986.

Leaving the parking lot, browse at a nearby information kiosk, then head for a stumpy lamppost onto a path leading to a two-story brick building. Known as the Quarters, it houses offices, a laboratory, a library, and researchers' living quarters. It's actually two buildings separated by a century. The left-hand wing was part of the plantation's slave quarters. The other wing and the linking portion were added in the 1940s.

As you walk through the link's arched passageway, check out the gift shop and information rack, and watch for the low-flying barn swallows that nest beneath the arch. Emerging, peruse the informative display case on the walkway wall to the right, then cross the flower-rimmed courtyard lawn on a short paved path. At the path's end, swing left across a broad, grassy, and tree-lined avenue to reach the Conifer Trail. There's a sign, but no trail as such. Rather, look for a series of numbered posts bordering a strip of conifers. No. 5 marks a weeping Norway spruce that's worth admiring. At 7 turn right and return to the avenue.

There, turn left and walk across the weathered, cacti-dotted bedrock that seems to have heaved up through the grass. Then scan grandly named but ephemeral Lake Georgette on your left. Next, head for a small green cinderblock structure, just beyond a ruined stone wall. Swing left in front of the wall and proceed gently uphill on an old road. On the left is a regal line of Sawara cypresses (native to Japan); on the right, though, next to the ruined wall, is a forlorn line of cypress stumps.

After the ground levels off and the road disappears, keep going across the grass and through a grove of black walnut trees. Then, turn left onto a gravel side road. For the next half-mile, you'll be close to the arboretum's southern property line, which is shrouded in a tangle of shrubbery. After the road ends in roughly 200 yards, keep going across the grass, edging right to pass through a single-chain gate set in a stone wall. This area is filled with magnolias, dominated by a huge cucumber tree, or cucumber magnolia (the young fruit are cucumberlike).

From there, traverse a tree-flanked meadow, staying to the right of center. Watch for numbered posts that mark the Broadleaf Trail. This route uses only a few of them, and out of sequence at that. After passing posts 11 and 4, veer right and around an unmowed area and proceed through wooded areas devoted to the rose family and pea family, then pass posts 5, 9, and 8.

At a gravel road—the Loop Drive—turn right and follow it out of the arboretum, into the open, and into the farming part of Blandy Experimental Farm. Stay on or near the one-way road's shoulder, and be alert for occasional vehicles approaching from behind. Cultivated fields and a few farm buildings surround you, with the Blue Ridge crestline as a hazy backdrop.

Turn right onto paved VA 628, which marks the farm's southern limit. It's lightly traveled, but cross and walk on the shoulder. Blandy fields is to your right, and a private cattle farm to your left. After about 0.8 miles, recross the road and turn right onto a gravel-surfaced lane that's part of the Loop Drive. Stay to one side as the lane winds through a research woodlot.

Mark the hike's halfway point by veering left to detour through a glorious grove of more than 300 ginkgo trees. Walk under a canopy of yellow flowers in spring, fan-shaped green leaves in summer, and bright yellow leaves in the fall. Beyond the native-to-China gingkos, at all seasons, the Tuleyries remains visible.

Back on the road, march down a handsome row of cedars of Lebanon (a nonnative species that's very rare in the metro area). At the side road after the one signposted "Parking," and especially if it's spring, take another short detour. Turn right onto the side road, climb a grassy slope, and circle through a scenic area of pines and azaleas. Then return to the Loop Drive.

Next, turn right onto Dogwood Lane. Lined with restored field-limestone walls and dazzling-in-spring dogwoods, it will take you past an amphitheater and the Quarters to the front end of the Loop Drive. Staying alert for cars, follow the drive as it traces an L-shaped course across wildflower-laced meadows for almost half a mile. Along the way, semicircle to the left to visit an ephemeral pond (Lake Arnold) and several huge and wonderful willows. Just before the Loop Drive leaves the arboretum, turn left to follow the fence line. Remain close to it for almost two miles, moving across gently rolling terrain and mowed-in-season terrain, and pass through several groves.

The first grove consists of maples that nicely slow down a fall hike. As you reach a corner of the arboretum, turn left and head down a gentle grassy slope toward a large woodpile. Beyond the pile, cut through a band of woods and veer to the right around a small pond. Then proceed gently uphill until you each a second arboretum corner. Turn left there and continue across the tree-dotted grassland and along the fence line. Depending on what creatures may be lurking in the grass, watch for hawks overhead (twice I've seen six little feet dangling beneath powerful wings).

En route, watch in particular for a princess tree, or paulownia (native to China) with its large, perfumed flower clusters; the tree has a cold-season habit of hanging on to its pecan-sized fruits while setting next season's flower buds. Pressing on, head for a gravel road (it's Loop Drive again). Swing right and follow the road about 100 yards back to the trailhead. For more information about the arboretum, contact Blandy Experimental Farm, (540) 837-1758 or www.virginia.edu/~blandy.

NEARBY/RELATED ACTIVITIES

Plan your arboretum visit to coincide with a scheduled program or event, such as the Garden Fair on Mother's Day Weekend in May, summer concerts in the amphitheater, or Arborfest in October. Call for details, (540) 837-1758. Visit the Burwell-Morgan Mill in nearby Millwood, (540) 837-1799.

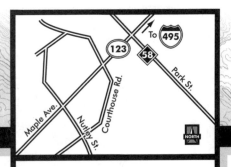

#58
W&OD Railroad
Regional Park

IN BRIEF

The W&OD Railroad Regional Park's ribbony trail enables hikers to get lots of exercise, scenery, and fresh air in the Vienna/Reston portion of deeply suburban Fairfax County.

DIRECTIONS

From Capital Beltway (Interstate 495) in Merrifield, Virginia, take Exit 49 onto I-66 heading west. Drive about 2 miles and take first exit (Exit 62). After 0.8 miles on exit ramp, access Nutley Street heading north toward Vienna. Drive 0.7 miles and turn right onto Courthouse Road. Drive 0.75 miles and turn right onto Maple Avenue (Vienna's portion of Chain Bridge Road) (VA 123). Drive 0.4 miles and turn right onto Park Street. Drive 0.2 miles and turn right into Vienna Community Center parking lot.

Or use Metro to get to trailhead. Take Orange Line train to Dunn Loring-Merrifield Metro station, take Metrobus 2C to Maple Avenue and Park Street, and then take to sidewalk for 0.2 miles to trailhead. Contact Metro, (202) 637-7000 or www.wmata.com.

DESCRIPTION

Much as a dachshund is three dogs long and half a dog high, so the Washington & Old Dominion Railroad Regional Park is several parks long and a tiny decimal fraction of a park wide. More precisely, it's 45 miles long and 0.0189 miles wide—as

KEY AT-A-GLANCE INFORMATION

Length: 13 miles

Configuration: Out-and-back

Difficulty: Moderate

Scenery: Woodlands, parklands, hedgerows, creeping-closer suburbia

Exposure: Mostly open; more so in winter

Traffic: Generally light; light to moderate on warm-weather evenings, weekends, holidays; heaviest in, near Vienna

Trail surface: Almost all pavement, with crushed-gravel option (see text)

Hiking time: 5–6 hours

Access: Open daily until dark

Maps: USGS Vienna; map in official W&OD trail guide

Facilities: Toilets, water, phones at, near trailhead, off-trail near half-mileposts 17, 18; toilet near post 15; water near post 16.5

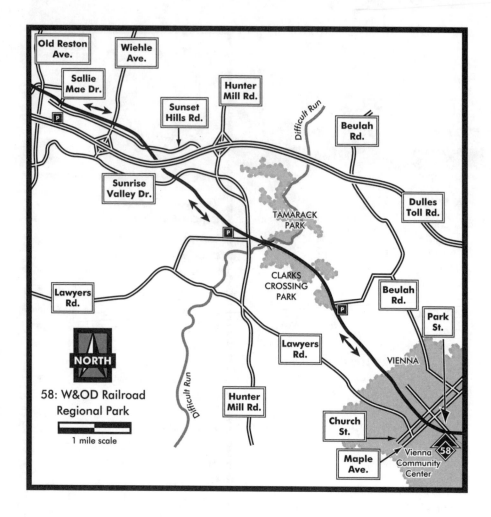

NORTH

58: W&OD Railroad
Regional Park

1 mile scale

can happen when an abandoned railroad
right-of-way becomes a park.

Owned and managed by the Northern Virginia Regional Park Authority
(NVRPA), the park extends across
northern Virginia between urban
Alexandria and exurban Purcellville. Its
chief attraction is an end-to-end, multi-
use, gently sloping, and well-maintained
paved path known as the W&OD Trail.

This hike uses the close-in and scenic
trail section between Vienna and Reston.
About 6.5 miles long, it's flanked by
other parks and unnamed parklands
that make the 100-foot-wide former

right-of-way seem broader and greener.
West of Vienna, the paved trail is paralleled by a crushed-gravel horse trail. The
paved trail is the most popular, largely
with cyclists and in-line skaters and especially in the Vienna area. Signs identify
the major thoroughfares along the trail.
Brown signposts and white numerals
painted on the trail every half-mile meas-
ure the cumulative distance from Alexandria (their locations also reflect careful
re-measurement of the trail in 2001).

By contrast, the gravel trail has little
signage, some hills, and sparse traffic
(mostly a few joggers and strollers, and

an occasional biker or equestrian). It also has thicker hedgerows, where wildflowers burst into scented bloom and the birds warble sweet in the spring.

Explore both trails (they're well-connected neighbors) at any time of year, but especially in the spring or fall, when the area is at its floral best. At all times, though, watch out for others and be attentive when crossing streets and roads.

To get started from the parking lot, head for the adjoining paved trail, turn right, and proceed. After about 0.2 miles, pass W&OD half-milepost 11.5 and then quickly reach Maple Avenue, Vienna's store-and-eatery-lined and traffic-clogged main street. Cross carefully at the traffic light (note the athletic figure on the crosswalk sign). Continuing, cross less-busy Church Street and reach the Vienna railroad station, one of six surviving W&OD stations. A modest wooden structure dating from around 1860, it's now leased by a model-railroading group. But park plans call for refurbishing it and adding a W&OD museum.

Then slip out of Vienna and into a landscape of hedgerows, parklands, woodlands, and sky. That's the hike's basic setting. But you'll also see some buildings, as well as overhead utility transmission lines.

After passing W&OD post 13, enjoy the first installment of Clarks Crossing Park. If it's spring, pause to take in the hike's lone and dazzling forsythia forest, next to a small parking lot. If it's summer, admire the hike's lone, gorgeous, and tree-sized hydrangea bush nearby. And (for contrast) note, on a treeless hill, the hike's lone mansion. Then press on, past a mile of the park's bottomlands.

After W&OD post 14, cross Difficult Run by bridge. It's the hike's lone significant stream, snaking northward across Fairfax County to the Potomac River.

Half a mile later, in spring, listen for the choral shrilling of spring peepers. Then, just past the hike's lone trailside outhouse, cross a paved road again for the first time in 3 miles. It's Hunter Mill Road, where the trail starts going uphill, mostly very gently, for nearly 2 miles.

After crossing Sunrise Valley Drive, duck under the Dulles Toll Road, just before W&OD post 16. Scan the open embankments for wildflowers. They help to visually offset the commercial buildings rising along the toll road. About half a mile later, on the far side of Sunset Hills Road, note the hike's lone water fountain, complete with a bowl for pets. It was donated by the nearby plumbing firm. The trail then levels off, having accumulated most of the hike's 500 feet of elevation gain.

Just after passing the hike's lone array of trailside fast-food outlets, you'll reach and cross busy Wiehle Avenue and start to see more of Reston's buildings. After going by a trail shelter and bulletin board, cross Old Reston Avenue. On the far side, head for a small, white-painted wooden hut. Just short of W&OD post 18, it's the hike's halfway mark and the former Wiehle station. Peering inside, note the half-door ticket counter, where the last ticket was sold in 1951.

Note the hike's lone convenience store nearby. Then recross Old Reston Avenue and return to the trailhead. For further information about the park and trail, contact the W&OD Trail office in Ashburn, (703) 729-0596, NVRPA, (703) 352-5900, or the Friends of the W&OD (FOWOD), www.wodfriends.org.

NEARBY/RELATED ACTIVITIES

If hit by post-hike hunger, head for the Sunflower Vegetarian Restaurant, (703) 319-3888, an inventive and inexpensive pan-Asian eatery on Chain Bridge Road a mile southwest of the trailhead.

#59
Wheaton Regional Park

Map showing Randolph Rd., Old Randolph Rd., Glenallan Ave., Georgia Ave., Kemp Hill Rd., #59, WHEATON REGIONAL PARK, 495

IN BRIEF

Wheaton Regional Park, in Montgomery County, Maryland, is packed with recreational opportunities. One is to use its trails to tour the rich array of facilities and renowned botanical garden.

DIRECTIONS

From Capital Beltway (Interstate 495), take Exit 31A and head north on Georgia Avenue (MD 97) for about 3 miles. Turn right onto Randolph Road, proceed for 0.3 miles, and then turn right onto Glenallan Avenue. Drive past Brookside Gardens parking lot, and then turn right into Brookside Nature Center parking lot (at 1400 Glenallan Avenue, about 0.6 miles from Randolph).

Or reach the trailhead by Metro and foot. Take Red Line train to Glenmont station. From corner of Glenallan and Layhill Road, walk southeast on Glenallan sidewalk for 1 mile, crossing Randolph, to nature center parking lot (no sidewalk for last 0.2 miles, so walk on left side of road). Contact Metro, (202) 637-7000 or www.wmata.com.

DESCRIPTION

When Birmingham Bud first visited Wheaton Regional Park, he was surprised: "What an incredible place! There really isn't much you can't do here." That quality also makes it an intriguing place to hike.

KEY AT-A-GLANCE INFORMATION

Length: 3.9 miles

Configuration: Modified loop

Difficulty: Easy

Scenery: Woodlands, exotic gardens, lake, recreational facilities, fields

Exposure: Shady, except near train tracks and in gardens; more open in winter

Traffic: Light on weekdays; moderate to heavy on weekends, holidays, especially in spring and gardens

Trail surface: About half dirt, half pavement

Hiking time: 2.5–3.5 hours (including slow amble through Brookside gardens)

Access: Open daily, sunrise to sunset (but gardens closed on December 25)

Maps: USGS Kensington; free park sketch map

Facilities: Toilets, water, phone at nature center, gardens, visitor center.

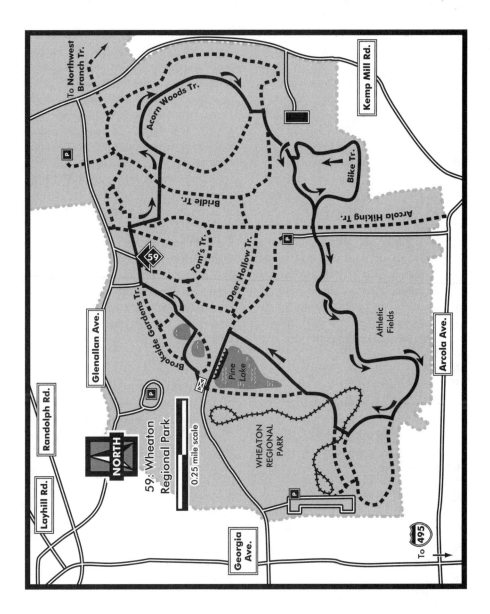

59: Wheaton Regional Park

0.25 mile scale

NORTH

Located a few miles north of Washington, it's best known as a place where people can skate; ride horses, bikes, a miniature train, and a carousel; and play indoor tennis and various outdoor team sports. It's other chief draw is Brookside Gardens, a world-class botanical garden.

However, much of the 534-acre park consists of trail-laced woodlands and fields, plus a lake. Oaks and hickories predominate. Wild orchids and other spring wildflowers thrive in the woods. Pinks, bluets, and other flowers splash color across the summer fields. Year-round, the park supports lots of wildlife, ranging in size from deer to bluebirds. But Brookside no longer serves meals to deer. An innovative fence installed in

1999 has enabled the gardens' roses, azaleas, and other plants to recover from long serving as browse.

This 3.9-mile hike winds through much of the park as a roughly clockwise loop with minimal elevation change. The first part lies in a woodland area where you may feel far removed from the urban world. The second part weaves through recreational facilities where you may be tempted to pause. The last part traverses 50 acres of exotic gardens where you may be astonished.

Begin the hike on a paved trail close to the information sign at the east end of the parking lot. Start by heading east into the woods and crossing a service road. Continue on a dirt-and-mulch trail to quickly reach a junction marked by a trail sign mounted on a big wooden post. There, turn right onto Tom's Trail (the park map calls it the Self-Guided Trail).

The dirt trail gains some elevation over 200 yards and then reaches a junction. There, turn left onto a connector trail. After crossing a horse trail, reach and turn left onto the scenic Acorn Woods Trail. Follow a stream for about 200 yards, and then let the trail carry you away as it makes a wide turn to the right.

Near the loop's southern end, you'll emerge into an open, narrow field. Turn left off the trail and head south across a field where plastic tubes grow (in fact, they protect tree seedlings from hungry deer). You'll soon reach a horse trail—the same one you crossed earlier.

Turn right onto the horse trail and follow it for about 200 yards. Watch for where it dips down, turns to the left, and crosses a culvert-encased creek. There, you should also see a very narrow, unmarked trail leading off to the left. Take it and cross the creek to a paved path. That's the Bike Trail.

Turn left and follow the Bike Trail in a counterclockwise loop through a magnificent stand of mature yellow poplars (tulip trees). Do the full loop, keep going west for about 200 yards, and cross the Arcola Hiking Trail. Continuing through more yellow poplars, you and the undulating trail will cross a paved road leading to the park's skating rink, off to the right. Then swing around the park's large athletic complex, on the left.

At another signposted intersection, at about the hike's 2.5-mile mark, turn to the right and follow the paved trail up a slight incline. As the trail begins to curve to the left, watch for a narrow dirt path heading off to the right and northward. Take it, and quickly reach the park's small-gauge railroad line. Cross the tracks carefully and twice (the line loops), emerging onto a rocky pathway running beside an open field.

Then cross a stream twice, first by bridge and then by foot, and head toward a stand of pine trees. As you approach, you'll see Pine Lake, fed by the stream. Proceed along the lake's eastern rim, and then once again step out into the open. At the next intersection, just over 3 miles into the hike, turn left onto a gravel road and cross the lake's dam. Then, watch for a paved and gated path on the right. Open the gate to step into another landscape, if not another world—that of Brookside Gardens. Roam through the 11 specialty gardens, gradually drifting northwest toward two greenhouses. There you'll find blooms in winter and yourself very close to the trailhead.

For more information on the park, contact the Montgomery County Department of Parks, (301) 680-3803. Also contact Brookside Gardens, (301) 949-8230 or www.mc-mncppc.org/parks/brookside/planning.htm.

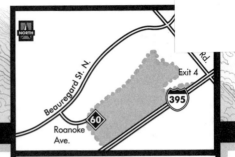

#60
Winkler Botanic Preserve

IN BRIEF

The Winkler Botanic Preserve is a private nature sanctuary hidden in western Alexandria. It's a lovely and unusual place to take a mini-hike both in the city and far from it.

DIRECTIONS

Access Shirley Memorial Highway (Interstate 395) heading southwest out of Washington. Exit at Exit 4, about 5.4 miles beyond 14th Street Bridge. There, turn right onto Seminary Road and drive northwest for 0.2 miles. At second traffic light, turn left onto Beauregard Street North. Proceed for 0.9 miles, counting off side streets on left. Take fifth one, Roanoke Avenue. Follow it for 0.1 miles and drive through gated entrance into preserve's parking lot. If lot is full, park along avenue outside gates.

Or get to preserve by using Metrobus or DASH service on Beauregard Street North, and then walking along Roanoke Avenue. Contact Metro, (202) 637-7000 or www.wmata.com; or DASH (703) 370-3274 or www.dashbus.com.

DESCRIPTION

The Winkler Botanic Preserve is an astonishing urban locale, especially for a first-time visitor. The trailhead lies at the edge of a meadow flanked by woods and what looks like a forest fire tower. The hike route's features include a lake, waterfall, mountain lodge, and even a

KEY AT-A-GLANCE INFORMATION

Length: 1.4 miles

Configuration: Loop

Difficulty: Very easy

Scenery: Small-scale woodlands, meadows lake, pond, streams

Exposure: Mostly shady; less so in winter

Traffic: Very light to light, increasing to moderate when school groups visit

Trail surface: Mostly wood-chip mulch or mulch and dirt; some gravel, grass

Hiking time: 1–2 hours (including dawdling)

Access: Open daily, 8:30 a.m.–5 p.m. (but closed on major holidays)

Map: USGS Alexandria

Facilities: Toilets in lodge (available when school programs not in progress)

Special comments: Remember that entrance gates close at 5 p.m.

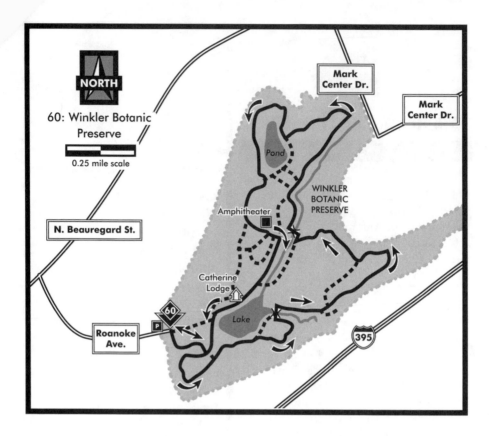

60: Winkler Botanic Preserve

Hobbit House, along with flora that validate the preserve's name.

It's astonishing that, in the mid-1970s, the property was an overgrown and refuse-strewn tract of neglected land along Shirley Memorial Highway. Its transformation began later that decade, when the Mark Winkler family decided to create a private botanic preserve.

It had to be built literally from below-ground up. The terrain itself was reshaped. Vast amounts of stone were trucked in to give the rock-poor tract some outcroppings and character. An integrated lake, pond, and stream system was created to control erosion and enhance the landscape. The Winklers decided that, as both a sanctuary and a research and educational institution, the preserve would specialize in plants native to the Potomac River valley. So, old trees

were saved, alien plants removed, and a long-term effort begun to plant hundreds of native species.

Catherine Lodge (named for a Winkler) was built to serve as the preserve's headquarters and as a meeting place for nature-oriented classes and other programs aimed at both schoolchildren and families. Trails were added. The public was invited. The preserve now has 70 species of trees and about 650 species of wildflowers and other plants. Its resident and transient wildlife population includes red foxes, small mammals and rodents, and red-shouldered hawks and lots of other birds.

This hike (the book's shortest) is a 1.4-mile loop covering much of the 44-acre property. The well-maintained trails are neither signposted nor blazed. Nor are the plants labeled. So, I focus on the route rather than details of what you see. If you're botanically curious, carry reference books. Do the same if you like birds; they're not labeled either.

The preserve is at its best during the warm-weather months, when tree leaves hide the nearby looming buildings, and the frog and insect chorus masks some of the ambient traffic noise. At all times, though, it's a wonderful place for introducing young children to both nature and hiking. But make sure that everyone stays on the trail—and that the family dog stays home.

From the parking lot, step onto the preserve's gravel-surfaced main path. Walk about 1.5 yards and then veer right onto a grassy meadow trail. Head downhill, cross a small gully, and then ascend on a mulch-covered trail to reach the wooden tower. The tower is actually a climbing wall for young would-be mountaineers.

Then take a mulched trail down to a very small pond that's the source of a very small brook. Just before turning left to head uphill, take a 20-foot detour on a covered bridge across the brook and back, the only covered bridge I know of in Alexandria and this book.

Clamber up the wooded slope; it's the steepest part of the hike, but, like all the other parts, it's short. Then, turn left and proceed along a fairly level dirt trail. Where the trail forks, go right. At the next junction, turn left and walk about 15 yards to a mini-overlook above the two-acre lake.

There, take in the mini-vista, including the far shore's Adirondacks-style lodge. Also watch for birds. Prick up your ears, too, and listen for the sound of a waterfall. You'll see the rock-girt pool from which the water leaves, but you won't see the fall or hear the pump.

Back on the main trail, turn left and follow a set of giant stone steps down to

The Winkler preserve has many surprises.

a stream. Cross on a rustic bridge, noting the tiered pools leading to the lake. On the far side, turn right, and head gently uphill through the woods on a mulched trail. En route, swing left at a fork. At the top, after passing some greenhouses, follow the trail as it turns sharp left. At the next fork, swing right and keep going, following the mulch. After turning right at a junction, cross a small stream by bridge, and eventually reach another junction. There, turn right onto the preserve's main gravel path.

Proceeding, cross a small open area and apple orchard (rescued from the Leesburg area) and then continue gently uphill through the woods. Watch for a mulched side trail on the left, marked by a small cube of stone 10 feet up on the left. Proceed along that uphill trail. At a junction, turn right and continue. Watch for a lovely small pond on your left. It's dotted with lily pads and half-hidden by an encircling band of trees, cattails, and wildflowers for part of each year.

You'll follow the trail past the pond counterclockwise, but mostly at a distance. Then, after following the trail sharp left, turn right at a junction and then right again at a fork. Next, go through an intersection, turn left and downhill at a fork, and then turn left at another junction. You'll then bisect a woodland classroom—a small amphitheater with a stone stage and flattened-log benches.

Continue down the trail to reach the main gravel path again. Turn right, and proceed to the lodge. Approaching it, watch for a gate. If you are inclined, turn in to visit the Hobbit House (it helps to be small, but you don't have to have furry feet or speak Elvish).

Then amble past the lodge to the lake. Take in the view, including, at last, the waterfall. Then, turn right and walk along a grassy lakeshore trail. Swing left at a junction, and pass a magnificent stand of staghorn sumac. Head across the meadow to the tower. From there, return to the trailhead—before 5 p.m. Contact the preserve for more information, (703) 578-7888.

RELATED/NEARBY ACTIVITIES
Arrange to return to take a guided tour of the preserve. Also consider combining this short hike with hike no. 25 (p. 87). You can tap into it at nearby Beauregard Street North and Morgan Avenue.

Appendices

Appendix A–Outdoor Shops

Appalachian Outfitters
2938 Chain Bridge Road
Oakton, Virginia
(703) 281-4324

Eastern Mountain Sports
2800 Clarendon Boulevard
Arlington, Virginia
(703) 248-8310

Fleet Feet
1841 Columbia Road NW
Washington, DC
(202) 387-3888

Galyan's
2 Grand Corner Avenue
Gaithersburg, Maryland
(301) 947-0200

12501 Fairfax Lakes Circle
Fairfax, Virginia
(703) 803-0300

Hudson Trail Outfitters
4530 Wisconsin Avenue
Washington, DC
(202) 363-9810

8525 Atlas Drive
Gaithersburg, Maryland
(301) 948-2474

1201 South Joyce Street
Arlington, Virginia
(703) 415-4861

L. L. Bean
8095 Tysons Corner Center
McLean, Virginia
(703) 288-4466

Mountain Trails
212 East Cork Street
Winchester, Virginia
(540) 667-0030

New Balance
5301 Wisconsin Avenue
Washington, DC
(202) 237-1840

Pacers
1301 King Street
Alexandria, Virginia
(703) 836-1463

Potomac Outdoors
7687 MacArthur Boulevard
Cabin John, Maryland
(301) 320-1544

REI
9801 Rhode Island Avenue
College Park, Maryland
(301) 982-9681

The Sports Authority
5425 Urbana Pike
Frederick, Maryland
(301) 696-0252

3701 Jefferson Davis Highway
Alexandria, Virginia
(703) 684-3204

Appendix B—Places to Buy Maps

ADC Map & Travel Center
1636 I Street NW
Washington, DC 20006
(202) 628-2608, (800) 544-2659

Appalachian Outfitters
2938 Chain Bridge Road
Oakton, Virginia
(703) 281-4324

Eastern Mountain Sports
2800 Clarendon Boulevard
Arlington, Virginia
(703) 248-8310

Tysons Corner Center
McLean, Virginia
(703) 506-1470

Hudson Trail Outfitters
12085 Rockville Pike
Rockville, Maryland
(301) 881-4955

94888 Arlington Boulevard
Fairfax, Virginia
(703) 591-2950

11750 Fair Oaks
Fairfax, Virginia
(703) 385-3907

Springfield Mall
Springfield, Virginia
(703) 922-0500

L. L. Bean
Tysons Corner Center
McLean, Virginia
(703) 288-4466

Potomac Appalachian Trail Club
118 Park Street SE
Vienna, Virginia
(703) 242-0693
7 p.m.–9 p.m., Monday–Thursday;
noon–2 p.m., Thursday and Friday

Rand McNally Map & Travel Store
7101 Democracy Boulevard
Bethesda, Maryland
(301) 365-6277

REI
9801 Rhode Island Avenue
College Park, Maryland
(301) 982-9681

3509 Carlin Springs Road
Bailey's Crossroads, Virginia
(703) 379-9400

US Geological Survey
Reston-Earth Science
Information Center
507 National Center
12201 Sunrise Valley Drive
Reston, Virginia
(703) 648-5953

Appendix C—Area Hiking Clubs

Appalachian Mountain Club
Washington DC Chapter
(202) 298-1488
www.amc-dc.org
(also check www.outdoors.org)

Capital Hiking Club
Bethesda, Maryland
(301) 229-5816
Caphiker@yahoo.com

Center Hiking Club
c/o Marion Knight
Alexandria, Virginia
(703) 751-3971
www.centerhikingclub.org

**Mosaic Outdoor Mountain Club
of Maryland**
P. O. Box 10410
Baltimore, Maryland 21209
www.momc-md.org

Mountain Club of Maryland
Baltimore, Maryland
(410) 377-6266
www.mcomd.org

Northern Virginia Hiking Club
(703) 440-1805
www.nvhc.com

Potomac Appalachian Trail Club
118 Park Street SE
Vienna, Virginia
(703) 242-0965
www.patc.net

Sierra Club
Metropolitan Washington Regional
Outings Program
(MWROP organizes outings for the
Maryland, Virginia, and New Columbia
(Washington, DC) chapters)
(202) 547-2326
www.mwrop.org

Wanderbirds Hiking Club
(301) 460-3064
www.wanderbirds.org
wanderbirds@aol.com

Washington Women Outdoors
Germantown, Maryland
(301) 864-3070
www.washingtonwomenoutdoors.org
wwo@patriot.net

Index

About the Author

Paul Elliott works as a writer/editor and plays primarily as a social and solo hiker. He has been leading hikes year-round in the Washington metro area and beyond since 1990, most recently for the Sierra Club and Appalachian Mountain Club. His forte is getting people with a taste for adventure to sample the pleasures and surprises of the area's remarkable array of hiking opportunities.

He discovered his hiking bone back in the late 1980s on a hike in DC's suburban parklands. Enjoying the physical exertion, as well as the vistas, wildflowers, and camaraderie, Paul's interest in hiking grew with each successive hike. Today, as an outdoorsman, hiking is Paul's chief outdoor avocation, and, as a writer, a vocation as well.